THE FINANCIAL POST

Smart Funds 1997

A Fund Family Approach to Mutual Funds

JONATHAN CHEVREAU

WITH STEPHEN KANGAS AND JOHN PLATT

FOREWORD BY ROB BELL

KEY PORTER BOOKS

Canadian Cataloguing in Publication Data

Chevreau, Jonathan
    The Financial Post smart funds 1997

ISBN 1-55013-751-4

1. Mutual Funds – Canada.   I Kangas, Stephen.   II Platt, John, 1959 – .
III. Title.   IV. Title. Smart Funds 1997.

HG5154.5.C44   1996   332.63'27   C96-932792-4

"Smart Funds" is a trademark of The Financial Post.

Key Porter Books Limited
70 The Esplanade
Toronto, Ontario
Canada M5E 1R2

Design(Interior): Daveral Prins Creative Network Inc.
Printed and bound in Canada

96 97 98 99 6 5 4 3 2 1

Contents

Foreword
by Rob Bell

The Canadian mutual fund industry has grown phenomenally in the past six years. From $35 billion in assets spread among fewer than 500 funds in 1990, the industry today manages nearly $200 billion in more than 1,300 funds. Given current growth figures, assets could easily exceed $600 billion by 2010.

It's easy to spot the trends behind these extraordinary numbers. With the constant threat of corporate downsizing and job rationalization in the 90s, many individuals are working longer and longer hours merely to keep their jobs. That leaves little time to learn the basics of financial planning and investing in a complex global economy. Meanwhile, the need to save and invest for retirement is more critical than ever, as demographics suggest generous government pensions may soon be a thing of the past. Increasingly, time-pressed Canadians are turning to professional money management for assistance, with mutual funds to fill the gap.

That leaves only one problem – which funds to buy. The choices are seemingly endless, from very conservative money market funds to bond funds, balanced funds, Canadian equity funds, international funds, emerging markets funds, resource funds, and so on. Complicating this chore is the fact that every year a few funds generate exceptional returns of 50% or 100% or more. But trying to pick which funds will do so next year is about as easy as trying to identify which stocks will double and triple – that is, it's next to impossible. There is really only one prudent method of investing in mutual funds: Find managers with proven expertise, determine the appropriate asset mix for your situation, invest and hold.

Smart Funds 1997 does 90% of the groundwork for you. It combines the considerable journalistic and research talents of Jonathan Chevreau of *The Financial Post* and Stephen Kangas and John Platt of Nesbitt Burns Inc., who have sifted through 150 fund management companies and 1,300 funds. The co-authors' approach is deliberate and rational: Research all fund companies to find those that offer the expertise, consistency and stability needed to meet investor objectives. Then focus on the funds within that family that have particular or unique strengths.

The co-authors have prepared a short list of 50 fund families and 125 "Smart Funds" which have proven their ability to earn above-average returns over time. They've also added more graphs, charts and colour, in order to provide a more distinctive and effective way of presenting the information.

Smart Funds 1997 is a must-read for any serious mutual fund investor. We all have a hundred other tasks that require our immediate attention. But the stakes are too high not to find the time to learn how to make more intelligent investment decisions – what you earn from employment determines your lifestyle today, but what you earn on your savings determines your lifestyle for the rest of your life.

Rob Bell is president of Bell Charts Inc., a Toronto-based firm that measures performance of Canadian mutual funds.

Preface to the Third Edition

In this third edition of the annual Financial Post guide to mutual funds – *Smart Funds 1997, A Fund Family Approach to Mutual Funds* – we've updated and expanded several features.

Last year's guide was essentially restricted to equity mutual funds but, given the volatility of stock markets in 1996, particularly in the United States, we thought it prudent to flesh out the many alternatives. In order to add more fixed income and other alternatives, we've boosted the number of Smart Funds to 125 from last year's 100. These include funds that invest in gold and precious metals, real estate and commodities as well as bonds, global bonds and the money market. And, in a further refinement to this edition, we've included comments on a few hundred more funds we consider "Noteworthy" within each fund family.

We've also expanded the number of fund families to 50, up from 30 in the previous edition. This year, they're arranged alphabetically, rather than grouped by load status. As well, we've introduced a more detailed fund family matrix that shows all funds in a family, including each fund's full name, management expense ratio (MER) and whether or not it's considered foreign content.

Smart Funds – those we believe offer investors the best value – are indicated with a star. Noteworthy Funds are shown with a triangle. All other funds offered by a family are in black. The more stars and triangles in a matrix, the greater the relative strength of that fund family.

To assist the three authors in culling the list of more than 1,300 mutual funds now available in Canada, we submitted a preliminary short list to a Smart Funds Selection Committee of six mutual fund specialists: Jon Kanitz, vice-president of Wood Gundy Inc., a broker and a contributing editor to *The FundLetter*; Patrick McKeough, editor of *The Successful Investor* newsletter, author of *Riding the Bull*, and a *MoneyLetter* contributor; Harland Hendrickson, editor of the *Market Trend Follower*, a market-timing newsletter specializing in load funds; Roger Cann, editor of *The CannFax*, a weekly market-timing service oriented to no-load funds; Elizabeth Tuck, vice-president, mutual funds research at RBC Dominion Securities Inc.; and Richard Christie, a mutual fund analyst at Brink, Hudson and Lefever Ltd. The authors made the final cut, however, so we cannot say that all the committee members necessarily endorse all the Smart Funds.

In the segment on asset allocation, we've retained the authors' philosophy of choosing two or three core fund families, but expanded the section to further emphasize our belief that diversification across asset classes, geographical areas and management styles is the best protection against market volatility. Mutual funds can, indeed, go down in value, and equity investments should be made with an understanding of the accompanying risks. Accordingly, the full page devoted to each Smart Fund includes important measures of the associated risks. If you do not feel comfortable with the risk level of a particular fund, do not invest in it. Find a more conservative fund that is more suited to your investment personality.

We've also included material on the more aggressive equity growth funds, notably technology and other sector funds and regional equity funds. And we still stand by many of last year's Smart Fund selections – 61 of which return from last year's 100 Smart Fund picks.

Mutual fund investors who are worried about the many contradictory predictions and advice that abound today will find plenty of new material here. But the underlying premise still holds true: own equities for the long term, diversify your assets, and pick your holdings from among the best fund companies and managers available.

How to Use This Book

Smart Funds 1997 is organized into four parts.

The first part shows how to assemble a portfolio of mutual funds tailored specifically to your own situation. It starts with the central philosophy of this book – that the most important step for fund investors is to first select two or three major fund families, then draw individual fund selections from those families. That way, you'll minimize fees, paperwork and confusion, while avoiding the over-diversification that may actually reduce your returns. This section explains the key attributes of the better fund families, such as having a full complement of fund types and management styles and an experienced money management team. In addition, this section contains a large section on various asset allocation strategies and how to use them to develop a portfolio that's just right for you.

The second part profiles seven top money managers – the smart managers behind the Smart Funds. (This year's selection supplements the twelve managers profiled in the first edition and the eight included last year.) Don't skip this section – after all the numbers are crunched and charts consulted, the manager or team of managers is still the most important factor in identifying a topnotch fund.

The largest part of this book is devoted to the major mutual fund families in Canada and the best individual funds, which we call Smart Funds, many sold by the families profiled in part three.

In the third part, you'll find profiles of the top 50 fund families, arranged alphabetically. A fund matrix at the beginning of each fund family shows at a glance which core and specialty funds it offers.

Finally, we list 125 Smart Funds, selected by the authors and the six-member selection committee from the more than 1,300 mutual funds available in Canada. Each listing contains comments on the fund and its manager, measures of the fund's risk, the portfolio's asset allocation as well as cumulative and year-over-year performance data going back ten years. The graph illustrates the growth of a $1,000 investment in the fund, the appropriate benchmark, and Canada Savings Bonds. You will also find the fund's quartile ranking, which shows how well the fund has performed relative to other funds in the same category.

Clearly, choosing fund families with several Smart Funds should increase the odds of creating a high-performance portfolio. We expect that readers, using this guide as a reference, will flip back and forth between the fund families and the Smart Funds, narrowing down first their choice of major fund families and then picking the most appropriate Smart Funds within each.

The Fund Family Approach To Building a Fund Portfolio

Industry observers expect that by the end of this century, there will be more than 1,500 mutual funds in Canada. Even now, the more than 1,300 funds available exceeds the 1,250 companies listed on the Toronto Stock Exchange. In the United States, the more than 7,000 available mutual funds surpasses the number of stocks listed on the New York and American stock exchanges combined.

The number of choices is daunting, not only for the casual mutual fund investor but even for financial planners and other investment professionals, some of whom maintain full-time staff dedicated solely to mutual fund research. The early 1990s' boom in fund investing resulted in a proliferation of exciting new funds. Unfortunately, it also led to many investors buying too many funds from too many fund companies.

But the task of sorting the wheat from the chaff is not as overwhelming as it appears. You can rapidly whittle down the selection to a reasonable number, armed with this book and, if you wish, a trusted financial adviser. But first you need to shift your focus from the merits and demerits of individual mutual funds and concentrate instead on fund families and, especially, the managers of those funds.

Too many investors start their fund search with the question, "What fund should I buy?" That's really the third question you should ask. Start, instead, with: "Should I be in mutual funds at all?" If you can't answer that objectively, find someone who can help you – and whose fortunes aren't tied to the mutual fund industry.

For most Canadians, the answer is yes, as more and more of us are being forced to take responsibility for our financial future. Surveys have shown the majority of Canadians in their 20s and 30s do not expect the federal or provincial governments to assume even partial financial responsibility for their retirement. At the same time, employers are getting out of the defined benefit pension business and putting the investment onus on employees through defined contribution plans or group RRSPs.

Many Canadians have realized that, in order to meet their financial goals, they must transform themselves from savers to investors. That means holding less money in bank accounts, GICs, Canada Savings Bonds and money market accounts, and more in domestic and foreign equity investments.

Although investing in equities can increase your return over time, it does mean taking on more risk. But, while most people still define investment risk as losing principal, many are beginning to recognize a bigger risk: not having enough money in the future to support themselves as their capital is eroded by inflation and taxes. The stark reality is that the biggest risk most Canadians face is outliving their income.

Over the long run, equity – or common stocks – is the only asset that will keep up with inflation and provide the kind of returns necessary to meet most goals. Mutual funds should be at least part of any properly diversified investment portfolio and they may even be your entire portfolio.

So, if you answered "Yes" to the question "Should I be in mutual funds at all?", you're ready to tackle the second question: "What core fund family or fund families should I choose?" This is the kick-off point of your overall investment strategy, and the first half of this buyer's guide is devoted to this essential question.

Last year, the accounting firm KPMG Peat Marwick reported that affluent Americans consider the reputation of a fund family to be the single most important factor in choosing a mutual fund. It cited a survey by U.S. Trust, a bank that serves affluent investors, which showed that 65% of wealthy investors consider the status of a fund's family the number one factor in their decision whether or not to invest. Only then do they consider a fund's future prospects, its past performance, and its expenses.

KPMG also found that, despite higher costs, funds sold through sales forces are most favored: 84% of the investors surveyed purchased funds that way. Of course, many do not restrict themselves to just one fund family: the typical investor used more than one distribution channel to assemble a portfolio.

That appears to be true in Canada as well: Even fund families that have built up a loyal clientele find their clients typically hold funds from at least three fund families. With more than 30 categories of mutual funds available in Canada, a single fund family may not provide enough variety. In fact, Jon Kanitz of our fund selection committee sees nothing wrong with a portfolio as large as 20 funds – as long as their individual investment styles and objectives vary.

Since many of the fund families outlined in this book offer more than 20 funds, it's quite possible to construct an entire fund portfolio from any one of these families. But, for most investors, owning funds from two or three fund families, with perhaps a specialty boutique family and the odd special-situation fund thrown in, makes the most sense. Sir John Templeton, founder of Templeton International and a pioneer of global investing, recommends most people diversify among eight or more funds spread among three fund families.

It's worth noting that if you ask a broker or financial planner to select your fund portfolio, he or she will usually choose your funds from, at most, six major fund families. Most investment advisers have two or three favourite fund groups, and there are a few families, such as Mackenzie, Trimark, Templeton and C.I. Mutual Funds, that crop up on many professionals' short lists.

Clearly, then, the most important decision is settling on one or two fund families. They will provide your core funds, as well as the base within which you will make any switches – from one fund to another, for instance, or from funds into cash (or a money market fund).

Most advisers agree the best way to pick your core fund family is to choose a reliable manager, or team of managers, with a solid track record of performance and an investment philosophy compatible with your own. You must also consider the number of fund types offered by each family; how many of these funds are highly rated (that is, Smart Funds); whether there are charges for switching from one fund to another in the same family; whether the family offers enough fund types to enable you to diversify by asset class, geography and management style; and if management expenses and other fees are reasonable.

Use the following five steps to decide on your core fund families:

1. Determine your best asset allocation

Although you're probably anxious to jump right in and start assessing fund families, there's a critical first step that's much closer to home. You must decide what percentage of your portfolio should be in each of the three major asset classes – equity (funds invested in the stock market, both domestic and foreign), fixed income (bond and mortgage funds) and cash (money market funds).

If your goal is long-term growth, for instance, and you can stand a little volatility along the way, then equity funds should comprise the largest portion of your portfolio. If, on the other hand, you're nearing retirement age and/or want your investments to generate income, you should put most of your portfolio into fixed income funds. The traditional range for the equity portion of a portfolio is 25% to 75%, as established by Benjamin Graham, author of the classic investment text, *The Intelligent Investor* (Harper & Row, New York, 1973 – 4th edition). To decide where you fall within that range, you can use a rule of thumb suggested by many advisers, which is to make the fixed income allotment equal to your age. That is, a typical 40-year-old would have 40% fixed income and 60% equities. If you are a little more aggressive, equities might rise to 65% or 70%; if you are on the cautious side, fixed income might rise to 45% or 50%. You may also have a small cash component, either because you need some money in the short term for another purpose, or because you haven't yet committed it to a specific investment. It's usually most convenient if you use a money market fund or funds from your core family or families to hold any cash.

If you're uncertain how to divide your portfolio, you can use balanced funds, asset allocation funds or asset allocation services – in which case one or more fund managers will make this decision for you. Asset allocation services like Mackenzie's STAR or Midland Walwyn's COMPASS, and many fund companies, such as TD Green Line, provide questionnaires that assess your personal financial situation and suggest the best asset mix. Or, you can rely on a professional investment adviser to make this recommendation.

Asset allocation strategies are discussed in more detail at the end of this section.

2. Pick a core Canadian fund family

Once you've got your asset allocation sorted out, you're ready to pick your first core fund family – your core *Canadian content* family.

Why? About half of all mutual fund dollars are invested in RRSPs. Since equity funds offer the best chance of growth and protection against inflation, and the federal government requires pensions and RRSPs to be 80% Canadian content, Canadian equity funds are naturally more popular than foreign equity funds. The top half of the fund matrices that begin each fund family profile show at a glance the Canadian funds available in each family.

Your core Canadian family should also be strong in fixed income products, since they'll also be an important part of your overall portfolio (and are subject to the same Canadian content rules).

Note: If you have investments outside your RRSP, be sure to arrange your holdings so fixed income funds – which are 100% taxable – are held inside your RRSP, and equity funds – which generate capital gains that are taxed at a more favourable rate – are held outside your RRSP. Look, also, for a strong dividend fund you can hold outside your RRSP in order to make use of the dividend tax credit, which reduces the tax payable on dividends from Canadian companies.

3. Pick a core international fund family

As the fund family matrices show, many fund families are strong domestically, many are strong internationally, but only a handful are strong in both.

If your core Canadian fund family is not also a strong international player, make sure your second core family has a strong global emphasis. That way, you can select funds for the 20% foreign content portion of your RRSP, as well as for your taxable (outside an RRSP) portfolio. (The bottom half of the fund matrices list the international funds offered by a family.)

Outside your RRSP, of course, you can invest as much as you want in global equities or bonds. Inside your RRSP, you or your adviser will have to decide whether maximizing foreign content is your main goal. If 20% is enough, most any fund family will do, provided it qualifies on other criteria. But you can have as much as 36% of your RRSP in foreign content if you include Canadian funds that invest the permitted 20% of their portfolios in foreign equity. And, finally, if your belief in Canada is so shaky that you want to fill your RRSP with 100% non-Canadian product, look for internationally oriented fund families that offer 100% RRSP-eligible bond funds, equity funds or balanced funds that are invested in foreign products through derivative-based strategies.

In the fund matrices, under the heading RRSP Eligibility, "RRSP" indicates a fund can be held in an RRSP without using any of the 20% foreign content limit, even if it appears to be a foreign fund. The entry "Foreign" indicates a fund must be counted as part of that valuable foreign content portion.

4. Diversify by management styles

Step 1 diversifies your portfolio among asset classes. Steps 2 and 3 diversify your holdings by geographical area. The next step is to diversify by management style.

No single fund family is perfect. One may have most fund types, for instance, but perhaps not all those funds are winners. But there's no point picking similar funds from more than one family – for instance, more than one Canadian equity fund – unless they're *complementary* or, to use the fund industry's jargon, *non-correlated* – that is, their performance fluctuates in different directions at the same time. The idea is to find pairs of funds in which one zigs when the other zags, so that overall performance is less volatile.

This is why it may make sense to pick a third fund family to supplement your core Canadian and core international families. Then pick from these three families at least two funds for each of your Canadian and international allotment: one a value investment style, the other a more aggressive growth style. Generally, growth funds are invested in small, startup firms that do best when the economy is growing rapidly or tending toward inflation, while value funds tend to emphasize out-of-favour blue chips that will out-perform at the end of a recession and during an economic recovery.

Some fund groups provide multiple investment styles. Mackenzie Financial has three different fund families, for instance: the value-oriented Ivy Family, the growth-oriented Industrial Group, and the globally oriented Universal Group, which has subadvisers under contract.

Some international specialists, such as Templeton and Fidelity, maintain a very consistent investment approach through in-house managers. Others, like C.I. Mutual Funds, 20/20 Funds Inc., Global Strategy Financial Inc., and Spectrum United Mutual Funds, diversify styles by contracting outside advisers. 20/20 Funds (now part of AGF Funds Inc.) uses the term *MultiManager*™ to describe its approach of employing different managers to oversee a specific investment strategy. Global Strategy Financial's *Multi-Adviser*™ approach uses three investment advisers within single funds. The Atlas Capital fund family is built on a style basis, with both growth and value versions of Canadian and U.S. equity funds.

5. Round out your portfolio with specialty funds

Once you've picked your core fund families, consider specialty funds. These higher-risk, higher-reward funds are usually volatile and should be restricted to no more than 5% or 10% of your portfolio. They include precious metals, commodity futures funds, technology and other sector funds and real estate funds (the latter should be held outside an RRSP). You can choose top-ranked funds that belong to the families you have already selected or funds from boutique-like firms that offer only one or two excellent funds, such as ABC Fundamental Value, Cundill Value or Marathon Equity.

HOW TO USE THE FUND FAMILY SECTION AND THE FUND MATRICES

Applying the fund family approach will be easier once you've studied the fund families. Representing more than half the content of this book, it presents 50 major Canadian fund families, arranged alphabetically. (In contrast to the 1996 edition, we have downplayed the difference between load and no-load. The distinctions between the two continue to blur – as evidenced by the "low load" and "level load" three-way pricing schemes used by companies such as AGF, while, at the same time, some previously pure no-load companies such as Atlas Capital have started to sell load versions through broker networks.)

Once you have selected, say, three core fund families, the next step is choosing individual funds from these families. Leading off each fund family profile is a "fund matrix" which shows at a glance all the Canadian and international funds available from any given fund group.

If one of the matrix entries shows a Smart Fund (indicated by a star), you'll find an analysis of that fund in the Smart Funds section at the end of this book. It presents 125 funds ranked as the best in their class by the experts involved with this book.

A second category, Noteworthy Funds, is new this year. Because there are so few Smart Funds compared with the more than 1,300 funds that are available, and because some fund families have relatively few Smart Funds, we've decided to include a few hundred other funds worthy of investor consideration. These funds, indicated in the matrices by triangles, are described in each fund family overview. We call this secondary list the "B Team." We believe that if you have narrowed your choice to two fund families, each having several Smart Funds, this "B team" provides other good funds, many of them first quartile (that is, among the top 25% in investment performance), that weren't selected as Smart Funds but can nevertheless be used to round out a fund portfolio.

BUY AND HOLD VERSUS FREQUENT SWITCHING

There are those who believe mutual funds should be bought and held for the long term, relying on the manager for all day-to-day tactical shifts. Theoretically, a single global balanced fund or asset allocation fund could be bought and held for decades, without the investor ever giving a thought to shifting stock and bond markets.

In practice, however, many investors want to take a hand in adjusting their fund portfolios. Given the bombardment of information through the media, newsletters, books, seminars and now even the Internet, it's little wonder such adjustments may seem necessary from time to time.

These two approaches illustrate the two main competing philosophies of mutual fund investing: market timing versus buy and hold. Both approaches can be executed in various combinations with load and no-load funds.

The mutual fund industry is sometimes accused of favouring the buy-and-hold approach for its own convenience. Money managers don't like frequent redemptions because they may be forced to liquidate positions at inopportune times. The switches also impose administrative costs which, they say, are borne by the buy-and-hold investors.

On the other hand, there are several fund dealers and newsletters that advocate frequent switching, both inside and between fund families. Examples of the latter include Harland Hendrickson's Edmonton-based *Market Trend Follower*, and Roger Cann's weekly *CannFax*. (Both men are on our Smart Funds Selection Committee.)

It's not for us to judge the pros and cons of switching. But, if you're not really sure what you're doing, there is an argument to be made for staying put and letting the manager do his or her job – particularly if you have a competent adviser who helped you buy the right funds in the first place.

Investors who attempt to second-guess the fund managers may end up being "whipsawed," that is, buying and selling at the wrong times. The odds are against you. Consider, for instance, the performance of the Standard & Poor's 500 Composite Stock Index (a U.S. market benchmark) from 1980 to 1989, a period that included 2,528 trading days. An investor in the market for the entire period (in other words, a buy-and-hold approach) received a total return of 17.5%, including dividends reinvested. If she missed the ten biggest gaining days, her return dropped to 12.6%. If she missed the 20 best trading days, her return would have been only 9.3%. If she missed the 30 best trading days, her return would have declined to 6.5%. And, if her market timing had her sitting in 30-day T-bills or a money market fund while missing the 40 best days (just 1.33% of the total trading days in that period), her return would have been an abysmal 3.9%.

If you're willing to put in the time and energy required to track the frequent oscillations in mutual funds' net asset values, then by all means engage in the switching game. But the same energy could be exerted directly in the stock and bond markets, without paying fund managers 2% annual management fees. Wasn't the whole idea of buying mutual funds to sit back and let someone else make these decisions?

There is, of course, a comfortable middle ground. Some investors want the diversification and convenience of funds and still want to switch funds occasionally, perhaps because current macroeconomic trends favour certain fund types over others, or perhaps simply to rebalance their asset mix.

For those who believe in market timing strategies – and even for those who want to make only occasional adjustments to their portfolio – there are some compelling arguments for sticking with just one fund family. This is particularly the case since many fund groups have now broadened their lineup of funds to cover different management styles, fund types and geographic areas. In addition, the growing trend to asset allocation services – such as AGF's service or Mackenzie's STAR – greatly expands the number of choices available for investors who prefer to stay within one family. But, most importantly, owning too many fund families can reduce your return. Each time you sell a fund from one family and replace it with a fund from another, you may have to pay redemption charges as well as sales commissions – all of which will reduce your net performance.

About 80% of load funds are sold with rear loads, that is, redemption fees payable on a declining schedule. These funds are commission-free when purchased, but, if you sell them within a few years, you'll have to pay a redemption fee of as much as 6%; the rate shrinks to zero over several years. Usually, though, you can switch from one fund to another in the same family, or to and from the family's equity or fixed income funds to money market funds, without charge. (Some brokers or dealers may still impose a sales commission of up to 2% to switch, although it's normally negotiable.)

There are no redemption charges if you sell a no-load fund and, if you have an account directly with a no-load fund company, you won't have to pay sales commissions on purchases or sales. However, some no-load companies, such as Altamira, limit the number of annual switches, and others charge a fee for more than a certain number of switches per year. Also, you may still have to pay sales commissions if you switch funds between no-load families and you hold the funds in a single account with a stockbroker or mutual funds dealer – which many people do in order to maximize foreign content in their RRSP.

The simplest course, then, would be to buy funds within a single fund family that offers 30 or more funds and stick with it. And many investors have done so, generally through the no-load funds of Altamira, Royal Mutual Funds or TD Green Line, or with the three fund families of load firm Mackenzie Financial.

Still, it is unlikely any one fund company will have winners across the gamut of a 30-fund portfolio. By choosing two or three core families, and owning a money market fund in each group in order to minimize redemption charges, it's possible to select excellent individual funds within all major fund types.

Whether you favour load or no-load, buy and hold or frequent switching, your approach will tend to fall within one of these four basic configurations:

1. Buy and hold with load funds

Most of the major load-fund groups, and the brokers and dealers that sell their funds, would like you in this camp. Ideally, you commit to a monthly pre-authorized withdrawal from your bank account in order to make regular purchases of funds from, say, three different fund families. In theory, you dollar-cost-average[1] your way to financial nirvana over the course of decades and retire happily ever after. The managers do what they do best and you lead your life, paying scant attention to daily market fluctuations.

If you diversify across asset classes, management styles and geographic regions, this tale should end happily. Once a year, in consultation with your financial planner, you rebalance your fund portfolio to return it to your original asset allocation. If your Far East equity fund, for example, did particularly well that year, you may redeem a portion of it to buy another fund in the same family that hasn't done as well. Thus, you end up "selling high" and "buying low," an eminently reasonable approach.

If you like the big brand-name load families, don't mind

---

[1] Dollar cost averaging is an investment method that requires you to invest the same amount of money at regular intervals. When fund prices are low, your investment buys more units than when prices are high, for the lowest possible average per-unit price over time.

paying for advice, and would rather do other things with your life than worry about fund portfolios, this approach may be for you. Alternatively, you could adopt the no-load version of this strategy (and settle for less advice), or a combination of both.

2. Buy and hold with no-load funds

This may be a bit of an oxymoron. The temptation to switch with no-loads seems to be irresistible. When markets went south in 1994, the no-load funds offered by the banks and fund groups such as Altamira took the brunt of redemptions, as nervous investors who held both load and no-load funds dumped the latter, rather than pay redemption fees.

Theoretically, this approach works the same as the first, but allows a little more flexibility to switch between families or to dump a family that turns out to be an out-and-out loser across the board. Outside an RRSP, it also provides greater flexibility to cash out with no penalty if you decide to use your investment funds to buy a cottage, a bigger house, or other major item. One hybrid strategy is to hold load funds inside your RRSP, where you're less likely to redeem them, and no-load outside. Or, you can buy load funds through discount houses such as Mutual Fund Direct (in London, Ont.) or Valenti Financial Services (in Ottawa). They sell most of the major load groups but do not charge loads, managing to live on only the yearly trailer or service fees[2]. Sounds like the best of all worlds! While full-service brokers claim these upstarts can't possibly provide the same quality of advice, they do provide newsletters and some counselling. They acknowledge, however, that they have to do ten times the volume of their full-service counterparts in order to build viable businesses. That tells you something about the service you may expect.

3. Frequent switching, load funds

This is Hendrickson's camp. He tends to prefer the performance of the load funds, but also likes to switch funds. This strategy calls for holding several fund families that do not penalize switching between their funds. (Although your broker may still charge a switching fee, it's generally negotiable.) If your market timing scenario calls for cash, switch all your equity and bond funds into the money market fund of each fund family. Thus, for example, in the Mackenzie

---

[2] Trailer fees are paid by a fund group to salespeople on an annual basis, continuing as long as an investor retains funds of that group sold by the salesperson.

group, you might switch to Industrial Cash Management; in Fidelity, to the Fidelity Canadian Short-Term Asset Fund.

The name of this game is to minimize switches between families in order to reduce fees. If you are disappointed with a particular family and want to bail out entirely, take advantage of the annual 10% free redemption that most permit and liquidate your position over some years. Or, stop new contributions to the family and wait several years for the declining redemption schedule to fall to zero.

4. Frequent switching, no-load funds

Because redemption fees inhibit switching, they sometimes protect investors from themselves. A 5% or 6% redemption fee is a powerful incentive to stay put and ride out market volatility, while individuals holding no-load funds may move back to cash at the slightest hint of market turbulence. Still, frequent switchers in the no-load camp can dump an entire no-load family in favor of another, with no penalty, at any time, as well as make frequent adjustments in line with their market outlook. In any case, the fund family approach still works for this group, if only because it reduces paperwork, potential confusion and delays.

But because "no load" generally also means "no advice," this camp puts a lot of onus on knowing what you're doing and being prepared to accept the losses along with the gains.

GLOBAL TACTICS

When choosing your core international fund family, it helps to know what kind of global investor you are. Here are the major types:

1. Regional

You have a strong interest in geography, politics and economics. Perhaps, you subscribe to *The Economist* as well as *The Financial Post.* When you think of the investment world, you can't help having a strong opinion that, for instance, the U.S. is overvalued and Asia is the economy of the future. You will likely gravitate to strong international fund families that let you invest in individual regions, either through single-country funds invested in countries such as India (20/20), Israel (Dynamic) or Germany (AGF), or funds invested in broader geographic regions (such as Asia, Europe or Latin America). The bottom half of each fund matrix is devoted to international funds, so you can see at a glance which approach a particular family takes. The regional investors include Altamira, Fidelity, C.I., Mackenzie, Spectrum United, Global Strategy, AGF, 20/20, and many of the bank groups.

2. Global

To you the world is a black box. You're all for maximizing foreign content but want to leave the specifics up to the fund managers. You prefer to let them decide how much, if any, to allocate to Latin America, Japan and so on. If you're this type, Templeton is the classic family for you. Or you might consider BPI, Trimark, and Phillips, Hager & North. In the fund matrices, these type of funds are shown as "all-global". Some families, such as AGF, C.I., Investors Group, and Mackenzie, provide both global and regional options.

3. Sectoral

You have strong opinions about how to invest your money. But you don't divide the investment world into geographic areas but into industries, or sectors – such as technology, resources or manufacturing. If you believe in sector funds, the classic family is GT Global Canada, which lets you invest in telecommunications, infrastructure, natural resources and health sciences around the world. In August, C.I. announced five similar "theme" funds. You can also buy science and technology funds from Altamira, CIBC, Royal Mutual Funds and TD Green Line, a telecommunications fund from Spectrum United, and a health care fund from Admax.

4. Non-domestic

You may fall into some or all of the above groups, but your overall concern is that Quebec is going to send Canada's stock and bond markets plunging. You want every penny of your RRSP outside Canada. If so, you need 100% RRSP eligible foreign funds provided by families such as Global Strategy, Mackenzie's Universal Family, C.I. Mutual Funds, BPI, Canada Trust and Scotia Excelsior. Look for the notation "RRSP" under the RRSP eligibility entry in the international half of the fund matrices.

5. Tax-averse

You have a large taxable portfolio. You don't mind having lots of Canadian content in your RRSP, but, globally, you want to move in and out of Asia, Europe, and so on as you see fit – without triggering capital gains. You should investigate the "umbrella" programs of AGF, GT Global and C.I.'s Sector Funds which allow you to defer capital gains.

MARKET TIMING VERSUS STRATEGIC ASSET ALLOCATION

Many of our Smart Funds are equity funds, because we believe they offer the best prospects for long-term growth. But that doesn't mean we think an investor should be invested in equities only, particularly in these turbulent times of record high North American stock markets, volatile gold prices and super-inflated new issues of junior resources and Internet companies. Equities go up and down. And while nobody complains about the ups, the downs sometimes test even the most dedicated investor.

The answer is to diversify your fund portfolio among the major asset classes: stocks, bonds and cash and, in some portfolios, gold or precious metals, real estate and perhaps even futures or derivatives (see 20/20 Managed Futures Value), through a strategy called asset allocation – which is simply the process of choosing a combination of investments that will achieve your financial goals with an accepted level of risk.

The power of asset allocation is that it establishes a framework within which all your investments are made. An appropriate mix of cash, bonds and equities in an investment portfolio will increase your return and decrease risk. This simple strategy can be enhanced by adding international bonds and stocks to the portfolio and by seeking out alternative money management styles – options made available through mutual funds to even the most modest investor. Not only can you diversify into different asset classes, geographic regions and management styles, but there are now asset allocation services available that try to identify the most optimal or efficient (in terms of risk versus reward) combination for each individual investor.

Asset allocation protects investors from their two worst enemies: themselves and media hype. It's not the same as market timing, which so many investors think is a "magic bullet" against risk and loss. The plaintive cry of those naive individuals typically goes like this:

"I need to find somebody or something to tell me which funds will go up, which ones will go down and when it's best to simply be in cash!"

For some professionals, market timing is a practiced science, but most are lazy about it. Without bothering to learn or practice a disciplined approach to investing, they try to convince themselves they can "make the perfect calls."

The manager profiles that follow this section provide both

points of view. Jean Pierre Fruchet, president of Guardian Timing Services Inc., is a disciplined market timer who believes stock crashes such as 1987's can be avoided. He uses just two asset classes: stocks or equity funds in bull markets, and cash in bear markets. Fruchet makes extreme switches: he's always 100% in, or 100% out of, the market.

At the other end of the spectrum is Gordon Garmaise, a classic strategic asset allocator. Garmaise developed academic research on modern portfolio theory (explained in more detail later in this section) into the commercially successful product, STAR, marketed by Mackenzie. A STAR questionnaire matches an individual's investing attitude and risk tolerance to one of 14 portfolios, each composed of seven-fund combinations selected from Mackenzie's roughly 34 funds. (The questionnaire was developed by a Ph.D. who happens to be Gordon Garmaise's partner and wife, Ena Garmaise.)

STAR portfolios tend to contain mostly equity funds for aggressive investors and a mix of bond and equity funds for more conservative investors. Cash is generally 10% to 15% or less, while gold and precious metals funds are used sparingly in some of the portfolios. The idea is to bundle complementary funds that, taken on their own, may be volatile, but are non-correlated when put together. (Non-correlated means the value of the assets fluctuate in different directions at the same time.) That means that when one type of asset is doing poorly, another type in the portfolio will typically be doing well. The resulting portfolio provides stable returns with reduced overall volatility.

The authors of this book are skeptical about market timing. The reality is that, for most people, investing and following the markets are immensely challenging chores. It's difficult and time consuming to keep up with the professionals. Finding the time to plan an investment strategy, to achieve short, medium and long-term goals, determine the best way to execute a plan and regularly monitor its success is a daunting task. Most people are just too busy – trying to work a double load at the office, grab a workout, spend some time with the kids, and enjoy a little peace and quiet with their significant other. As a result, too many put off the need to plan, execute and maintain an appropriate investment strategy.

Asset allocation, on the other hand, is not a fad. There is a strong foundation for the principles of asset allocation. The most often-cited research in this area is "Determinants of Portfolio Performance" (*Financial Analysts Journal*, July-August 1986, pp. 39-44), a study conducted in 1986 by three investment professionals, Gary P. Brinson, L. Randolph Hood, and Gilbert Beebower. The authors examined the returns of 91 large U.S. pension plans for the period 1974-1983. They examined the variation in quarterly returns over that 10-year period and determined that:

• On average, 93.6% of the total variation in the actual plans' return was explained by the investment policy (that is, asset mix) alone.

• Market timing, when combined with investment policy, "added modestly to the explained variance" – it raised it to 95.3%. Adding the selection of individual stocks accounted for 97.8% of the variance.

This study, which was updated in 1991, shows that the emphasis must be on selecting the right asset mix and sticking with it. Clearly, asset allocation is important; more important, in fact, than picking the right stocks.

MODERN PORTFOLIO THEORY AND THE NOBEL PRIZE

Behind the concept of asset allocation is years of work by two prominent professors: Harry Markowitz and William Sharpe. Beginning in the mid-1950s, they developed the hypothesis that became known as Modern Portfolio Theory, which examines the correlation of assets. Their work was recognized with the Nobel Memorial Prize for Economics in 1990.

When the values of two assets fluctuate in the same direction at the same time they are said to be "correlated." The degree to which they are correlated can be measured mathematically. If two assets have a correlation measure equal to 1, their values fluctuate by exactly the same amount at exactly the same time. If you own both these assets, you have not helped your portfolio. You would do just as well or poorly by owning either one.

If you can combine assets that are non-correlated (those that have a correlation measure of less than one) you have diversified your portfolio. More importantly, by using this approach, you can add riskier (and potentially more rewarding) assets to your portfolio and still lower the overall risk of your combined assets. In theory, you can continue to do this until your portfolio is "optimized" – that is, it combines the highest potential reward with the lowest potential risk.

Computer programs analyse past returns of asset classes (using benchmarks, such as the TSE 300 composite index for Canadian equities) and calculate correlation measures in order to combine assets into an "optimal" or "efficient" portfolio. Given the almost infinite number of possible combinations of risk and return preferences, an almost infinite number of portfolios can be generated. Plotting all these portfolios on a graph of risk and return produces a line known as the efficient frontier.

An Efficient Frontier

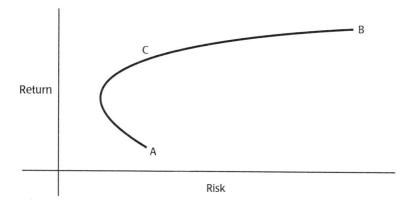

On this graph, point A is usually representative of a portfolio consisting entirely of T-Bills, and point B, a portfolio entirely of equities. People who have never seen this graph are often surprised by its shape. It clearly shows that if their portfolio is at point A, they can move all the way up to point C (that is, increase their return) without taking any more risk. This movement could be accomplished with the addition of a combination of bonds and stocks. Even more significant is the fact they can move to any point on the frontier between A and C and increase their return while decreasing their risk.

While the concept of the efficient frontier is appealing, the question remains, "How do I get on the curve?" And, more importantly, "Where on the curve is the best place for me?"

Determining the exact answers to these questions is a difficult task. The efficient frontier is, after all, a theory. Computers generate efficient frontiers using historical data (that is, past performance) and expected returns based on forecast data. In practice, the efficient frontier is a moving target wholly dependent on the data fed into a computer. Indeed: "The sensitivity analysis we performed with optimizations ... should convince anyone that the output is indeed very sensitive to minor changes in the input variables," wrote

Roger C. Gibson in *Asset Allocation – Balancing Financial Risk,* Irwin Professional Publishing, 1990, pg. 176.

The more appropriate task for individual investors is to try to get as close as possible to the optimal portfolio. There are two ways to do that: strategic and tactical asset allocation. Strategic asset allocation defines the appropriate limits of each asset class for a type of portfolio and sticks with those limits regardless of market conditions. Tactical asset allocation focuses more on market conditions and varies the proportions of each asset class in an effort to have more of the portfolio in any class that appears ready to outperform the others. In other words, TAA is a form of market timing.

Strategic Asset Allocation (SAA)

The simplest form of strategic asset allocation is a fixed balanced fund. Such funds have restricted limits on how much can be invested in equities and fixed income. A neutral stance is 50% of each asset class, with limits for each typically 40% to 60%. That means that even if a fund manager believes equities are going to outperform bonds, she could never invest more than 60% of the portfolio in equities or, vice versa, less than 40% even if she believes the market is due for a correction. (A variation of this is a "fund of funds" in which a fund company pools two or more of its funds, say one equity fund and one bond fund, to create a balanced portfolio with similar stringent allocation allowances).

Examples of fixed balanced funds are:

Royal Trust Advantage Balanced
Royal Trust Advantage Growth
Royal Trust Advantage Income
United Canadian Portfolio of Funds
Dynamic Managed Portfolio
Investors Retirement Growth Portfolio
Investors Retirement Plus Portfolio
Investors Income Portfolio
Investors Income Plus Portfolio
Investors Growth Plus Portfolio
Investors Growth Portfolio
Investors World Growth Portfolio

Recently, the mutual fund industry began recommending personalized portfolios of mutual funds with different investment objectives, with the mix of funds based on investor responses to questionnaires. The idea behind these questionnaire-driven services is that personal asset allocation depends on four factors: objectives, time horizon, ability to tolerate risk, and financial situation.

A number of SAA services exist, based on a similar process. A questionnaire is given to assess these factors, and the resulting score identifies the investor as a particular type (income, balanced, growth and so on). An investor with a maximum income profile will be matched with a portfolio that is heavily, if not entirely, invested in fixed income. The maximum growth investor, on the other hand, will be shown a portfolio with a substantial equity portion. And there are any number of variations in between – for example, emerging market funds have a place in a growth portfolio, but not in a maximum income portfolio.

The mix, once allocated, does not change unless the investor's profile changes (for example, through job loss, approaching retirement or inheritance). The portfolio is rebalanced periodically, however, to maintain the initial allocation if one asset group does particularly well relative to the rest.

Tactical Asset Allocation

Tactical asset allocation (TAA) is a form of market timing. These types of services or mutual funds offer the small investor a one-stop investment vehicle that:

1. Tries to overweight whichever asset class is deemed by the manager to be undervalued and likely to outperform over the near term, and;

2. Avoids market downturns by moving to safer assets before one occurs.

The following are the more prominent TAA funds available in Canada:

> AGF Asset Allocation Service
> Dynamic Partners Fund
> Dynamic Global Partners Fund
> First Canadian Asset Allocation Fund
> 20/20 American Tactical Asset Allocation Fund
> 20/20 Canadian Asset Allocation Fund
> 20/20 European Asset Allocation Fund
> Universal World Asset Allocation Fund

The performance of most of these funds is, so far, merely average. That's because even the most sophisticated market timing models, coupled with highly experienced managers, are up against big odds of not getting it right. And, as we saw earlier in the example of the Standard & Poor's best trading days, missed opportunities can have a significant effect on portfolio return.

The other problem with tactical asset allocation funds is they are not tailored to the individual investor. The manager's market calls might be too aggressive for some investors, at other times not aggressive enough. For most investors, the alternative – strategic asset allocation – is more appropriate.

Successful investing is not only about choosing the right investments (even if they are Smart Funds). Success comes only when quality investments are included in a quality financial plan. The success of David Chilton's *Wealthy Barber* is testimony to the fact that developing a successful plan is not difficult. However, it does take some time and a willingness to learn. If you have an ample supply of both, go it alone. If not, get a financial adviser – if you find a good one, it will be money well spent.

Forget about product until you have accurately determined your personal objectives and risk tolerance within a disciplined financial plan. Then, finding the product will be easy. And, if mutual funds are what you seek, the balance of this book will serve that purpose well.

Money Manager Profiles

MARATHON EQUITY'S WAYNE DEANS

Marathon Equity Fund is the top-performing Canadian equity fund of the 1990s, with a five-year compound annual growth rate of 40.6% to June 30, 1996 – numbers generated first by Bob Disbrow and, more recently, by Wayne Deans.

Deans operates out of Vancouver, from his own firm, Deans, Knight Capital Management Ltd. His west-coast connections, including those forged during eight years with Vancouver-based pension fund manager M.K. Wong & Associates, ensure that his pick of hot new Vancouver Stock Exchange issues as well as those generated in the resource sector and by fund sponsor First Marathon are top-notch. As a result, Deans bought both Diamond Fields Resources and Bre-X Minerals – last year's most exciting junior resource success stories – before they took off. The same connections also allow him to steer clear of less attractive offerings. "We know the white hats from the black hats," he says.

Unfortunately, First Marathon Securities Ltd. closed Marathon Equity to new investors last spring when the fund reached $300 million in assets. But investors can buy nearly identical funds also managed by Deans: the O'Donnell Canadian Emerging Growth Fund, offered by O'Donnell Investment Management; the Navigator Value Investment Retirement Fund, from Navigator Funds Ltd.; and the Atlas Canadian Emerging Growth, from Atlas Capital Group.

Mind you, one or more of those funds may also have been closed off to new investors by the time this book reaches your hands. When he started, Deans believed it might be necessary to cap when total assets under management in the three funds reached $500 million. By spring the total had hit $650 million. Deans now expects the funds will have to be closed to new investors well before $1 billion is gathered.

With a still-trim physique at age 50, slicked-back hair and investment-banker suspenders, Deans radiates confidence. Divorced and childless, he loves sports, especially auto racing, skiing, biking and running. Like most fund managers, he's also a voracious reader of investment research as well as varied magazines and books.

Deans was born in Montreal in 1946. He studied commerce at Sir George Williams University (now called Concordia), working for Royal Bank as a teller during the summers, then full-time as a management trainee after graduating in 1968. Eventually, Deans returned to school, fast tracking a one-year MBA at Hamilton's McMaster University, with emphasis on securities analysis. An on-campus interview led to a job at the Bank of Canada in Ottawa in 1970, assessing the impact of bank policies on the stock market. Deans was also part of a team that managed the bank's pension plan, a third of which was in stocks. He was given the responsibility of managing those stocks.

"That was my introduction to money management," says Deans, although he was somewhat restricted in his choices by the deputy governor's preference for household names in the portfolio. In 1979, Deans was sent to observe U.S. federal reserve operations. While there, he met many central bankers – contacts he maintains today. He also learned "that macroeconomic top-down research was useless, that central bankers with the best financed research departments and the best people were highly inaccurate in their economic forecasts."

Later, Deans grew equally disenchanted with large-cap Canadian equity funds. He left the Bank of Canada in 1980. "I learned a lot but didn't see myself as a civil servant. Performance measurement is not high on their list," says Deans.

He was offered two jobs in the investment business, one with Wood Gundy, the other with the then-A.E. Ames & Co. He chose Ames. Deans started trading bonds on the fixed-income desk, planning to move to Vancouver. But Ames was soon in trouble and Deans reactivated his contacts with Wood Gundy. He landed a bond trading job in Vancouver. There he became friends with his boss, Peter Campbell, who was well known as a fixed-income specialist.

Campbell convinced Deans to return to Toronto to work with Jim Beqaj, then president of Wood Gundy. It was the era of the "bought deal," invented by Gordon Capital, and Deans worked a few years on innovative fixed-income deals for Gundy.

During that period, Deans became friends with Vancouver money manager Milton Wong, who approached him in 1984 when he started his investment counselling business, M.K. Wong & Associates. Deans returned to Vancouver as a partner in M.K. Wong. This, he says, "was where my education in money management began."

By 1985, M.K. Wong was managing $3 billion, surpassing such older well-known firms as Phillips Hager & North Ltd., also of Vancouver. But Milt Wong's investment returns in 1986-87 were less than impressive and by 1988 it started to lose business. Wong made Deans president in a drastic attempt to turn the firm around. Deans trimmed the staff to 18 from 50, and increased the emphasis on small-cap growth stocks. The performance numbers bounced back and, by 1990, so did assets under management. But Wong and other senior partners weren't believers in Deans' small-cap approach, and Deans and fellow money manager Doug Knight were bought out in 1992.

Deans now says the five years he ran M.K. Wong "were the most miserable of my life." But they allowed him to hone his small-cap investment approach. Although he's convinced small and medium-cap stocks give "the biggest bang for the buck," Deans doesn't automatically pick small caps. Rather, he screens stocks for 11 characteristics and says, "It turns out that very few big cap companies pass the screens."

Deans and Knight started Deans, Knight Capital Management with no clients, not a lot of money, and a plan to invest only in small-cap Canadian growth stocks and high-yield corporate bonds. Their first break came two weeks after setting up shop, when Northstar Energy of Calgary, looking for a more aggressive approach for its pension plan, turned to the new firm. Soon, Placer Dome asked them to do the same for its plan.

That set the stage for managing mutual funds. In September 1994, First Marathon asked Deans to manage its one in-house fund, Marathon Equity. He also took on virtual clones at Atlas Capital Group and Navigator Funds, which had just lost manager Irwin Michael, who had left to start his own firm.

Deans is in the investment industry for the long haul. "Guys in our business don't know how to do anything else," he says. "Everyone I know who is serious about this business loves doing it, and will do it till the day they die. I'll be around as long as I can be."

ELLIOTT & PAGE'S NEREO PITICCO

In 1993, when Elliott & Page Ltd. lost Canadian equity manager John Zechner to rival C.I. Mutual Funds, it seemed a major disaster. While E&P has always espoused a team approach to investing, it was also among the first investment counsellors in Canada to endorse the marketing stratagem of the "star" manager. Suddenly the star was gone.

Three years later, the star-manager syndrome has grown to epidemic proportions, as major Canadian equity managers indulge in an apparent game of musical chairs. Zechner still maintains high visibility through C.I., where the funds he manages have more or less equalled the return of the TSE 300 composite index.

At the top of the performance heap, ironically, is the manager E&P picked to succeed Zechner: Nereo Piticco. The E&P Equity Fund achieved a 20% return in the year ended June 30, 1996.

Piticco's father immigrated to Canada from Italy in 1952 to work as a miner in Noranda, Quebec. Piticco's mother joined him in 1954 and Nereo was born the following year.

Piticco, who speaks English, French and Italian, grew up in Noranda, studied business at Concordia University and completed his bachelor of commerce in finance and economics at the University of Montreal. Upon graduating in 1977, he joined Royal Trust in Montreal, starting in the pension investments division. While there, he completed the Canadian Securities Course, the chartered financial analyst (CFA) program and the other necessary credentials for a portfolio manager. As more and more co-workers left – frequently for Toronto – Piticco inherited more responsibility, and was exposed to a wide variety of account experience, from endowments to corporate pension funds.

Following a Royal Trust reorganization, Piticco moved to Toronto in 1986, where his mentor was Peter Larkin, head equity strategist at Royal Trust. After 12 years at the firm, Piticco gambled on a shot to become a full-fledged investment counsellor, joining Barclays McConnell (formerly E.J. McConnell & Associates) in 1989.

Piticco joined Elliott & Page in December 1993. There, his classic investment style is embraced by a team that works in a open-office "bullpen" structure not unlike that seen in the hit television series Traders. He works closely with colleagues and fellow money managers Peter Jackson, Ted Macklin and Jack Campbell. Because Piticco also runs pension and institutional portfolios in addition to mutual funds, he's responsible for more than $1 billion in Canadian equities. He's also manager of E&P sister funds, such as the Cornerstone Funds. In the summer of 1996, Piticco and two partners formed their own PCJ Investment Counsel, with E&P as its first and most important client.

Piticco is known as a "top-down sector rotator" manager. That sounds like a mouthful, but it simply means that he prefers to pick stocks depending on which sector of the economy is expected to outperform, rather than following the "bottom-up" approach of picking a company first, regardless of which industry it's in. His style also calls for either over- or under-weighting various sectors of the TSE, favouring, say, resource stocks rather than consumer stocks, and changing those weightings – or "rotating" – from sector to sector as he sees fit.

In addition, the E&P Equity Fund is one of the few top-performing funds that doesn't concentrate on small-cap stocks. "We've identified the fact we can generate added value by staying with large stocks and making concentrated sector bets and actively trading, taking advantage of volatility in the market," Piticco says. "We don't have to step down (a level) and discover the next Bre-X or Diamond Fields to outperform."

Since Piticco is not a market timer, cash is kept to a minimum, both in the pure equity funds and the E&P Balanced Fund.

Ironically, given E&P's early role in creating the "star" fund-manager concept, Piticco warns investors that "people should be very careful about buying the star concept. Wayne Gretzky is a great hockey player but lots of general managers wouldn't want him on their team. They'll take Mark Messier every time."

Piticco believes in keeping in constant touch with his clients, "the ultimate buyer of the products," meeting with many every few months. "I've never operated in a vacuum," says Piticco. "There's always been a greater link to the ultimate recipient of my good performance or with people who (will be hurt by) my poor performance. That's helped me maintain a perspective on the fact egos can inflate very quickly in this business. Just because someone can generate a big return in the market, it isn't necessarily indicative of intelligence or infallibility."

Piticco has another touchstone as well: his RRSP is 100% invested in the E&P Equity Fund, as is his wife's. The couple lives in Mississauga, Ont., with their twin 13-year old sons and 11-year old daughter. At age 41, Piticco sports a touch of gray, a moustache and a tan. Like most fund managers, he rises early, and is at his desk shortly after 7 a.m.

Elliott & Page's "star" manager doesn't pretend his childhood ambition was to be a mutual fund manager. "That just evolved.

but there's nothing in the world I'd rather do," he says. "This is the greatest job in the world. You're exposed to so many things and people. No two days are ever the same."

TRIMARK'S VITO MAIDA

When Trimark Investment Management Inc. was searching for someone to replace high-profile money manager Dina DeGeer and manage its $5-billion worth of Canadian equities, it came up with two names unknown to the average investor.

But Vito Maida and Wally Kusters were plucked from the world of pension fund management in 1995, like DeGeer before them, who came from Confederation Life, because they were exactly the sort of managers Trimark chairman Robert Krembil believed would fit the Trimark mould.

Maida, 36, met Krembil many years before he beat out heated competition for the Trimark job. When Maida first started in the industry, as an investment analyst at the Ontario Municipal Employees Retirement System (OMERS), he researched the top portfolio managers in Canada and called on Krembil. The Trimark chairman agreed to an initial meeting and the two kept in touch. For Maida, the meeting was yet another step in a determined assault on the investment industry that had started years earlier.

Vito Maida, the eldest child and only boy in a family of five first-generation Canadians, born of Italian parents who immigrated in the mid-1950s, wasn't exposed to high finance in his youth. But he considered education the best way to get ahead and was subscribing to *Business Week* and *Fortune* by the time he was 17 years old. When just 12 years old, he began saving for university, aided by a part-time job as a department-store stock boy.

Maida completed a BBA at Wilfrid Laurier University, an MBA at the University of Western Ontario, and finished his CFA in 1990. But at Trimark, he's learning things they didn't teach at school. "It's more of a philosophy, the character-type things, the subtleties of what is a good business and what isn't. In the end, this comes down to judgment," he says.

Maida thinks it's dangerous for managers to rely on computers to spit out recommendations and numbers. "You have to look at how the numbers are derived and, ultimately, the people managing the operation."

At Trimark, managers are expected to visit the companies they recommend. Maida estimates he and Kusters visited 50 to 60 companies in their first four months on the job. More often than not, they decide against investing. "The important decision is what you don't invest in, as opposed to what you do," he says.

Maida landed his first investment job after completing his BBA. He was a financial analyst in corporate and government banking at Bank of Montreal. There, he converted accrual accounting statements into cash flow statements, a "wonderful grounding" that aids his work at Trimark. Another important progression in his career was from small-cap manager to medium-cap manager at OMERS.

But when Maida got the call from Krembil, he was happily settled at Hamblin Watsa Investment Council Ltd., a corporate pension and high-net-worth counsellor he had joined late in 1992. As with Krembil, Maida had been no stranger to founder Prem Watsa. From Watsa he learned "the whole idea of portfolio concentration: having a short list of 20 names or so," – which is also a prime Trimark trait. In addition, he learned to "never leave a stone uncovered."

Like most portfolio managers, Maida puts in long hours. But, either at the beginning or the end of the day he tries to find time for his four-year-old son and two-year-old daughter. He married an accountant in 1989, whom he had met on a blind date set up by their sisters. Today, except for a little hockey and the church, the investment business is his main interest. And, when he gets the time, Maida is also an amateur historian of investment history.

While a firm believer in the benefits of mutual funds, Maida nevertheless advises fund buyers to do their homework on a fund before investing. "How long has it been around? What's the reputation of the manager and the long-term track record? How does the manager attain his record? What is the reputation of the overall fund company itself? The fund investor should do all that because of the great number of new funds out there," he says.

Maida regards himself as "blessed" and says Trimark has been fortunate to have assets entrusted by almost a million Canadians. "It's an awesome responsibility that has been given to us and we take it quite seriously. Every time we make an investment decision we make sure we do our homework. We're not always right but in the long term, given the homework we do and the prices we buy at, you should get an above average return."

FIDELITY'S ALAN RADLO

Anywhere else, 38-year-old Alan Radlo might be considered the new kid on the investment block. But after 11 years at industry giant Fidelity Investments, currently as lead manager of Canadian small-cap stocks at the Canadian subsidiary, Radlo is an experienced hand. "I used to be the young whippersnapper on everyone's heels at Fidelity. Now they're on my heels," Radlo reflects in an interview, some months before the well-publicized hiring of ex-AGF star manager Veronika Hirsch.

Still, Radlo's career path doesn't quite fit the Fidelity stereotype. A typical Fidelity manager is young, well-educated and ambitious: the credentials are often an MBA from an Ivy league school, Fidelity as the first job out of school, and then the well-worn path of junior analyst, senior analyst and, finally, portfolio manager – first, a small fund then, if you do well, a larger one.

But, although Radlo grew up in the Boston area in which Fidelity is based, Fidelity wasn't his first investment job, nor was his family affluent enough to send him to the typical Fidelity-type school. His father was an engineer for the state of Massachusetts, and his mother raised three children. Alan wanted to be a doctor but his pre-med grades weren't quite high enough, in part because he had to commute to Brandeis University in the suburbs and pay for his tuition by stringing tennis rackets every night.

He shifted his pre-med studies to economics. During the transition, "I had to take a lot of philosophy and psychology. I started reading the Wall Street Journal to keep awake and realized that to succeed I had to get into business. I used to read every story and company: who was successful, who wasn't, what makes a good company and what makes a bad one."

Radlo put some of his college fund into the stock market. He did well on his first few oil-stock flings, including a "half flyer," Canada Southern Petroleum. But, other than a family vacation in Quebec when he was 13, Canada would stay in his future.

After receiving his BA, Radlo went straight to the University of Massachusetts in Amherst for his MBA, "where I got my stock knowledge," he says. "We studied stocks 24 hours a day." Unlike the ivory-tower dwellers in the Ivy league, his professors were rooted in the real world, with strong connections to Wall Street. At the same time, Radlo was playing the market to help with school expenses. "If 100 shares of a stock went up a quarter point, that used to be two nights pay. I was leaving classes to make (phone) calls. I thought this stuff was easy."

But he also learned to be conservative from a grandfather who had been through the Depression, and his first stock loss is still etched in his mind. "When you have crap in your portfolio and the market goes up you can still make money," says Radlo, "but if the market goes down and you have crap you have nothing."

Radlo applied to work at Fidelity upon graduating in the early 1980s, but "didn't make the cut." Instead, he ended up in the treasury department of Bank of Boston. Soon, he'd snagged an assistant's job trading small-cap stocks for the bank's pension fund and, later, when a colleague left, Radlo found himself – at age 25 – managing a $100-million fund. "Younger even than the Fidelity hot shots," he points out.

But the pension business gave Radlo a more conservative perspective than most Fidelity managers. "I had great numbers but (my bosses) started chastising me for portfolio turnover. The corporate treasurer at the bank told me to participate fully in the market, 'but don't lose us money. These are people's retirement savings.'" Even today, Radlo tends to hold a little more cash than average, either for liquidity or in case of market downdrafts.

After three years with the bank, Radlo finally cracked the Fidelity lineup, and joined the firm in 1985. He was re-introduced to Canada in 1987, working for Fidelity International, a global fund based in Bermuda that had a 3%-4% weighting in Canada. As part of his duties, Radlo visited some oil companies in western Canada – among the first U.S. fund managers to do so. Later, Radlo moved to Fidelity Management Research, where he ran the Fidelity Canada fund for U.S. investors wanting exposure to Canada.

Radlo's early successes with Canadian stocks led to the creation of the subsidiary Fidelity Canada, first under John Vivash, then John Simpson. Radlo left Fidelity Canada for a few years, leaving George Domolky as the chief Canadian equity manager. He returned for the 1995 launch of Fidelity Canadian Growth Company, the small-cap fund (that is, restricted to companies with a market capitalization of $300 million or less) he currently runs. He also heads the equity portion of the Canadian asset allocation fund.

Radlo, a bachelor, makes frequent trips between Boston and Toronto, and travels across Canada in search of small-cap Canadian stocks. "This business is a sacrifice. I admit the job hurts me socially," he says. Radlo describes most Fidelity fund managers as "stock jocks who know every company in every industry. They're walking encyclopedias. It's a 24-hour-a-day thing … You have a report card every day." This isn't to say the women managers at Fidelity aren't stock jocks too – as Radler says, they "are as hard-driven as the guys are."

Radlo considers himself a value manager, even if his fund carries the growth name. "It's not an oxymoron. There can be value in growth stocks," he says. In fact, he's finding so many quality Canadian stocks at bargain prices he doesn't even try to fill the permitted 20% foreign content.

He admits Quebec is "still casting a serious pall over the market, but I'm assuming that Quebec stays." Nevertheless, Radlo says he didn't sleep for two weeks in October before the Quebec referendum. Had the separatists won, he says, "it would have been short-term devastation."

Currently, Radlo views the Canadian market, and particularly small caps, as extremely undervalued relative to the U.S. – especially the NASDAQ exchange, home of most American small-cap stocks. But he doesn't like the growing numbers of non-voting stocks and tangled intercompany ownerships. "It seems an improper way of doing business. I think there should be one share, one vote." These practices have held back the Canadian market, "especially in Quebec, where management owns 10% of the underlying stock but controls 90%. As a result, many of these companies are illiquid to start with," says Radlo.

"Investing in Canada has been very easy for me this cycle. Everything that happened in the U.S. happened in Canada one and a half years later: industrial streamlining, divestitures." And, given the growing belief that government safety nets will no longer bail people out in retirement, major Canadian pension plans are likely to start beefing up their stock portfolios, he says. And that, in turn, "will have a huge positive effect on the market."

ALTAMIRA'S WILL SUTHERLAND

To paraphrase Rodney Dangerfield, bond fund managers just don't get any respect. Not compared with the more glamorous field of equity managers, anyway.

So laments Will Sutherland, who is to Altamira's bond operation what colleague Frank Mersch is to equities. In fact, in 1995, while Mersch and most Canadian equity managers struggled to narrowly beat the Toronto Stock Exchange, Sutherland and other bond managers racked up returns of more than 20% – to much less acclaim.

Despite the lower public profile, Sutherland – an Altamira vice-president who started with the firm the same year as Mersch –

has always preferred the logic of the bond market. "Bonds are math," he says. "I've also found bonds a lot easier to value because interest rates can't go to 50% or fall below zero."

Sutherland's ready smile always seems about to break into laughter. He admits his sardonic sense of humour also serves as a defence mechanism against the pressures of his job, even though, after 20 years in the business, he's well past his apprenticeship.

Born in 1952 on a farm outside Owen Sound, near Georgian Bay, Ont., Sutherland was educated in a one-room schoolhouse until grade 7 and attended high school in Owen Sound. He went to the University of Toronto's University College in 1970, graduating with a B.Comm degree in 1975. For his first job, he had his pick of an advertising agency or Canadian Imperial Bank of Commerce. The bank offered $100 more a year and Sutherland's career in money management was launched.

At CIBC, he acquired a thorough grounding in the art of bond trading as he bid on municipal bonds for the bank. At that time, many towns and villages in Canada issued their own bonds, and Sutherland researched such places as Lucky Lake, Sask., and Flamborough, Ont. He was also exposed to various provincial and federal debt securities.

Sutherland went on to manage the pension assets of CIBC employees. In 1982, he moved to Royal Bank. His arrival coincided with the beginning of a new era of financial instruments – the forerunners of today's derivatives – which included financial futures, strip bonds, asset swaps and the first collateralizations. It was also the period during which "I first saw bonds go up in value," says Sutherland, who recalls how bonds had developed a bad reputation as their value kept falling with successive interest rate increases. Back then, "wags would call them ... a prudent way to lose money," he says. In the early '80s, Sutherland also acquired his chartered financial analyst designation.

By 1987 Sutherland was ready to put the fruits of his apprenticeship to work, joining Ron Meade and Frank Mersch at the then-tiny ($100 million in assets) Altamira. In the early years of the firm, Sutherland, like Mersch, recognized the importance of developing a unique personal style. For a bond manager, that meant diverging from the ScotiaMcLeod bond index benchmarks, much as an equity manager might diverge from the sector weightings of the TSE 300 composite index when assembling a stock portfolio. So, if 40% of the benchmark bond index is in one- to five-year bonds, for instance, Sutherland invests as much as 80% of his portfolio in one- to five-year bonds, or as little as zero. With this "structured active" approach, Sutherland manages 70% of the portfolio in a conservative manner, but extends the average duration of the balance of the portfolio – thus increasing both risk and potential reward.

Given today's extremely volatile interest rates, an aggressive bond manager can add 5% or 10% in value to a bond fund by anticipating interest rate movements. As interest rates rise, the value of existing bonds falls – creating capital losses for bond holders – because new, higher-coupon issues are more attractive. Conversely, if interest rates fall, the value of existing bonds increases – creating capital gains – because new issues carry a lower coupon rate. The longer the duration – remaining time to maturity – of a bond, the more this effect is accentuated.

Most bond managers are comfortable varying duration to four or six years, but Sutherland extends duration out as far as 30 years in some cases. Such a gambit depends, of course, on the successful application of a strategy known as interest rate anticipation. Such second-guessing "is something we do every day," says Sutherland. Over time, managers draw on "an accumulation of mistakes and a recognition of patterns in the market that develop our intuitive grasp of where the markets are going."

In order to balance his aggressive approach, Sutherland reduces credit risk by using only Government of Canada bonds, thus avoiding the risk of defaults, that is, corporate bankruptcies, among a portfolio's holdings.

Today, the once-innovative style pioneered by Altamira is rapidly becoming the norm. Many bond managers would describe themselves as interest rate anticipators, but of those, many vary duration by only a year or so. There are a few, such as Norm Bengough at Dynamic, however, who have pushed the Altamira model even further.

Altamira employs five people on its bond desk, who scrutinize the market constantly for opportunities. "In the bond market, the real profits are made from periods of excessive negativity," he says. "Similarly, when it seems to be the perfect time to buy bonds and people think everything is OK, you have to force yourself to be cautious.

"We try to look at the longer-term level of interest rates, and buy bonds above the longer-term average and sell bonds below the longer term, and not get involved in the day-to-day noise. We will trade the portfolio and do quite aggressively during the market noise, but that's just small value added."

The noise became deafening in 1994, however – the worst bond market in 40 years. It was the first time in 25 years that

Altamira Income Fund lost money (the fund preceded the establishment of Altamira in 1987). Sutherland took it to heart. "My name goes on that negative year. The reponsibility to clients and institutions is something we all have to bear. We made our first mistake by not getting out of the market. Our biggest fear was making a second mistake by selling at the bottom." As the market stabilized, Altamira went longer term, and Sutherland feels vindicated by the 20% returns of 1995.

When he drives home to North Toronto about 5:30 p.m. each evening, the Altamira fixed-income team is either up or down $50 million on their $5-billion fixed-income portfolios (including mutual funds and institutional clients). His own financial holdings are relatively simple: Altamira Income Fund exclusively in his RRSP, cash outside his RRSP, and the private stock of Altamira itself. Leisure hours are few, and spent mostly "being dad" to two young sons, five and seven, although he fits in the occasional mystery novel or game of bridge.

Despite his passion for the bond market, Sutherland admits that "There are times when I don't like the bond market ... when I'd love to own Hong Kong stocks and never a bond. But, as money managers we recognize (our clients) already own Hong Kong stocks and want to own bonds for a reason, so we own bonds for them." And, so far at least, their clients are glad they do.

MACKENZIE'S GORDON GARMAISE

Gordon Garmaise, the architect behind Mackenzie Financial's successful STAR asset allocation service, thrives in the limbo between pure academic research and its commercial application. While not technically a fund manager, his computer-generated model portfolios of Mackenzie-managed funds have as much or more impact as any one fund manager.

Garmaise, 48, started his independent consulting firm, Garmaise Investment Technologies, in 1977, after years of rigorous investment-oriented academic studies and three or four jobs in which he sought to combine investment theory with practise.

Born in Montreal, Garmaise graduated in economics and political science from McGill University in 1969. That's where he met his wife Ena, who later joined the firm.

Gordon subsequently went to the Massachusetts Institute of Technology for an MBA in finance and economics. While there, he met such greats in the field as economists Paul Samuelson and Bob Merton. Specializing in investment theory, he finished the program in 1973.

After a few management consulting jobs in Toronto, including at Ernst & Young, he stumbled across the now-defunct Canavest House, a brokerage house that specialized in investment theory. For Garmaise, it was a dream job. "It was unique in North America. I couldn't believe it when I discovered it in Toronto." Soon, however, he was overcome with the entrepreneurial urge and started his own firm, "partly from my pathetic savings" and partly with financing from Loewen Ondaatje & McCutcheon. Garmaise bought out Loewen's share in 1987.

Garmaise then "fulfilled every sophomore's dream" by hiring a former MIT professor to write two computer optimizers that were based on modern investment theories, yet could be applied to real-world portfolios. But he had made the mistake of putting the product cart before the marketing horse; the firm's bread and butter was a more mundane bimonthly periodical on capital markets. Garmaise put the highly theoretical work on a back burner for a while, in favour of developing more administrative products, including portfolio accounting software, that people were willing to buy.

By the early 1980s, Garmaise was compiling forecasts on securities for major brokerage houses and evaluating their accuracy. He found a ready market in 35 institutional clients. As an MIT graduate, Garmaise believed in efficient markets (that is, the theory that at any given time the price of a stock represents its best valuation because all factors affecting a stock are known or expected and thus reflected in the price), and his forecasting work seemed to vindicate that belief. He continued to develop innovative investment products – at one point he created an optimized portfolio for a pension plan that resembled modern derivative-based products.

By the mid 1980s, Garmaise had gained international recognition by developing one of the first personal computer-based bond portfolio management programs. Soon he was managing two index funds for TD Green Line funds: one in the U.S. and one in Canada. But his hope that index funds would catch on in Canada as they had in the U.S. was not fulfilled.

Meanwhile, Ena finished a Ph.D. in management at the University of Toronto. Her research into investor attitudes toward risk culminated in the questionnaire that produces the main inputs in Mackenzie's STAR portfolios. Both Garmaises believe in a long-term approach that does not depend on short-term market moves, whether positive or negative. "In the short term, people seem to overreact to recent events, which is especially characterized by the stock market," says Ena, whose research found six different ways in which investors misinterpret and handle uncertainty. "People overreact to recent news, are overconfident about forecasts, and are not able to accept the element of chance in investment returns." Or, as Gordon puts it, people "try to impute meaning to what are largely random events."

Garmaise developed his asset allocation models further in the 1990s when he introduced a product through Marathon Brokerage called Select Fund Portfolio, in partnership with then-Marathon president Paul Bates. A precursor to STAR, it used funds sold through TD Green Line. For the program, Garmaise created seven- or eight-fund optimized portfolios that typically outperformed balanced funds by three to four percentage points a year, yet with lower risk. In 1994, Mackenzie asked him to do the same thing exclusively within its three fund families (Industrial, Ivy and Universal).

The STAR portfolios use as many as seven asset classes, selected from Canadian equity, U.S. equity, international equity, Canadian bonds, international bonds and a variety of mortgage, precious metals and dividend funds. The program measures several risk indicators for each fund and classifies each fund's style. Garmaise has found that seven funds provides the optimal trade-off between diversification and administrative complexity.

STAR does not use market timing. The portfolios are balanced annually to bring the asset allocation back into line, but never in anticipation of market moves.

Inevitably, competitive products that resemble STAR are cropping up, such as Bank of Montreal's MatchMaker. Later this year, Mackenzie and Garmaise plan to extend STAR beyond the Mackenzie funds to include funds from other families, even though, from an "efficient frontier" perspective, Mackenzie's 35-odd funds offer sufficient diversity to optimize a portfolio for virtually any investor. In fact, says Garmaise, a portfolio selected by STAR from Mackenzie funds is "almost as efficient as that [selected] across 25 fund families."

Gordon walks to work from his Toronto home, putting in roughly a 9 a.m. to 7 p.m. day when he isn't on the road. He's logged plenty of air miles, making 170 STAR presentations for Mackenzie in 1995. And there's no sign the pace is about to slow, as more and more investors come to appreciate the value of asset allocation. For Garmaise, the difficult combination of academia and commerce seems to have paid off.

GUARDIAN TIMING'S JEAN-PIERRE FRUCHET

As a dedicated market timer, Jean-Pierre Fruchet tries to re-read John Kenneth Galbraith's "The Great Crash: 1929" at least once a year.

"Just to remind myself," says the charming European-born president of Toronto-based Guardian Timing Services Inc. (unrelated to the Guardian Group of Funds). "It's a very good reminder of the horror of what a bear market really means. It's my European background: it's your money; you should protect your capital."

Fruchet's job is to make sure his clients are in cash during major bear markets, as they were ten days before the crash of 1987, most of 1990 and mid-way through 1996. Fruchet doesn't rely on his own instincts, but on a computer model he developed decades ago on computer punch cards, and which now exists in a refined version on a Lotus 123 spreadsheet.

Fruchet, born in southwestern France in 1939, spent most of the 1960s in various universities, completing his certificate in math and physics at the Faculté des Sciences in Paris, then graduating in engineering in 1963 from Switzerland's Federal Institute of Technology of Zurich. Then followed post-graduate work at the European Institute of Business Administration and, finally, an MBA in 1967 at Harvard, with emphasis on finance, marketing and international business.

He started his investment career in North America, first at Morgan Guaranty Trust Co. in New York from 1967 to 1969, then the first half of the 70s at Arnhold and S. Bleichroeder Inc. of New York, as an adviser to foreign investors. There he also acted as a research analyst for legendary money manager George Soros, and managed two offshore funds, using both technical and fundamental analysis.

After seven years in New York, Fruchet was ready to leave but didn't want to return to France. By then married with two young sons, he decided to move to Montreal, his wife's home town. In 1974, he landed a job at Royal Bank, and spent the next ten years in management positions in the areas of corporate planning, capital budgets, acquisitions, global finance and government lending. Fruchet eventually came to Toronto, where he founded Guardian in 1984 as an investment counsellor emphasizing market timing, portfolio insurance techniques, index funds and mutual funds.

Fruchet had been refining his market timing approach

with his own money for 13 years before he started Guardian. Even today, his personal assets are mostly invested in his own funds. Among his first clients was Guardian Trust Co., which gave him space, support staff, a line of credit and $3 million to invest.

Fruchet doesn't believe in bonds or gold. When his model is bullish, based on more than 20 variables, he is 100% in equity funds, selected stocks or index futures. When the model is bearish, he is 100% out, safely earning his clients the modest returns of money market funds. He's justifiably proud of his record: close to the market in up periods and positive money market returns during bear markets, when those invested in equities lose money – such as in 1990, when his Protected American was up 10.7% while the TSE 300 lost 14.8%.

"Market timing means protecting wealth in bear markets," Fruchet says. It's not a get-rich-quick scheme, he insists. Rather, "it's for an investor who is extremely conservative and realizes that making back his losses is really a waste of time." Investors have spent 65 of the last 95 years losing money in bear markets and making back their money, he says, which means two-thirds of the time is wasted.

"If you had been brilliant enough to buy at the bottom, sell at the top, go short at the top and buy back at the bottom, and you did that for each of the 30 major bull and 30 major bear markets this century, $1,000 would be worth $65 billion, versus $60,000 for the buy-and-hold investor. Even if you were right just 75% of the time, you would still be worth $400 million. That's the carrot."

To execute his market timing moves, Fruchet operates "switch accounts" that move his institutional clients in and out of the equity funds of Trimark and Altamira. His own Canadian Protected and Protected American funds are run on similar principles. Fruchet considers mutual funds ideal trading vehicles, since no-load funds or switches within load families entail no trading costs.

The results have not always been admirable. As Fruchet once told *Investor's Digest*, "you have to be humble enough to understand that the computer is smarter than you are." Indeed, Fruchet had to eat humble pie in 1995, when in his fourth-quarter report he apologized to First American Fund unitholders for returning just 4.9% while the Standard & Poor's 500-composite stock index rose 34.1%. Fruchet wrote that he was "disappointed and embarrassed" by the results, and outlined steps he'd taken to avoid similar mistakes.

Today, Fruchet defends the model and the timing signals it gave in 1995. The problem was the human implementation of those signals, he says ruefully. The model was bullish but, because of Fruchet's concern about overall valuations, he invested only half the portfolio in equities. Then he compounded this miscalculation by investing mostly in Canadian rather than U.S. equity funds, disregarding the model. The U.S. market, of course, rose much higher than Canada's that year.

"The drawback of what I do is significant," Fruchet says, "Sometimes the market is going up and I'm out ... and clients get terribly upset. I say to them, 'Look, you have to remember this is not a get-rich-quick scheme. You have to have a time horizon of five or ten years. If you just look at monthly figures, you should not be my client because you don't understand what I'm doing. I'm managing risk ... which means sometimes I'm going to be wrong.'"

The Major
Fund Families

1. ADMAX INTERNATIONAL MANAGEMENT LTD. LOAD

Strengths: Asian equity funds
Admax Global Health Sciences Fund
Weaknesses: Performance of North American funds
High management expense ratios
Web Site: www.admaxregent.com **Toll Free:** 1-800-667-2369

CANADIAN	Category	Rating	Fund Name	M.E.R.%	RRSP/Foreign
Money Market:		■	Admax Cash Performance Fund	1.18	RRSP
Equity:	Mid- to Large-cap	▲	**Admax Canadian Performance Fund**	2.67	RRSP
Multi-asset:	Asset Allocation	■	Admax Asset Allocation Fund	2.54	RRSP

FOREIGN	Category	Rating	Fund Name	M.E.R.%	RRSP/Foreign
Fixed-Income:		■	Regent World Income Fund	2.20	RRSP
Global Equity:	All-global	▲	**Regent International Fund**	2.67	Foreign
	Specialty	★	**Admax Global Health Sciences Fund**	7.16	Foreign
Regional Equity:	Far East	▲	**Regent Korea Fund**	3.54	Foreign
		▲	**Regent Tiger Fund**	3.37	Foreign
		▲	**Regent Dragon 888 Fund**	3.02	Foreign
	Japan	▲	**Regent Nippon Fund**	3.14	Foreign
	Europe	■	Regent Europa Performance Fund	3.46	Foreign

It seems that every year a unique fund from this small specialty
shop hits the top of the charts. In 1995, the Admax Global Health

Sciences Fund beat all comers with a spectacular return of 66.3%.

A year earlier, the Admax Regent Korea and Regent Tiger funds were top performers. These two funds (as well as Altamira's Asia Pacific fund) shared Peter Everington as fund manager. Both funds are volatile, at times leading the pack, then lagging, and as a result their relative performance over the past five years is spread over all four quartiles. In the summer of '96, Everington and his firm, Regent Pacific Group of Hong Kong, were replaced by Invesco of Denver, as manager of the health fund.

Admax chairman Lou Voticky was among the first to introduce innovative new fund types and then sell the wheels off them. Admax was established in 1987 with a core group of three funds: Canadian equity, American equity and Canadian bonds. By 1992, it had seven North American funds, serving such market niches as health sciences and market timing. The North American funds tended to languish in the fourth quartile most of the time, however. Admax avoids Latin America, believing the economic growth prospects of Asia are more attractive.

The 14th fund in the family was Regent Dragon 888, launched in April 1994. It specializes in mainland China, one of just three such open-end funds in Canada (the others are from Sagit and AGF). These funds are volatile, of course, and this one was in the fourth quartile of Asian funds for the two years ended May 31, 1996.

Generally, it seems the further Admax strays from Asia, the worse it does. In December 1995, Admax American Performance Fund was merged into the Health Sciences fund. Its Regent Europa Performance Fund has been consistently in the fourth quartile for three years.

In addition, management expense ratios are among the highest in the industry.

While Invesco is strong in Asia, expect to see more consistent, less volatile performance from Admax in the future. New funds will tap into Invesco's strong "theme" or industry-specific family, with a science and technology fund likely as the next new offering.

Smart Funds:

Admax Global Health Sciences Fund

Noteworthy Funds:

Admax Canadian Performance Fund. Although this fund had lagged its competition, it's recently picked up under new money manager Kevin Elliott of Laketon Investment Management, which manages the fund for Admax. Formerly with Canada Life, Elliott's focus on "best ideas" stocks should give this fund family the core equity product it's been lacking. The managers earn a performance bonus if they exceed the TSE 300 total return index.

Admax International Funds. Admax severed its five-year relationship with Regent Fund Management of Hong Kong and, specifically, its high-profile manager Peter Everington. While Admax chairman Lou Voticky recognized Everington as "brilliant," his big-bet style of management led to relatively poor performance. Admax has passed the management to Invesco, the managers of the Global Health Science Fund, who manage money for clients around the world and have impressive performance numbers. At the time of writing, however, the U.S. mutual fund newsletter, Morningstar, is not rating similar funds in the U.S. very high.

Availability

Only through brokers and dealers.

2. AGF FUNDS INC. LOAD

Strengths:	Bonds and asset allocation		
	Unique single country funds		
Weaknesses:	Fallout from 20/20 executive departures		
Web Site:	www.AGF.com	**Toll Free:**	1-800-268-8583

CANADIAN	Category	Rating	Fund Name	M.E.R.%	RRSP/Foreign
Money Market:		■	AGF Money Market Account	0.97-1.47	RRSP
		■	20/20 Money Market Fund	1.05	RRSP
Fixed Income:	Long-term	★	**AGF Canadian Bond Fund**	1.25-1.75	RRSP
	Short-term	■	**AGF High Income Fund**	1.45-1.95	RRSP
	Mixed-term	■	20/20 Income Fund	1.98	RRSP
Equity:	Mid- to Large-cap	■	AGF Canadian Equity Fund Ltd.	2.52 (Ser A)	RRSP
		■	20/20 Canadian Growth Fund	2.57	RRSP
	Small-cap	★	**AGF Growth Equity Fund Ltd.**	2.43 (Ser A)	RRSP
		■	20/20 RSP Aggressive Equity Fund	2.51	RRSP
		▲	**20/20 RSP Aggressive Smaller Companies**	2.25+	RRSP
	Resource	★	**AGF Canadian Resources Fund Ltd.**	2.64 (Ser A)	RRSP
	Other	★	**20/20 Managed Futures Value Fund**	3.00+	RRSP
Tax-advantaged:	Dividend	★	**20/20 Dividend Fund**	1.98	RRSP
Multi-asset:	Balanced	■	AGF Growth & Income Fund Ltd.	1.35-2.00	RRSP
	Asset Allocation	■	AGF Asset Allocation Service		RRSP
		■	AGF U.S. Asset Allocation Service		Foreign
		■	20/20 Canadian Asset Allocation Fund	2.50	RRSP

FOREIGN	Category	Rating	Fund Name	M.E.R.%	RRSP/Foreign
Money Market:		■	AGF U.S. Dollar Money Market Account	0.64 (Ser A)	Foreign
		■	AGF U.S. Income Fund	2.01-2.54	Foreign
Fixed-Income:		■	AGF Strategic Income Fund	1.91-2.48	RRSP
		▲	**AGF Global Government Bond Fund**	1.35-1.85	Foreign
		■	20/20 World Bond Fund	1.99	Foreign
		■	20/20 Foreign RSP Bond Fund	2.02	RRSP
		■	20/20 U.S. Short-term High Yield Fund	2.49	Foreign
Global Equity:	All-global	■	AGF World Equity Fund	2.50+	Foreign
		★	**20/20 International Value Fund**	2.89	Foreign
		■	20/20 Aggressive Global Stock Fund	2.35+	Foreign
Regional Equity:	US Large-cap	■	AGF American Growth Fund	2.36 (Ser A)	Foreign
		■	20/20 Aggressive Growth Fund	2.54	Foreign
	U.S. Small-cap	■	AGF Special Fund	2.42 (Ser A)	Foreign
	Latin American	★	**20/20 Latin America Fund**	3.22	Foreign
	Emerging Market	■	20/20 MultiManager Markets Fund	3.50	Foreign
	Far East	★	**AGF Asian Growth Fund**	2.47 (Ser A)	Foreign
		■	20/20 Asia Pacific Fund	2.67	Foreign
	Japan	▲	**AGF Japan Fund**	2.59 (Ser A)	Foreign
	Europe	▲	**AGF European Growth Fund**	2.65-3.2	Foreign
	Other	▲	**AGF China Focus Fund**	2.65-3.2	Foreign
		▲	**AGF Germany Fund**	2.50+	Foreign
		■	20/20 India Fund	3.49	Foreign
Global Balanced:		■	20/20 World Fund	2.60	Foreign
		■	20/20 RSP Int'l. Equity Allocation	2.52	RRSP
		★	**20/20 Amer. Tactical Asset Allocation**	2.64	Foreign
		■	20/20 European Asset Allocation Fund	2.62	Foreign

Late in 1995, one of Canada's senior fund companies, AGF Management Ltd., stunned the industry by acquiring 20/20 Funds Inc. for $100 million in cash and stock. To many, it seemed a model marriage, combining the pedigree of the Goldring family with the aggressive innovations of 20/20 co-founder John Wood. At a single stroke, AGF was catapulted into the No. 5 position in industry assets, arguably where it should be after some 40 years in the business.

But by April '96 the honeymoon was over. Majority shareholder Warren Goldring fired Wood and three other senior 20/20 executives, resulting in *The Financial Post* headline, "Has AGF lost its 20/20 vision?"

Then, in August, AGF's attempt to turn around its disappointing AGF Canadian Equity Fund with new appointee Veronika Hirsch backfired when she jumped ship to Fidelity. Still, AGF has always been strong on the domestic bond front – fixed-income specialists Warren Goldring and Clive Coombs are among the best in the business.

AGF has never been a slouch in international equities, either. Goldring believes successful fund products depend on strong markets. Thus, AGF was participating in the American market (AGF is the acronym for American Growth Fund) when the most exciting high-tech developments consisted of colour television, new wonder drugs and jet airplanes. It has also been strong in Asia overall, as well as in individual countries such as Japan and China.

The fund matrix is somewhat overwhelming, but only because it reflects the offerings of two companies. (We have simplified it by not listing all of the load versions of each fund or the U.S. dollar versions.) The company plans to combine and streamline its fund offerings as well as make changes in fund management. The new lineup is due to be released in November 1996, with full transferability between all funds available in January '97.

For international equity investors with taxable (non-RRSP) portfolios, AGF, like C.I. and G.T. Global, is an especially attractive fund family. With the addition of the Germany Fund, there are now nine funds in the AGF International Group. Investors can switch between these funds without triggering a capital disposition, which also maximizes foreign content capacity in an RRSP or RRIF, because the book value of the investment doesn't increase unless you leave the group. Also available is the new all-global World Equity Fund.

The 20/20 subadvisory relationships greatly strengthened AGF's hand. Now AGF has an all-India fund (which suffered the dubious distinction of being among the worst performers of all funds in 1995), a commodity futures fund and two excellent fund managers, with distinctly different styles, in Charles Brandes and Richard Driehaus. Brandes is a classic value investor while Driehaus is a momentum investor, a style aptly summarized in the name of the fund he manages – 20/20 Aggressive Growth Fund.

Asset allocation is a strong suit of both AGF and 20/20. The latter has always emphasized regional tactical asset allocation funds; AGF pioneered an asset allocation service that selects from its domestic equity, bond and money market funds. The service's performance was in the first quartile on average for the five years to May 31, 1996, although it was third quartile for the last three years. The more recent MAP personal computer-based asset allocation program is a questionnaire-based asset allocation service that uses modern portfolio theory to maximize return and minimize risk, using all the AGF funds.

Most AGF funds tend to be managed in-house, while the 20/20 Funds are not. 20/20 trademarked the term MultiManager to describe its approach of contracting with external money managers around the world to manage its funds. This increases management expense ratios but also makes it easier to fire underperforming managers. 20/20 saw its role as "managing the managers." It did so early in 1996 when it replaced WorldInvest Ltd. with STI Capital Management and Durkee Capital Advisors as the managers of the

20/20 World Fund, a global asset allocation fund that lost money over the two years ended May 31, 1996.

The combination of AGF and 20/20 has created one of the strongest fund families in Canada. Once the streamlined fund lineup is unveiled, the only remaining administrative detail will be inclusion of the 20/20 international funds under the AGF International Group umbrella.

Smart Funds:

20/20 American Tactical Asset Allocation, 20/20 Dividend, 20/20 International Value, 20/20 Latin America, 20/20 Managed Futures Value, AGF Asian Growth, AGF Canadian Bond, AGF Canadian Resources, AGF Growth Equity.

Noteworthy Funds:

AGF China Focus. The two-year-old China Focus is a promising fund for investors willing to overlook short-term volatility for long-term gain. The fund is not quite as country-specific as it first appears. Rather, it invests around the world in companies that stand to benefit from the explosive economic growth China is expected to generate over the next two decades (its economy grew 11% a year in 1994 and 1995, compared with just 3% in the U.S). The fund fell back 8.5% in 1995, which means it's not too late to get in on the ground floor of the China play.

AGF European Growth. This was a first-quartile performer for the two years to May 31, 1996. Manager John Arnold, of AGF's Dublin arm, uses a value-oriented investment strategy, moving across the continent between large- and small-caps depending on the values he finds.

AGF Germany. Formerly a closed-end fund, this is the only pure Germany play available in Canada. But it has been third and fourth quartile relative to other global funds and there are better growth stories in other regions in the world. Managed by Deutsche Asset Management.

20/20 Aggressive Smaller Companies Fund. This is a small-cap version of the similarly run 20/20 RSP Aggressive Equity Fund, which was closed to new investors March 1, 1996. It appears to be off to a good start, investing in companies with a market capitalization between $200 million and $1.5 billion. It, too, will eventually be capped, 20/20 says. The fund is managed in Richard Driehaus's classic momentum style.

AGF Japan. The oldest Japan fund in Canada (inception: January '69), this fund is one of the best that focuses solely on Japan.

Nomura Investment Management of Tokyo, one of the region's biggest securities dealers, advises the fund managers.

AGF Global Government Bond. A Smart Fund last year, this fund has performed well but does not qualify for another year in that select group. The bond management team of Warren Goldring and Clive Coombs is one of the best on the street, so this fund should provide good returns.

Availability:

Only through brokers and dealers.

3. AIC LIMITED   LOAD

Strengths:	Investing in the wealth industry
	Warren Buffet style equity investing
Weaknesses:	Lacks mainstream funds like fixed income
	Sales & Marketing
E-mail:	aic@moonstar.ca	**Toll Free:** 1-800-263-2144

CANADIAN	Category	Rating	Fund Name	M.E.R.%	RRSP/Foreign
Money Market:		■	AIC Money Market Fund	1.00	RRSP
Equity:	Mid- to Large-cap	★	AIC Advantage Fund	2.55	RRSP
		★	AIC Diversified Canada Fund	2.70	RRSP

FOREIGN	Category	Rating	Fund Name	M.E.R.%	RRSP/Foreign
Global Equity:	All-global	■	AIC World Equity Fund	2.75	Foreign
Regional Equity:	US	▲	AIC Value Fund	2.65	Foreign
	Emerging Market	■	AIC Emerging Markets Fund	2.75	Foreign

Based in Hamilton, Ont., AIC Ltd. could be called the "little boutique" that grew. The firm is the brainchild of Michael Lee-Chin, who realized years ago that investing in the mutual fund industry or, more broadly, the "wealth management" industry, might be a better bet than the general economy. Based on the performance of the AIC Advantage Fund, he was right on the money. AIC Advantage is the Canadian version; there are also U.S. and world versions that combine wealth management companies with high-tech picks. The key manager on these funds is Jonathan Wellum, who was profiled in the 1995 edition of this book, and was declared Fund

Manager of the Year in 1995 by the trade newspaper Investment Executive.

AIC is an equity shop, offering no fixed-income or balanced funds, and only one money market fund to placate the market timers in its customer base. Lee-Chin, Wellum and the other managers are unabashed followers of the Warren Buffett school of investment: Buy good companies for the long term and hold them. Berkshire Hathaway, Buffett's famous holding company, features prominently in the funds' portfolios and an AIC team has been attending the company's annual meetings in Omaha for years.

With just six funds in the family, AIC is not suitable as a core fund family for most investors, but one or more AIC funds could add some oomph to the performance of other North American equity holdings.

Smart Funds:

AIC Advantage, AIC Diversified Canada.

Noteworthy Funds:

AIC Value. This U.S. version of the Advantage Fund has also been in the top quartile for most of the last five years. In addition to wealth management firms, it invests in consumer product and telecommunication companies. The management expense ratio is 2.65%. Overall, it's a good fund but there are better choices for RRSP foreign content.

Availability:

Only through brokers and dealers.

4. ALTAMIRA INVESTMENT SERVICES INC.   NO-LOAD

Strengths:	Canadian equities				
	Service & unitholder education				
Weaknesses:	Dependence on Frank Mersch				
	Increasing size of more popular funds				
Web Site:	Altamira.com		**Toll Free:**	1-800-263-2824	

CANADIAN	Category	Rating	Fund Name	M.E.R.%	RRSP/Foreign
Fixed Income:	Long-term	■	Altamira Bond Fund	1.31	RRSP
	Medium-term	★	**Altamira Income Fund**	1.00	RRSP

		Rating	Fund Name	M.E.R.%	RRSP/Foreign
Equity:	Short-term	■	Altamira Short Term Gov't. Bond Fund	1.33	RRSP
	Mid- to Large-cap	▲	**Altamira Capital Growth Fund Limited**	2.02	RRSP
		★	**Altamira Equity Fund**	2.31	RRSP
	Small-cap	■	Altamira Special Growth Fund	1.82	RRSP
	Gold/Precious Metal	▲	**Altamira Precious & Strategic Metal Fund**	2.32	RRSP
	Resource	■	Altamira Resource Fund	2.31	RRSP
		▲	**AltaFund Investment Corp.**	2.38	RRSP
Tax-advantaged:	Dividend	▲	**Altamira Dividend Fund Inc.**	1.64	RRSP
	Labour-sponsored	■	Triax Growth Fund		RRSP
Multi-asset:	Balanced	■	Altamira Balanced Fund	2.00	RRSP
		★	**Altamira Growth & Income Fund**	1.41	RRSP

FOREIGN	Category	Rating	Fund Name	M.E.R.%	RRSP/Foreign
Fixed-Income:		■	Altamira Short Term Global Income Fund	1.22	RRSP
		■	Altamira Global Bond Fund	1.83	RRSP
		■	Altamira Speculative High Yield Bond Fund	2.10	Foreign
Global Equity:	Specialty	▲	**Altamira Science & Technology Fund**	2.37	Foreign
Regional Equity:	US Large-cap	★	**Altamira U.S. Larger Company Fund**	2.36	Foreign
	US Small-Med	▲	**Altamira Select American Fund**	2.32	Foreign
	NAFTA/NA	■	Altamira North American Recovery Fund	2.31	RRSP
	Emerging Market	■	Altamira Global Discovery Fund	3.13	Foreign
	Far East	■	Altamira Asia Pacific Fund	2.38	Foreign
	Japan	▲	**Altamira Japanese Opportunity Fund**	2.38	Foreign
	Europe	■	Altamira European Equity Fund	2.41	Foreign
Global Balanced:		■	Altamira Global Diversified Fund	2.00	Foreign

Altamira is the company brokers love to hate, since it combines several excellent funds with no-load status – meaning it pays no or minimal fees to brokers. But more than a quarter million unit holders are very happy with Altamira, which is a first-class act no matter how you cut it.

The performance of Frank Mersch's equity funds is still the dominant attraction, but there's plenty more. Ian Ainsworth has done a fine job with the U.S. Larger Companies Fund and, so far, with the new Science & Technology Fund. Will Sutherland (see profile in Chapter 2) is one of Canada's top bond fund managers. Sue Coleman is making a comeback in small caps after a disappointing 1994 and 1995 and has gained a new profile as the manager of the Triax labour-sponsored fund.

Altamira's commitment to education is second to none – as evidenced by its unitholder communications, extensive seminar program, its pivotal role in the No-Load Fund Association, and its pioneering web site on the Internet, since copied by most of the major companies in the Canadian fund industry.

Even in the area of corporate philanthropy, Altamira has made its mark with president Philip Armstrong's support of 1995's summer "no-load opera" concert at Toronto's Harbourfront, repeated in 1996.

Both in its unitholder communications and seminars, Altamira emphasizes portfolio creation. It stresses proper diversification by asset type, economy, large and small market capitalization, sector and, in the case of bonds, maturity. Frequent switching is discouraged, even if no-load investors are more inclined to indulge in it than load investors who face redemption fees. Because Altamira counsels buying and holding funds for the long haul, it limits switches to ten a year, even if clients take their business elsewhere as a result.

For investors whose Altamira portfolios have blossomed to $500,000 or more, Altamira's private client services department offers more personalized service, although the funds and fees are the same.

Altamira's management expense ratios are reasonable: lower than many load fund rivals, but higher than Elliott & Page, Trimark and no-load competitors such as Sceptre, Scudder, and Phillips, Hager & North.

Excellent funds, no commissions and ongoing investor education – sounds good. But there are a couple of caveats. Although there is a wide choice of funds, some are only average performers: the Global Diversified fund has long been sub-par (in the fourth quartile for ten years), while Peter Everington's Asia Pacific Fund suffered from his bet against Hong Kong in 1995. For RRSP or RRIF investing, you can beat the 20% foreign content on the fixed-income side with the short-term global income fund and the global bond fund, but the family offers no 100% RRSP-eligible equity or balanced funds, which leaves RRSP investors with a high degree of reliance on the Canadian equity market for growth. This won't be of concern to high-net-worth investors with ample assets outside an RRSP, however.

The risk with an all-Altamira portfolio lies in how long Mersch and other key managers stay with the team. It's common knowledge among industry insiders that Altamira has been looking for a buyer, perhaps a bank (TD Bank was said to be close to a deal, but the parties walked away from the altar in June 1996) or a foreign group wishing to acquire Altamira's goodwill and unit holders. Many of the founder/managers are well off and could easily leave, should they choose to escape the stress of the investment industry. Manager Normand Lamarche has already left, after a one-year "sabbatical." Eventually, Altamira may also go public, giving its founding team the chance to cash out of the dynasty.

All in all, though, if you're serious about no-load investing, Altamira is the standard by which all others are judged.

Smart Funds:

Altamira Equity, Altamira Growth & Income, Altamira Income, Altamira U.S. Larger Company.

Noteworthy Funds:

New Altamira Value. This is actually a closed-end fund, which is bought and sold like a stock. Managed by Frank Mersch, it's small (about $120 million), so it provides him with trading opportunities not readily available to the large Altamira Equity fund. The fund is aggressive and not suitable for everyone.

Altafund Investment Corp. This fund, managed by David Taylor, is heavy on western Canadian resource stocks and its performance has been first quartile for most of the past five years.

Altamira Capital Growth. A 1996 Smart Fund, this core equity fund is still first quartile over ten and five years, though it has slipped recently. Manager Ian Joseph took over from Frank Mersch, with Ian Ainsworth providing up to 20% in foreign, mostly U.S., equities.

Altamira Precious & Strategic Metals. This new gold and precious metals specialty fund is managed by Frank Mersch; it was first quartile for the year to May 31, 1996.

Altamira Science & Technology. This new high-tech fund run by Ian Ainsworth is mostly invested in U.S. computer hardware, software and communications firms, but also life sciences and biotechnology, and it's big on Internet issues. It's a good fund, but Green Line's is the bellwether in this sector.

Altamira Select American. A small- to medium-cap U.S. equity fund, it was first quartile over the three years to May 31, 1996, although it's been in the second quartile more recently. It's been coming on strong in early 1996, though, as small caps came back into vogue in the U.S. It's managed by Wellington Asset Management.

Altamira Japanese Opportunity Fund. Managed by Regent Management of Hong Kong, this fund enjoyed a spectacular year relative to other Japanese funds, due to Regent's currency hedging strategy. Altamira policy limits hedging to a maximum 50%.

Altamira Dividend Fund Inc. A Smart Fund last year, this remains a high-quality dividend fund most suitable for non-registered accounts or for those seeking a conservative equity fund.

Availability:

Directly from Altamira or from some brokers and dealers on request.

5. ATLAS ASSET MANAGEMENT INC. NO-LOAD

Strengths: Style diversification (value and growth)
Access to many external advisors
Weaknesses: Complexity of fund types
Limited availability
Web Site: none   **Toll Free:** 1-800-463-2857 (ATLS)

CANADIAN	Category	Rating	Fund Name	M.E.R.%	RRSP/Foreign
Money Market:		■	Atlas Canadian Money Market Fund	1.12	RRSP
		■	Atlas Canadian T-Bill Fund	1.28	RRSP
Fixed Income:	Long-term	■	Atlas Canadian Bond Fund	2.10	RRSP
	Short- to Med-term	★	**Atlas Canadian High Yield Bond Fund**	1.93	RRSP
Equity:	Mid- to Large-cap	▲	**Atlas Canadian Large Cap Growth Fund**	2.56	RRSP
		■	Atlas Canadian Large Cap Value Fund	2.72	RRSP
	Small-cap	▲	**Atlas Canadian Emerging Growth Fund**	2.47	RRSP
		■	Atlas Canadian Emerging Value Fund	2.72	RRSP
	Other	▲	**Atlas Managed Futures Fund**	12.23	RRSP
Multi-asset:	Balanced	■	Atlas Canadian Diversified Fund	2.32	RRSP
		■	Atlas Canadian Balanced Fund	2.31	RRSP
	Asset Allocation	■	Hercules Global Allocation Service		

FOREIGN	Category	Rating	Fund Name	M.E.R.%	RRSP/Foreign
Money Market:		■	Atlas American Money Market Fund	1.18	Foreign
Fixed-Income:		★	**Hercules World Bond Fund**	2.10	RRSP
		▲	**Hercules Global Short-Term Fund**	1.50	RRSP
		■	Hercules Emerging Markets Debt Fund	2.12	Foreign
Global Equity:	All-global	■	Atlas Global Equity Fund	2.73	Foreign
Regional Equity:	US	■	Atlas American Emerging Value Fund	2.69	Foreign
		■	Atlas American Large Cap Growth Fund	2.68	Foreign
		■	Atlas American Large Cap Value Fund	2.68	Foreign
	NAFTA/NA	■	Atlas NAFTA Value Fund	2.73	Foreign
	Latin American	▲	**Hercules Latin American Value Fund**		
	Far East	■	Hercules Pacific Basin Value Fund	2.83	Foreign
	Europe	■	Hercules European Value Fund	2.80	Foreign
Global Balanced:		★	**Atlas American Advantage Fund**	2.67	Foreign

The Atlas Group's 25 funds bring a style-based approach to a competitive market, with both value and growth versions in many fund categories and, in some cases, small- and large-cap versions too. But there is such a thing as too much choice. Most people would require the advice of a financial planner to construct a workable portfolio from this complex family.

The Atlas and Hercules funds were created in 1994, when Atlas Asset Management Inc., formerly Finsco Investment Management Corp., became a subsidiary of brokerage firm Midland Walwyn Capital Inc. Originally, the Atlas funds focused on North America, while Hercules covered Latin America and the rest of the world. To minimize confusion, both families are now under the Atlas Capital umbrella. Eight of the funds were renamed in late 1995.

New president Sue Dabarno (formerly of Canada Trust), is transforming the Atlas group into hybrid no-load/low-load funds available through an increasing number of dealers. New in 1996, the low-load option declines from 3% the first two years to 2% the third year, and zero thereafter. Six free switches a year are permitted, with a fee of $50 a switch thereafter.

The Atlas funds work well with Midland Walwyn asset allocation services. Investors who mix Atlas funds with other load families can use Midland's COMPASS asset allocation service, or, with an all-Atlas portfolio, an asset allocation service run by Morgan Stanley.

Investors could choose Atlas as either a Canadian or American core family, or both, and supplement it with funds or families with strength outside North America, such as Templeton. The Hercules family nicely complements any North American-focused fund families, such as Trimark, or even the Atlas funds.

The funds are managed externally by a variety of advisers around the world. Most of the Atlas Canadian Funds are former Finsco funds, and have established track records. Subadvisers on the domestic funds include T.A.L. Investment Counsel Ltd., Bissett Associates of Calgary and Deans, Knight Capital Management Ltd. of Vancouver. U.S.-based advisers include Salomon Brothers Asset Management Ltd. and Fisher Investments Inc. Global managers include Bankers Trust Co. and Edinburgh Fund Managers.

Investors who want an all-global fund can choose Atlas Global Equity, managed by IAI International Ltd. Those who like to pick regions can do so through Hercules funds focused on Europe, the Pacific Basin and Latin America. All are value funds. There is also a 100% RRSP-eligible global short-term debt fund and a 20% RRSP-eligible emerging market debt fund.

Smart Funds:

Atlas American Advantage, Atlas Canadian High Yield Bond, Atlas Hercules World Bond.

Noteworthy Funds:

Atlas Canadian Emerging Growth. A Smart Fund in 1996, this is managed by Wayne Deans of Deans, Knight, who also manages the Marathon Equity Fund, the O'Donnell Canadian Emerging Growth and the Navigator Value Investment Retirement Fund (poorly named in our opinion). This would have been a Smart fund again but the manager intends to cap the portfolio at $125 million, and it was already at $105 million at the time of writing.

Atlas Managed Futures. This is one of only two managed futures funds available in Canada, a new type of mutual fund, based on derivatives, that is not highly correlated with stocks and bonds and thus can diversify a portfolio. This was a Smart Fund in 1996 but has underperformed the 20/20 Managed Futures Value Fund since.

Atlas Canadian Large Cap Growth. Run by Calgary's Bissett, whose Canadian equity fund is a Smart Fund this year. Note that the latter is available from Bissett with a lower management fee.

Hercules Global Short-Term Fund. This is managed by Salomon Brothers, acknowledged global leaders in international fixed income.

Hercules Latin American Value. The Mexican peso crisis left this fund with a 42% loss in its debut year ended March 31, 1995. Managed by Bankers Trust, who have a big presence in Latin America, this fund has rebounded recently.

Availability:

Primarily through Midland Walwyn Inc., Financial Concepts Group, and some others.

6. BEUTEL GOODMAN MANAGED FUNDS INC. LOAD OR NO-LOAD

Strengths: Pension fund origins and orientation
American equities
Weaknesses: Limited global fund line-up
Web Site: none　　　　　　　Toll Free: 1-800-461-4551

CANADIAN	Category	Rating	Fund Name	M.E.R.%	RRSP/Foreign
Money Market:		■	Beutel Goodman Money Market Fund	0.59	RRSP
Fixed Income:	Mixed-term	▲	**Beutel Goodman Income Fund**	1.32	RRSP
Equity:	Mid- to Large-cap	■	Beutel Goodman Canadian Equity Fund	2.26	RRSP
	Small-cap	■	Beutel Goodman Small Cap Fund	2.50	RRSP
Multi-asset:	Balanced	■	Beutel Goodman Balanced Fund	2.20	RRSP

FOREIGN	Category	Rating	Fund Name	M.E.R.%	RRSP/Foreign
Global Equity:	EAFE	▲	**Beutel Goodman Int'l. Equity Fund**	2.60	Foreign
Regional Equity:	US	▲	**Beutel Goodman American Equity Fund**	2.70	Foreign

For Beutel Goodman, mutual funds are almost a sideline. The seven funds it offers to retail investors account for just $90 million of the $10 billion in assets run by this huge pension fund manager with nearly 30 years in the business. Most of the funds share the managers and philosophy of the much larger segregated pension portfolios.

As subsidiary Beutel Goodman Managed Funds Inc. was formed in 1990 to offer retail mutual funds, several now have five-year performance records. The best are second quartile over that period, as noted below. The funds are sold with a front load up to 4% or with no load if bought direct. A sliding scale reduces management fees as unitholder assets rise; most of the equity funds start at 2%.

Noteworthy Funds:

Beutel Goodman American Equity. One of the more promising funds in the family, it's been second quartile over the five years to May 31, 1996, with an average compound annual growth rate of 15.2% over that period. The small, $4-million fund is managed from Toronto and uses research from Houston-based Beutel Goodman Capital Management.

Beutel Goodman Income. This bond fund also has second-quartile status in the five years to May 31. Volatility has been slightly higher than average but so has performance. An MER of 1.32% is also attractive.

Beutel Goodman International Equity. This newer EAFE (Europe, Australia and the Far East) fund appears to be back on track after a couple of rough years in 1994-95. The portfolio is evenly split between Europe and the Far East, with a dash of Latin America.

Availability:

Through selected brokers and dealers, or direct.

7. BISSETT & ASSOCIATES   NO-LOAD

Strengths:	Low MERs, No-Load
	Small-cap equities
Weaknesses:	Limited availability
Web Site:	none **Phone:** (403) 266-4664

CANADIAN	Category	Rating	Fund Name	M.E.R.%	RRSP/Foreign
Money Market:		■	Bissett Money Market Fund	0.50	RRSP

Fixed Income:	Mixed-term	■	Bissett Bond Fund	0.75	RRSP
Equity:	Mid- to Large-cap	★	Bissett Canadian Equity Fund	1.35	RRSP
	Small-cap	▲	Bissett Small Cap Fund	2.00	RRSP
Tax-advantaged:	Dividend	★	Bissett Dividend Income Fund	1.50	Not RRSP eligible
Multi-asset: Portfolio of Funds		▲	Bissett Retirement Fund	0.85	

FOREIGN	Category	Rating	Fund Name	M.E.R.%	RRSP/Foreign
Global Equity:	All-global	▲	**Bissett Multinational Growth Fund**	1.50	Foreign
	EAFE	■	Bissett International Equity Fund	1.50	Not RRSP eligible
Regional Equity:	US	■	Bissett American Equity Fund	1.50	Foreign

One of Alberta's largest pension and private investment managers expanded into the Ontario market in 1996. While few investors are familiar with Bissett & Associates Investment Management Ltd., its combination of low management expense ratios, no-load status and several top-quartile funds make it a compelling alternative to many better-known fund groups.

Calgary-based Bissett manages more than $750 million for institutional pension plans and wealthy individuals. It also advises several other funds managed by others, including Atlas Canadian Growth and Canada Trust Everest Special Growth.

Over the past two years, assets of Bissett mutual funds have increased substantially, and the push into eastern Canada should accelerate that trend. The company rarely advertises – although David Bissett is frequently quoted in the business press. As a result, minimal marketing expenditures translate into very reasonable management fees: 1% for most of the equity funds (1.5% for the small cap and 2% for the international equity fund), 0.75% for the bond fund and just 0.5% for the money market fund. There are no switching fees.

Bissett's emphasis is on North American equities. Its Canadian content tends to centre on western Canada and, to some extent, the oil sector, which makes the group attractive for investors wishing to "Quebec-proof" their portfolios. Bissett has an EAFE fund, the Bissett International Equity Fund, which is advised by Jardine Fleming Investment Management of Hong Kong.

This company did not go unnoticed last year, but its limited availability made it difficult to recommend.

Smart Funds:

Bissett Canadian Equity, Bissett Dividend Income.

Noteworthy Funds:

Bissett Retirement Fund. Top quartile for the three years to May 31, 1996, as well as most of the more recent periods, this is a balanced fund or "fund of funds" that invests in other Bissett funds. The management fee is low, at 0.85% a year.

Bissett Multinational Growth Fund. This new fund was first quartile to May 31, 1996. It invests primarily in U.S.-based global multinationals, but fully a third of the portfolio is non-U.S. companies. The management fee of 1% is one of the lowest of all global equity funds. All stocks in the fund pay consistently increasing dividends, which smoothes out volatility.

Bissett Small Cap Fund. Consistently second quartile over three years, this fund invests in small- and medium-cap companies throughout North America, but with an emphasis on western Canada. This area is David Bissett's forte and his risk-adjusted performance is very competitive with others in this asset class.

Availability:

Direct from the company for investors in Alberta, British Columbia and Ontario. The firm is investigating third-party distribution channels.

8. BANK OF MONTREAL FIRST CDN. FUNDS   NO-LOAD

Strengths:	Declining fees for large volume of assets
	MatchMaker asset allocation service
Weaknesses:	Lack of 100% RRSP eligible global funds
	Some equity fund performance
Web Site:	www.fcfunds.bomil.ca **Toll Free:** 1-800-665-7700

CANADIAN	Category	Rating	Fund Name	M.E.R.%	RRSP/Foreign
Money Market:		■	First Canadian Money Market Fund	1.10	RRSP
		■	First Canadian T-Bill Fund	1.11	RRSP
Fixed Income:	Long-term	■	First Canadian Bond Fund	1.51	RRSP
	Mortgage	★	**First Canadian Mortgage Fund**	1.18	RRSP
Equity:	Mid- to Large-cap	■	First Canadian Growth Fund	2.27	RRSP
	Small-cap	■	First Canadian Special Growth Fund	2.28	RRSP
	Index	▲	**First Canadian Equity Index Fund**	1.57	RRSP
	Resource	▲	**First Canadian Resource Fund**	2.28	RRSP
Tax-advantaged:	Dividend	■	First Canadian Dividend Income Fund	1.85	RRSP
Multi-asset:	Asset Allocation	■	First Canadian Asset Allocation	1.98	RRSP

FOREIGN	Category	Rating	Fund Name	M.E.R.%	RRSP/Foreign
Fixed Income:		★	**First Canadian International Bond Fund**	1.96	Foreign
Global Equity:	EAFE	▲	**First Canadian International Growth Fund**	1.95	Foreign
Regional Equity:	US	■	First Canadian U.S. Growth Fund	2.23	Foreign
	NAFTA/NA	■	First Canadian NAFTA Advantage Fund	2.15	Foreign
	Emerging Market	■	First Canadian Emerging Markets Fund	2.07	Foreign
	Far East	▲	**First Canadian Far East Growth Fund**	2.03	Foreign
	Japan	■	First Canadian Japanese Growth Fund	2.01	Foreign
	Europe	■	First Canadian European Growth Fund	2.08	Foreign

Like most of its bank competitors, Bank of Montreal's First Canadian Funds made considerable strides this past year, particularly on the sales front. The biggest announcement, early in 1996, was the launch of the MatchMaker strategic asset allocation service, derived from the successful STAR service of Mackenzie Financial Corp. (See profile of Gordon Garmaise, Chapter 2).

Investment research shows that asset mix accounts for more than 90% of the variance in an investor's returns. MatchMaker uses a questionnaire to match investor objectives and risk tolerances to one of twelve "optimized" portfolios consisting of various combinations of First Canadian funds. (Despite its name, The First Canadian Asset Allocation Fund, which is not managed with an optimization strategy, has been a below-average performer since inception.)

Other First Canadian funds have provided mixed returns. Among its domestic products managed in-house, First Canadian's greatest strength is in fixed-income funds: Canadian Bond Rating Service rates the First Canadian T-Bill, Money Market and Mortgage funds AAA, or superior quality.

The large-cap Canadian equity fund, First Canadian Growth, has almost matched the Equity Index fund. Investors might ask whether the 2.27% MER of the managed fund adds much value, compared with the index fund's MER of just 1.57%.

The special Canadian equity funds seem to have justified their management fees, however. The small- to medium-cap Special Growth Fund and the Resource Fund have been above-average performers.

The bank is starting to take some positive steps on the investment management front. Its domestic funds are managed internally, while its global funds use Dunedin Fund Managers (recently acquired by Edinburgh Fund Managers) and Chicago's Harris Investment Management Inc. In February, Bank of Montreal Investment Counsel (BOMIC) merged with Jones Heward

Investment Counsel Inc. (to be known as Jones Heward Investment Management), thus combining BOMIC's strength in fixed income with Jones Heward's expertise in Canadian equities.

Internationally, the relationship with Harris Investment Management that began with the innovative NAFTA Advantage Fund was extended to include the First Canadian U.S. Growth Fund. It is now managed by Donald Coxe, known to many Canadian investors through his regular newspaper column. He has his work cut out for him: under BOMIC, U.S. Growth was a fourth-quartile fund, returning just 5.7% in the year ended May 31, 1996 and 8.5% compounded over two years. NAFTA Advantage returned 21.7% in its debut year, with co-management by Harris, Bancomer S.A. and Jones Heward's Rick Betts (a former manager on the 20/20 Canadian Growth fund).

One big advantage for high-net-worth investors is the declining management fee schedule, which starts to kick in at $50,000 invested in a fund. U.S. Growth's 2% management fee, for instance, falls to 1.6%, then 1.4%, 1.2%, 1.1% and finally, 1.0% on amounts greater than $1 million.

Smart Funds:

First Canadian International Bond, First Canadian Mortgage.

Noteworthy Funds:

First Canadian Equity Index. One of few Canadian equity index funds, it has been in the second quartile most of the last three years, and third quartile over five years. The M.E.R. is 1.52%.

First Canadian Resource. New in 1993, this resource fund has been consistently in the second quartile.

First Canadian Far East Growth. Launched in August 1994, this Asian (excluding Japan) equity fund has been a top-quartile performer since inception. Managed by Edinburgh Fund Managers, its M.E.R. of 2.07% is lower than many rival Asian funds.

First Canadian International Growth. One of the few no-load, non-North American funds, it has a strict Europe, Australia and Far East mandate and therefore carries a heavy weighting in Japan (at time of writing it was 45.3% of the portfolio).

Availability:

Bank of Montreal branches, Nesbitt Burns and Investorline Discount Brokerage Service.

9. BPI CAPITAL MANAGEMENT CORP.   LOAD

Strengths: Small-cap equities
Many 100% RRSP eligible global funds
Weaknesses: Load structure tends to be high
MERs high but coming down
Web Site: BPIFUNDS.COM   **Toll Free:** 1-800-263-2427

CANADIAN	Category	Rating	Fund Name	M.E.R.%	RRSP/Foreign
Money Market:		■	BPI T-Bill Fund	0.65	RRSP
Fixed Income:	Long-term	■	BPI Canadian Bond Fund	1.54	RRSP
Equity:	Mid- to Large-cap	■	BPI Canadian Equity Value Fund	2.74	RRSP
	Small-cap	★	**BPI Canadian Small Companies Fund**	2.38	RRSP
	Resource	▲	**BPI Canadian Resource Fund Inc.**	2.60	RRSP
	Other	▲	**BPI Canadian Opportunities RSP Fund**	2.50	RRSP
Tax-advantaged:	Dividend	★	**BPI Income Fund**	1.23	RRSP
Multi-asset:	Balanced	■	BPI Canadian Balanced Fund	2.75	RRSP

FOREIGN	Category	Rating	Fund Name	M.E.R.%	RRSP/Foreign
Fixed Income:		■	BPI Global RSP Bond Fund	1.70	RRSP
Global Equity:	All-global	■	BPI International Equity Fund	2.72	Foreign
		■	BPI Global Equity Fund	2.78	Foreign
	Small-cap	★	**BPI Global Small Companies Fund**	2.52	Foreign
	Specialty	■	BPI Global Opportunites Fund	2.50	Foreign
Regional Equity:	US	▲	**BPI American Equity Value Fund**	2.67	Foreign
	US Small-cap	★	**BPI American Small Companies Fund**	2.93	Foreign
	Emerging Market	■	BPI Emerging Markets Fund*	2.49	Foreign
Global Balanced:		■	BPI North American Balanced RSP Fund	2.91	RRSP
		■	BPI Global Balanced RSP Fund	2.53	RRSP

* formerly BPI Global Real Estate Securities

BPI made headlines in 1994 when it became the minnow that swallowed the whale, by acquiring Bolton Tremblay Funds Inc., a company then five times larger than itself. But one year later, the executive who engineered that gutsy deal, BPI's visionary but youthful founder, Mark Bonham, was ousted and replaced by fellow cofounder Jim McGovern.

The sales- and marketing-oriented McGovern has taken several steps to address some of the major criticisms against BPI, including its high management expense ratios. These are being reduced.

BPI's strength is small-cap funds, both in Canada and the United States and, to a lesser extent, globally. The U.S. and global funds are managed by its New York adviser, Lazard Frères Asset Management.

When the company was founded in 1987, it began with

regional equity funds in Europe and the Far East. Over time, it abandoned this top-down approach and fashioned its current bottom-up, value-driven strategy. Thus, unlike many of its rivals in the global fund arena, it no longer offers regional funds. Instead, its products tend to be global or international, similar to the Templeton group's strategy. BPI has three all-global funds: an international equity fund run by Lazard Freres a global small-cap fund and a new emerging markets fund born in May 1996 from the ashes of the BPI Global Real Estate Securities Fund. Also new in 1996 was the BPI U.S. Money Market Fund.

In 1995, BPI targeted high-net-worth investors with new funds run much more aggressively than is usual for mutual funds. First, a hedge fund, BPI Global Opportunities, was launched, followed by the Canadian version, BPI Canadian Opportunities RSP Fund. The fund generated an astounding 222% return in its first year, beating all other funds sold in Canada to July 31, 1996. These two funds are not for the faint of heart or pocketbook. Marketed under sophisticated investors guidelines, they require minimum investments of $150,000 in most provinces. The eye-popping returns are achieved by engaging in such aggressive tactics as leveraging, short selling and arbitrage.

As noted in the company matrix, BPI has struggled in the fixed-income area. The BPI Canadian Bond has been mired in the fourth quartile most of the last five years. (In June '96, BPI announced that fixed-income manager Michael Labinowich had resigned.) While it is possible to construct an all-BPI portfolio of funds, the authors favour picking some of the better performers to round out the portfolios of other fund families.

As BPI drives management fees down, however, more and more of its funds will start to look attractive. In addition, the company offers high-net-worth investors some alternatives not readily available elsewhere.

Smart Funds:

BPI American Small Companies, BPI Canadian Small Companies, BPI Global Small Companies, BPI Income.

Noteworthy Funds:

BPI Canadian Opportunities RSP: First quartile for the first half of 1996, this hedge fund has so far delivered high returns. Run by in-house managers Steven Misener and Frederick Dalley, its M.E.R. is 2.50%. As with most hedge funds, there is a performance bonus, with the managers collecting 20% of any returns exceeding 10%. The similarly run BPI Global Opportunities Fund was also first quartile in the year to May 31, 1996. Lazard Freres' Michael Rome and Joe Ainsberg are the managers. M.E.R. is 2.50%.

BPI Canadian Resource Fund Inc. Managed by Fred Dalley since BPI acquired it from Bolton Tremblay, this has been a good fund in its class. Small-cap manager Steve Misener's suggestions have helped as well.

BPI American Equity Value: Lazard manages this larger-cap fund for the less risk tolerant.

Availability:

Only through brokers and dealers. Note that BPI Capital Opportunities Funds are subject to large minimum investment requirements under regulators' sophisticated investor guidelines, which vary by province.

10. C.I. MUTUAL FUNDS INC. LOAD

Strengths:	John Zechner & Emilio Bassini	
	100% RRSP eligible global funds	
	Sector Funds for global switchers	
Weaknesses:	Latin & Emerging Markets slump	
Web Site:	www.cifunds.com	**Toll Free:** 1-800-268-9374

CANADIAN	Category	Rating	Fund Name	M.E.R.%	RRSP/Foreign
Money Market:		■	C.I. Money Market Fund	0.75	RRSP
Fixed Income:	Long-term	■	C.I. Canadian Bond Fund	1.65	RRSP
Equity:	Mid- to Large-cap	▲	**C.I. Canadian Growth Fund**	2.40	RRSP
Tax-advantaged:					
	Labour-sponsored	■	C.I. Covington Fund	3.93	RRSP
Multi-asset:	Balanced	▲	**C.I. Canadian Balanced Fund**	2.35	RRSP
	Dividend/Bonds	▲	**C.I. Canadian Income Fund**	1.90	RRSP

FOREIGN	Category	Rating	Fund Name	M.E.R.%	RRSP/Foreign
Money Market:		■	C.I. U.S. Money Market Fund	0.50	Foreign
Fixed Income:		▲	**C.I. World Bond Fund**	2.05	Foreign
		▲	**C.I. New World Income Fund**	2.15	Foreign
		▲	**C.I. Global Bond RSP**	2.05	RRSP
Global Equity:	All-global	▲	**C.I. Global Fund**	2.50	Foreign
		▲	**C.I. Global Equity RSP**	2.50	RRSP
Regional Equity:	US	★	**C.I. American Fund**	2.45	Foreign

	■	C.I. American RSP Fund	2.45	RRSP
Latin American	■	C.I. Latin American Fund	2.85	Foreign
Emerging Market	■	C.I. Emerging Markets Fund	2.85	Foreign
Far East/Large-cap	▲	**C.I. Pacific Fund**	2.55	Foreign
Far East/Small-cap	■	C.I. Emerging Asian Fund	2.85	Foreign
Europe	■	C.I. European Fund	2.50	Foreign
Global Balanced:	★	**C.I. International Balanced RSP Fund**	2.50	RRSP

C.I. Mutual Funds (C.I. is an acronym for Canadian International) was early on the global funds bandwagon but concentration on Latin American and emerging markets hurt it in late 1994 and much of 1995. Its previous track record, quality marketing and strong wholesaler support helped minimize redemptions, however.

C.I. continues to plow the field pioneered by Global Strategy: that of 100% RSP-eligible foreign equity funds. Notable among its new products is one that would have been especially timely had it been available early in 1995, when U.S. markets were soaring: a 100% RRSP-eligible U.S. equity fund called the C.I. American RSP Fund, run by BEA Associates' Bill Priest. BEA has one of the most sophisticated derivatives teams in the business, and complemented its already strong money management group with the addition of Bill Sterling, formerly head of international economics at Merrill Lynch and now spearheading C.I.'s global investment strategies. New C.I. funds, introduced August 1996, are five specialty sector funds in telecommunications, health care, resources, financial services and technology. The resource fund is managed by John Zechner, the rest by BEA.

BEA is strong in Latin American and emerging markets, under star manager Emilio Bassini. But since Bassini's funds were heavily weighted to Mexico, they've had a rough ride since the Mexican peso crisis of late 1994. C.I. Latin American Fund was fourth quartile for the two years to May 31, 1996 and has lost money since inception, while C.I. Emerging Markets is third quartile over two and three years. But the bad news doesn't end there. C.I. European has also been a laggard the past three years and the management of this fund has been taken away from TCW and given to Hansberger Global Investors Inc. And, while the flagship C.I. Global Fund still has a solid second-quartile record over ten years, it too has sagged the last three.

C.I. was the first to introduce a fund structure that allows investors to switch between certain of its funds without realizing a capital disposition. (AGF and G.T. Global have followed suit.) Each of these "sector" funds, which represent about 12% of

C.I.'s total asset base, is identical to the non-sector fund of the same name and should be considered by investors looking at the C.I. fund family.

In a positive move from a fund family perspective, C.I. is trying to bring the magic of Sir John Templeton – albeit some steps removed – to its investors. The launching of the "Hansberger Value Series," managed by former Templeton boss Thomas Hansberger, provides investors with an alternate investment style to those practiced by BEA and Zechner. Hansberger, based in Ft. Lauderdale, founded Templeton with Sir John, but left shortly after it was acquired by Franklin Resources, Inc. He has been out of the business due to a non-competition contract he signed on leaving but now, within sight of the Templeton offices, he is rounding out a global management team that will practice the same value style of management that has made the Templeton funds so successful. At the time of writing, the Hansberger series includes only international funds and is not part of the Sector family, but there are plans to introduce a Canadian manager within the Hansberger series and make these funds part of the Sector group. In September, C.I. announced that Jonathan Baird would be running a new value-oriented Canadian equity fund and a new dividend fund.

Smart Funds:

C.I. American, C.I. International Balanced RSP

Noteworthy Funds:

C.I. Canadian Balanced: John Zechner's reputation lies mostly in Canadian equities but he's no slouch in bonds, either. This balanced fund allows him to manage both and the result has been first quartile over the three years to May 31, 1996, but third quartile the past two. Early in the spring of '96 he had 30% in bonds and 34% in cash, a rather cautious stance.

C.I. Canadian Growth/Sector Canadian: A Smart Fund in 1996, John Zechner's flagship Canadian equity vehicle is second quartile over the three years to May 31, 1996. But assets have passed the $1-billion mark and performance has slipped to the second and third quartile more recently. We expect this fund to recover as sales slow and Zechner travels less.

C.I. Canadian Income: Launched October 1994, this is a new hybrid fund that invests mostly in bonds but will put as much as one-third of the portfolio into solid Canadian dividend-paying blue-chip stocks. Also run by Zechner, it's in the first quartile for the year to May 31, 1996.

C.I. Global Bond RSP Fund, C.I. New World Income, C.I. World Bond: The fixed-income and derivative expertise of Greg Diliberto and BEA has made these funds strong contenders in their asset classes. The World Bond Fund has one of the best risk-adjusted returns in its category.

C.I. Global/Sector Global/Global Equity RSP: Look for this fund group to maintain its upward momentum now that Bill Sterling is running the global asset allocation.

C.I. Pacific/Sector Pacific. A Smart Fund in 1996, this fund is one of the longest-running and most successful Asian funds, and still first quartile over ten years. Now a billion-dollar fund, its performance has been second quartile the past five years. More aggressive investors, seeking smaller Asian companies, might investigate Hansberger Asian (formerly C.I. Emerging Asian) as a complement or alternative.

Hansberger Value Series: These funds should eventually look and behave in a very similar way to the funds offered by Templeton.

Availability:

Only through brokers and dealers.

11. CIBC SECURITIES INC.   NO-LOAD

Strengths:	Leadership of Paul Starita
	T.A.L. in-house management
Weaknesses:	CIBC Canadian Equity Fund
Web Site:	www.cibc.com **Toll Free:** 1-800-465-3863

CANADIAN	Category	Rating	Fund Name	M.E.R.%	RRSP/Foreign
Money Market:		■	CIBC Canadian T-Bill Fund	1.20	RRSP
		■	CIBC Premium Canadian T-Bill Fund	0.58	RRSP
		■	CIBC Money Market Fund	1.20	RRSP
Fixed Income:	Long-term	■	CIBC Canadian Bond Fund	1.50	RRSP
	Short-term	▲	**CIBC Canadian Income Fund**	1.35	RRSP
	Mortgage	★	**CIBC Mortgage Investment Fund**	1.60	RRSP
Equity:	Mid- to Large-cap	■	CIBC Canadian Equity Fund	2.05	RRSP
	Small-cap	■	CIBC Capital Appreciation Fund	2.40	RRSP
	Resource	■	CIBC Canadian Resources Fund	2.30	RRSP

| Tax-advantaged: | Dividend | ■ | CIBC Equity Income Fund | 2.10 | RRSP |
| Multi-asset: | Balanced | ■ | CIBC Balanced Income and Growth Fund | 2.25 | RRSP |

FOREIGN	Category	Rating	Fund Name	M.E.R.%	RRSP/Foreign
Money Market:		■	CIBC U.S. Dollar Money Market Fund	1.20	Foreign
Fixed Income:		■	CIBC Global Bond Fund	1.80	RRSP
Global Equity:	All-global	■	CIBC Global Equity Fund	2.35	Foreign
	Specialty	■	CIBC Global Technology Fund	2.25	Foreign
Regional Equity:					
	US Large-cap	■	CIBC U.S. Equity Fund	2.25	Foreign
	US Small-cap	■	CIBC U.S. Opportunities Fund	2.25	Foreign
	Emerging Market	■	CIBC Emerging Economies Fund	2.50	Foreign
	Far East	★	**CIBC Far East Prosperity Fund**	2.85	Foreign
	Japan	■	CIBC Japanese Equity Fund	2.60	Foreign
	Europe	■	CIBC European Equity Fund	2.25	Foreign

A year ago, we commented that the departures of John Vivash and Keith Sjogern left a leadership vacuum at CIBC Securities Inc. That was soon filled by the colourful Paul Starita, whose cross-country seminars with Royal Trust Mutual Funds some years back helped build that franchise along with the image of no-load investing through banks and trust companies.

Starita loves a challenge and CIBC should fit the bill. The bank has suffered the indignity of running several long-term, fourth-quartile funds. The most prominent underperformer is the Canadian Equity Fund, a fourth-quartile fund over the past five years, as is Balanced Income & Growth. Over the past three years, Capital Appreciation and Equity Income have also been fourth quartile.

Starita and fellow Royal Trust alumnus Don Rolfe, now president and CEO at CIBC Securities, have certainly shaken things up. They ran a campaign to lower management expense ratios with a "performance commitment" to boost results. That makes CIBC the first no-load major to respond to the aggressively lower MERs of foreign newcomer Scudder Investor Services Canada.

The first problem Starita and Rolfe tackled was CIBC Canadian Equity, as the core, large-cap Canadian equity category is critical to fund marketing. In mid-1995 they appointed a new manager, Maurice Hebert, and changed the management style from sector rotation to an emphasis on value. That fund was also the first to drop its MER: to 2.05% from 2.25%.

They also introduced several aggressive global equity funds, as Starita had at Royal Trust with such innovative offerings as the Zweig U.S. equity funds. The most interesting of the new CIBC products is a global technology fund – following the earlier lead of

Green Line, Altamira and Royal Mutual Funds – and an Emerging Economies fund. Regional equity funds were also introduced for Japan, Europe and U.S. small caps, and a Canadian resource fund was unveiled. In August '96, CIBC added four new funds; index funds for Canada and the U.S., a precious metals, and an energy fund. Three more were added in September, including a "demographics" fund.

With 28 funds now in the CIBC stable, the family offers a well-rounded lineup. (The experimental Hyperion load family, which targeted more affluent sophisticated investors, was sold to Talvest Fund Management Inc.)

Most of the no-load funds are now managed by T.A.L. Investment Counsel Ltd., the country's largest pension manager, which in 1994 was acquired by CIBC. T.A.L. runs all the funds except for CIBC Far East Prosperity and the new Japanese Fund, which are both managed by CEF Investment Management Ltd. of Hong Kong, also owned by the bank through Talvest.

Smart Funds:

CIBC Far East Prosperity, CIBC Mortgage Investment Fund.

Noteworthy Funds:

CIBC Canadian Income. This differs from CIBC Bond Fund in that the average term of bonds in the portfolio will not exceed five years, thus reducing interest rate volatility. It's been first quartile the last two years and the M.E.R. is 0.86%.

Availability:

CIBC branches, Wood Gundy and CIBC's Investor's Edge Discount Brokerage.

12. CLEAN ENVIRONMENT MUTUAL FUNDS LTD.   LOAD

Strengths:	Profits in the environment business
	Ethical/socially conscious investing
Weaknesses:	Limited family of funds
	Limited availability
Web Site: none	**Toll Free:** 1-800-461-4570

CANADIAN	Category	Rating	Fund Name	M.E.R.%	RRSP/Foreign
Equity:	Mid- to Large-cap	▲	Clean Environment Equity Fund	2.99	RRSP

| Multi-asset: | Balanced | ▲ | **Clean Environment Balanced Fund** | 2.99 | RRSP |
| | Dividend/Bonds | ■ | Clean Environment Income Fund | 2.49 | RRSP |

FOREIGN	Category	Rating	Fund Name	M.E.R.%	RRSP/Foreign
Global Equity:	All-global	■	Clean Environment Int'l. Equity Fund	3.23	Foreign

Clean Environment mutual funds provide more than just a clean conscience for investors concerned about the environment. Two of the family's four funds, the Equity and Balanced funds, are first-quartile performers for the three years ended Apr. 30, 1996.

These funds are run just like any other mutual fund, except certain "screens" are used to eliminate companies judged to be destructive to the environment. But Clean Environment is a little broader than that: it seeks companies that can grow and profit from the environment business itself. It uses the term "sustainable growth" to define companies that develop technologies that "meet the needs of the present without compromising the ability of future generations to meet their own needs." It therefore finds companies that redesign processes, use alternative techniques, preserve, recycle and reduce raw material consumption, increase efficiency and reduce pollution – since, in theory at least, damaging "unethical" stocks should ultimately underperform.

Alternatively, you could invest in any high-growth mutual fund, and donate a percentage of the proceeds to ethical or environmental causes.

The family is small and young, founded in 1992 by president Ian Ihnatowycz, the main stock picker, and recently departed principal Robert Swan.

As the matrix shows, there are just four funds in the Clean Environment stable, but they cover a fairly wide scope: Canadian stocks, bonds and global equities, as well as a basic balanced fund.

Noteworthy Funds:

Clean Environment Equity Fund. The flagship Canadian equity fund has outperformed the TSE since its inception in 1991. Given its mid-cap mandate, the higher performance is not surprising, but the manager has achieved it with reasonable volatility. It had a 21.3% return in 1995 and 26% for the year ended May 31, 1996. The M.E.R. at 3.01% is on the high side.

Clean Environment Balanced Fund. Also above-average for its category, it has a credible 12% compound average growth rate to May 31, 1996. The M.E.R. of 2.99% is higher than average.

Availability:

Only through brokers and dealers.

13. CANADA TRUST EVEREST FUNDS   NO-LOAD

Strengths:	100% RRSP eligible global funds
	Some good global funds
Weaknesses:	Key executive departures
	Innovation appears on hold
Web Site:	www.canadatrust.com **Toll Free:** 1-800-386-3757

CANADIAN	Category	Rating	Fund Name	M.E.R.%	RRSP/Foreign
Money Market:		■	Everest Money Market Fund	1.12	RRSP
Fixed Income:	Long-term	■	Everest Bond Fund	1.36	RRSP
	Mortgage	■	Everest Mortgage Fund	1.61	RRSP
Equity:	Mid- to Large-cap	■	Everest Stock Fund	1.86	RRSP
	Small-cap	▲	**Everest Special Equity Fund**	2.19	RRSP
Tax-advantaged:	Dividend	▲	**Everest Dividend Income Fund**	1.94	RRSP
Multi-asset:	Balanced	■	Everest Balanced Fund	2.13	RRSP

FOREIGN	Category	Rating	Fund Name	M.E.R.%	RRSP/Foreign
Fixed Income:		■	Everest International Bond Fund	2.43	RRSP
Global Equity:	EAFE	■	Everest International Equity Fund	2.91	Foreign
Regional Equity:	US	■	Everest U.S. Equity Fund	2.28	Foreign
		■	Everest AmeriGrowth Fund	1.51	RRSP
	NAFTA/NA	■	Everest North American Fund	2.35	Foreign
	Emerging Market	▲	**Everest Emerging Markets Fund**	4.00	Foreign
	Far East	★	**Everest AsiaGrowth Fund**	2.44	RRSP
	Europe	▲	**Everest EuroGrowth Fund**	2.29	Foreign

For years, Canada Trust was one of the more innovative of the large no-load fund groups offered by financial institutions. But many of the visionaries who developed the solid Everest family of funds have departed. President Sue Dabarno left to head Atlas Capital. Former Trimark marketing manager Richard Hamm came and went in less than a year, and John Mulvihill's Mulvihill Capital Management Inc. is gradually being phased out of its advisory role on many of the North American funds. Canada Trust is centralizing its investment management and mutual fund services under a new umbrella structure, CT Investment Management Inc., but it's not yet clear what, if any, benefits this will provide the approximately 500,000 unit holders.

A main attraction of the Everest Funds are the three 100%

RRSP foreign equity funds, managed externally by David Patterson of Newcastle Capital Management Inc. in Toronto. For investors whose main financial assets are in their RRSP and who want more than 20% of their portfolio invested outside Canada, AmeriGrowth, EuroGrowth and AsiaGrowth provide a way to do that. The International Bond Fund is also 100% RRSP eligible, and managed by Schroder Capital Management International Inc. of New York.

The four other foreign equity funds are eligible only for the 20% foreign content portion of an RRSP. C.T. has a no-fee foreign content monitoring service that will notify investors as their foreign content exceeds 20%.

Investors with core portfolios in other fund families will find the three index funds the most interesting, while those who use other Canada Trust products and services, such as GICs, certificates of deposit, financial planning, high-net-worth services and tax advice, may find the Everest Funds a convenient complement.

Smart Funds:

Everest AsiaGrowth.

Noteworthy Funds:

Everest EuroGrowth. This is one of the few all-Europe 100% RRSP-eligible global equity funds, like Global Strategy Diversified Europe. As with the AmeriGrowth and AsiaGrowth funds, the Canada Trust version is managed by Newcastle.

Everest Dividend Income. New in October 1994, this maximizes after-tax income outside an RRSP or RRIF. It has been first quartile for most periods since its launch.

Everest Special Equity. The mandate of this fund was recently modified to maximize the 20% permissible foreign content while still maintaining 100% RRSP eligibility. Three new managers were selected to replace John Mulvihill: Bissett's David Bissett, Guardian's Gary Chapman and an as-yet unnamed manager from Warburg Pincus.

Everest Emerging Markets. Launched in January 1995, this fund is managed by Montgomery Asset Management Inc. of San Francisco, but it carries a hefty 4.00% management expense ratio.

Availability:

Canada Trust branches and EasyLine. Not available in the Northwest Territories.

14. DESJARDINS FUNDS NO-LOAD

Strengths: Long track record of conservative growth
Two new 100% RRSP global funds
Weaknesses: Limited appeal outside Quebec
Web Site: none   **Toll Free:** 1-800-361-6840

CANADIAN	Category	Rating	Fund Name	M.E.R.%	RRSP/Foreign
Money Market:		■	Desjardins Money Market Fund	1.14	RRSP
Fixed Income:	Long-term	▲	**Desjardins Bond Fund**	1.68	RRSP
	Mortgage	■	Desjardins Mortgage Fund	1.68	RRSP
Equity:	Mid- to Large-cap	■	Desjardins Equity Fund	1.99	RRSP
	Small-cap	■	Desjardins Growth Fund	2.01	RRSP
	Other	■	Desjardins Environment Fund	2.20	RRSP
Tax-advantaged:	Dividend	■	Desjardins Dividend Fund	1.99	RRSP
Multi-asset:	Balanced	■	Desjardins Balanced Fund	2.01	RRSP
	Asset Allocation	■	Desjardins Diversified Secure Fund	0.95	RRSP
		■	Desjardins Diversified Moderate Fund	0.59	RRSP
		■	Desjardins Diversified Audacious Fund	0.50	RRSP

FOREIGN	Category	Rating	Fund Name	M.E.R.%	RRSP/Foreign
Global Equity:	All-global	▲	**Desjardins International Fund**	2.39	Foreign
Regional Equity:	US	▲	**Desjardins American Market Fund**		RRSP
Global Balanced:		■	Desjardins Worldwide Balanced Fund		RRSP

Montreal-based Desjardins launched two new funds in 1994, and five more in 1995, expanding its fund family to 14 offerings. Both the Worldwide Balanced and American Market funds are 100% RRSP-eligible global funds, filling a gap for investors who wish to minimize Canadian content.

The additions also address another problem: Before those new funds were unveiled, most of the family was devoted to Canadian funds, managed by Canagex Associates Inc. (a subsidiary of the Laurentian Group and adviser on most of the Laurentian funds). But many of the Canadian equity managers at Canagex have left in the past couple of years, including BPI's Steven Misener.

Desjardins American Market Fund is similar to Canada Trust's successful AmeriGrowth Fund and C.I.'s new C.I. American RSP Fund. It invests 20% directly in U.S. stocks and the balance in stock futures on the Standard & Poor's 500 index, backed by Canadian Treasury Bills.

The Desjardins Worldwide Balanced Fund is split equally between stocks and bonds. Securities are divided between Europe, Japan and the Pacific Rim, and the United States, with slightly more emphasis on the U.S.

Desjardins has been in the mutual fund business for four

decades. The Desjardins Equity Fund was formed in 1956 and the bond fund and International fund in 1959. The funds are sold primarily in Quebec, and the manager and trustee for the Desjardins Funds is Desjardins Trust Inc., a Mouvement Desjardins company. The in-house portfolio manager is Desjardins Investment Management Inc.

Desjardins offers four Canadian equity funds, including the environmentally conscious Environment Fund (see also Clean Environment Funds above). A dividend fund was also launched in 1994. The long-established large-cap Canadian equity fund, Desjardins Equity Fund, has achieved a 7.9% average 10-year compound annual growth rate to May 31, 1996, virtually the same as the category average. The new mid-cap Desjardin Growth Fund has underperformed the older flagship.

In January 1995, Desjardins launched three strategic asset allocation funds, all with the prefix Desjardins Diversified, and with the increasingly aggressive suffixes "Secure," "Moderate," and the oddly named "Audacious," which is half invested in equities.

Obviously, French language proficiency makes this fund family a strong candidate as the domestic fund family of choice for investors in Quebec.

Noteworthy Funds:

Desjardins International: This fund has been one of the group's top performers, and is seventh among global equity funds for five-year performance, with a 13.6% average compound annual growth rate to May 31, 1996. For years Desjardins' only international product, it has as subadviser Henderson Financial Management Ltd. of Britain (which manages some of Mackenzie's international funds).

Desjardins Bond: Consistent first-quartile performance for the ten years to May 31, 1996, with 10.8% 10-year compound annual growth, well above the 9.3% category average. More than half the portfolio is in Government of Canada bonds. "Quebec-proofers" should note that 26% is invested in Quebec provincial bonds and Hydro Quebec.

Desjardins American Market Fund: One of a handful of the increasingly popular 100% RRSP-eligible American equity funds, achieved through S&P 500 index stock futures. (The prototype for the genre is Canada Trust's AmeriGrowth and, more recently, C.I.'s American RSP Fund.)

Availability:

Desjardins Trust branches, some Caisses Desjardins branches and financial planners.

15. DYNAMIC MUTUAL FUNDS   LOAD

Strengths: Geological and gold expertise
Bonds and asset allocation
Global specialty funds
Weaknesses: No 100% RRSP eligible global equity funds
Web Site: www.Dynamic.ca   **Toll Free:** 1-800-268-8186

CANADIAN	Category	Rating	Fund Name	M.E.R.%	RRSP/Foreign
Money Market:		■	Dynamic Money Market Fund	0.59	RRSP
Fixed Income:	Long-term	★	**Dynamic Income Fund**	1.68	RRSP
	Short-term	■	Dynamic Government Income Fund	0.83	RRSP
Equity:	Mid- to Large-cap	■	Dynamic Fund of Canada	2.51	RRSP
	Small-cap	■	Dynamic Canadian Growth Fund	2.55	RRSP
	Gold/Precious Metal	★	**Dynamic Precious Metals Fund**	2.57	RRSP
Tax-advantaged:	Dividend	■	Dynamic Dividend Fund	1.61	RRSP
		▲	**Dynamic Dividend Growth Fund**	1.81	RRSP
Multi-asset:	Asset Allocation	▲	**Dynamic Partners Fund**	2.45	RRSP
	Portfolio of Funds	■	Dynamic Team Fund*	0.98	RRSP

FOREIGN	Category	Rating	Fund Name	M.E.R.%	RRSP/Foreign
Fixed Income:		★	**Dynamic Global Bond Fund**	1.94	RRSP
Global Equity:	All-global	■	Dynamic International Fund	2.79	Foreign
	Specialty	▲	**Dynamic Global Resource Fund**	3.42	Foreign
		▲	**Dynamic Global Precious Metals Fund**	(new)	Foreign
		★	**Dynamic Real Estate Equity Fund**	3.70	Foreign
		■	Dynamic Global Millennia Fund**	3.12	Foreign
Regional Equity:	NAFTA/NA	▲	**Dynamic Americas Fund*****	2.59	Foreign
	Far East	■	Dynamic Far East Fund	3.50	Foreign
	Europe	■	Dynamic Europe Fund	2.70	Foreign
	Other	■	Dynamic Israel Fund (closed-end)		Foreign
Global Balanced:		■	Dynamic Global Partners Fund	2.68	Foreign

* formerly Dynamic Managed Portfolio
** formerly Dynamic Global Green Fund
*** formerly Dynamic American Fund

Think of Dynamic Mutual Funds and the image of a team of rowers surging across a lake may immediately come to mind. That's no accident. The company's television ad campaign was meant to emphasize its team approach. In addition, its asset allocation fund is called "Partners," and its Managed Portfolio of Funds has been renamed the "Dynamic Team Fund."

Indeed, while its profile may be lower than that of household names like Trimark or Mackenzie, Dynamic Mutual Funds has become one of the stronger alternative independents. Many brokers and customers have been voting with their wallets: in the past two years Dynamic has moved from thirteenth to ninth in asset size (now $4.2 billion), without buying smaller rivals. It was second in terms of sales and asset growth in 1995.

Dynamic is completely different from fund companies that subcontract fund management to external advisers. With Dynamic, you're buying a small, tightly knit team of seasoned in-house stock-picking and bond-trading talent, and a coherent investment philosophy across an entire family of funds. Dynamic's team members thinks for themselves – as is apparent from their detailed quarterly market commentaries and the non-conformist portfolio allocations in their funds. (The Far East is under-represented in Dynamic's international fund, for example, while its Europe Fund has twice as much devoted to Sweden than Britain.)

Dynamic downplayed the role of individual "star" managers after Jonathan Baird departed late in 1995. Nevertheless, the heart of the firm is the father-and-son team of chairman Ned Goodman and Jonathan Goodman.

Certifiable "gold bugs," the Goodmans literally wrote the book on gold, *Investing in Gold*, in partnership with author Steven Kelman. They believe the price of gold will pass US$700 by 2000 (it was US$383 at time of writing). Even so, the team is still trying to live down its famous "pass" on both Diamond Fields Resources and Bre-X Minerals, two stocks that should have been right up their alley.

Goodman & Co. is a unit of Dundee Bancorp., a diversified asset management company with particular expertise in precious metals. The management team is supported by six investment analysts who specialize in specific sectors. They take a traditional value approach to stockpicking, seeking undervalued situations not yet recognized by the market at large.

Dynamic is also a strong fixed-income manager, led by partner Norm Bengough, an investment veteran with 27 years in the business. His aggressive "interest rate anticipation" approach is supplemented by spread-trading techniques that enhance returns. As with stocks, Dynamic seeks undervalued bonds, providing their credit quality is acceptable.

Dynamic has also introduced new fund products that are not available from most of its rivals, such as the closed-end Dynamic Israel Growth Fund, and global resource, real estate and precious metals funds.

Investors who like the Goodman team's approach will find this large family of funds will serve well as a viable core fund family, both domestically and globally. Those who have a core family elsewhere may want to supplement it by cherry-picking some of the stronger Dynamic specialty funds described here.

Smart Funds:

Dynamic Precious Metals, Dynamic Global Bond, Dynamic Income, Dynamic Real Estate.

Noteworthy funds:

Dynamic Global Resource. Launched in May 1995, the fund has been first quartile ever since, returning 65.7% in the year ended April 30, 1996. More than half the portfolio is invested in Canadian resource stocks. Lead manager Jonathan Goodman and the Dynamic team collect a performance bonus of up to 2.25% if they beat the Morgan Stanley index. Nevertheless, it's not a good idea to tie up foreign content in your RRSP with this or the Global Precious Metals fund.

Dynamic Global Precious Metals. The Goodmans have doubled their bet on gold by introducing a global version of the Dynamic Precious Metals Fund that will focus on Australia, Latin America and Indonesia – where many new discoveries are being made. Jonathan Goodman and his team receive an incentive bonus if they beat the Financial Times Gold Mines Index.

Dynamic Americas. Formerly Dynamic American Fund, the fund has been renamed to reflect a broader mandate allowing Latin American stocks and a slightly reduced emphasis on the U.S. market. This fund has been climbing the charts since Anne MacLean took over management in January 1995. Her value approach should make this fund less volatile in the event of a U.S. market correction.

Dynamic Partners: This is another long-term first-quartile fund that has slipped the past two years. It was a Smart Fund in 1996.

Dynamic Dividend Growth: The more aggressive of the two dividend funds offered by Dynamic, it is a conservative Canadian equity fund suitable for non-RRSP accounts out to generate income.

Availability:

Only through brokers and dealers.

Strengths: Canadian equities
Sector rotation style
Weaknesses: Low visibility
No 100% RRSP eligible global funds
Web Site: www.fundlib.com/ellpag.html   **Toll Free:** 1-800-363-6647

CANADIAN	Category	Rating	Fund Name	M.E.R.%	RRSP/Foreign
Money Market:		▲	E&P Money Fund	0.23	RRSP
		■	E&P T-Bill Fund	2.12	RRSP
Fixed Income:	Long-term	▣	E&P Bond Fund	1.68	RRSP
Equity:	Mid- to Large-cap	★	E&P Equity Fund	1.89	RRSP
Multi-asset:	Balanced	★	E&P Balanced Fund	1.93	RRSP

FOREIGN	Category	Rating	Fund Name	M.E.R.%	RRSP/Foreign
Fixed Income:		★	E&P Global Bond Fund	1.67	Foreign
Global Equity:	All-global	▲	E&P Global Equity Fund	1.60	Foreign
Regional Equity:	US	▲	E&P American Growth Fund	1.41	Foreign
	Emerging Market	■	E&P Emerging Markets Fund	1.80	Foreign
	Far East	■	E&P Asian Growth Fund	1.69	Foreign
Global Balanced:		■	E&P Global Balanced Fund	2.34	Foreign

Elliott & Page has a long history of managing money – in 1949, it became the first investment counsellor registered in Ontario. Today, it's a member of the Manulife Group of financial service companies and manages $7 billion for corporations, unions, pension funds, foundations and individual investors. Mutual funds are an important part of that – at the end of February 1996, E&P passed the $1-billion milestone in mutual fund assets.

For most investors, E&P is a contender as a Canadian-oriented core fund family, particularly for those individuals who want a solid balanced fund or strong equity participation. Not all its funds have been winners, though: Elliott & Page Bond has languished in the fourth quartile for most of the past five years.

Globally, E&P offers a mixed and relatively unproven bag of goods. Its U.S. equity fund, Elliott & Page American Growth Fund, is fourth quartile over the last five and ten years. But, in 1993, Elliott & Page contracted with Goldman Sachs Asset Management as sub-advisors for the fund, and recently the relative performance of the fund has improved, moving up to the third quartile.

The company raised its profile considerably in late 1994 when it doubled its stable of funds by unveiling five new global funds, advised by one of the most respected investment managers in the world. The Global Equity, Global Balanced, Global Bond and Emerging Markets funds are managed by Fleming Investment Management Ltd. in London and the Asian Growth Fund by Jardine Fleming in Hong Kong.

Investors should take care in choosing the load structure. In addition to the unusual low-load option of 0% to 2% (typically coupled with higher MERs on the funds sold with this option), E&P's rear-load option has a novel declining redemption schedule that can start anywhere from 2% to 6% in the first year, declining to nil after seven years.

In January '96, the mutual fund world was saddened by the news that Elliott & Page president Morton Patrontasch passed away. His successor is Jim Crysdale, head of the fixed income team, who has been with E&P since 1986.

Smart Funds:

Elliott & Page Balanced, Elliott & Page Equity, Elliott & Page Global Bond.

Noteworthy Funds:

E&P Global Equity. This new global equity fund, advised by Robert Fleming, was first quartile in the year to May 31, 1996. This fund invests in both the U.S. and Japan and tends to stick close to benchmark index weightings.

E&P Money. A consistent first-quartile money market fund for most of the last ten years, it has been managed by vice-president Maralyn Kobayashi since its inception in 1984. She uses an interest rate anticipation style. The fund has an extremely low MER.

E&P American Growth. This fund is improperly named. It is managed by Goldman Sachs, which actually employs a bottom-up value style of management rather than growth. This style has not been rewarded by U.S. markets lately, which explains the lagging performance the fund has experienced. But this is a more conservative holding for those worried about a U.S. market correction.

Availability:

Only through brokers and dealers.

17. ETHICAL FUNDS INC.

Strengths: Funds for investors with a conscience
Weaknesses: Availability
Web Site: None   **Toll Free:** 1-800-267-5019

CANADIAN	Category	Rating	Fund Name	M.E.R.%	RRSP/Foreign
Money Market:		■	Ethical Money Market Fund	1.30	RRSP
Fixed Income:	Medium-term	■	Ethical Income Fund	1.66	RRSP
Equity:	Mid- to Large-cap	▲	**Ethical Growth Fund**	2.24	RRSP
	Small-cap	■	Ethical Special Equity Fund	2.68	RRSP
Multi-asset:	Balanced	▲	**Ethical Balanced Fund**	2.21	RRSP

FOREIGN	Category	Rating	Fund Name	M.E.R.%	RRSP/Foreign
Fixed Income:		■	Ethical Global Bond Fund	1.97	RRSP
Regional Equity:	NAFTA/NA	▲	**Ethical North American Equity Fund**	2.55	Foreign
	Far East	■	Ethical Pacific Rim Fund	2.60	Foreign
Global Balanced:					

* no load through credit unions; varies with funds

This family sets itself the lofty goal of meeting normal investment objectives while operating within certain ethical and moral bounds. The managers seek companies that are progressive in their labour and race relations, or embrace positive environmental practices. They also avoid companies that derive "a significant portion" of their revenue from tobacco, nuclear power or military goods.

While that might appear to limit potential returns, in fact, some of the funds have done just as well or better than average, allowing investors to sleep well at night both morally and financially.

The family increased from five funds to eight with three new product launches in January 1995: the 100% RRSP-eligible Ethical Global Bond Fund and Ethical Special Equity (a Canadian small-cap fund), and the foreign-content Ethical Pacific Rim Fund.

All the funds are managed externally. Vancouver-based Connor, Clark & Lunn Investment Management Inc. runs the flagship Canadian equity fund, while small-cap specialist Howson Tattersall Investment Counsel Ltd. of Toronto (see Saxon Funds) runs Ethical Special Equity. Global managers include Alliance Capital Management, Hambros Pacific Fund Management Ltd. and Hambros Bank Ltd.

The commission structure is a bit quirky. The five original funds are no-load if purchased from participating credit unions, and no front or rear load fees are applicable on the three new funds, including those bought through brokers or dealers.

Noteworthy Funds:

Ethical Growth Fund: Managed by well-known pension fund managers Connor, Clark & Lunn, this fund has been an above-average performer since inception.

Ethical North American Equity: Managed by Alliance Capital, this fund is an average performer in the category and volatility has been low.

Ethical Balanced: Managed by the lesser known Co-operators Investment Counselling Ltd., this fund is still third quartile over a five-year period but it's improving: it was second quartile in the past three years and first quartile for the past two.

Availability:

Primarily from a local credit union. Not available in Quebec.

18. FIDELITY INVESTMENTS CANADA LTD. LOAD

Strengths:	Clout of world's largest fund company
	Massive research & standardized
Weaknesses:	Size of some funds
	Much shuffling of equity fund managers
Web Site:	www.fidelity.ca **Toll Free:** 1-800-387-0074

CANADIAN	Category	Rating	Fund Name	M.E.R.%	RRSP/Foreign
Money Market:		■	Fidelity Short-Term Asset Fund	1.25	RRSP
Fixed Income:	Long-term	■	Fidelity Canadian Bond Fund	2.03	RRSP
	Short-term	■	Fidelity Canadian Income Fund	1.25	RRSP
Equity:	Mid- to Large-cap	■	Fidelity Capital Builder Fund	2.58	RRSP
		★	**Fidelity True North**		RRSP
	Small-cap	★	**Fidelity Cdn. Growth Company Fund**	2.64	RRSP
Multi-asset:	Asset Allocation	▲	**Fidelity Cdn. Asset Allocation**	2.59	RRSP

FOREIGN	Category	Rating	Fund Name	M.E.R.%	RRSP/Foreign
Money Market:		■	Fidelity U.S. Money Market Fund	1.25	Foreign
Fixed Income:		■	Fidelity RSP Global Bond Fund	2.31	RRSP
		■	Fidelity North American Income Fund	1.75	Foreign
		■	Fidelity Emerging Markets Bond Fund	2.35	Foreign
Global Equity:	All-global	★	**Fidelity International Portfolio**	2.75	Foreign
Regional Equity:					
	US. Large-cap	★	**Fidelity Growth America Fund**	2.40	Foreign
	US. Small-cap	■	Fidelity Small Cap America Fund	2.69	Foreign
	Latin American	■	Fidelity Latin American Growth Fund	3.40	Foreign

Emerging Market	▲	**Fidelity Emerging Markets Portfolio**	3.50	Foreign
Far East	★	**Fidelity Far East Fund**	2.83	Foreign
Japan	▲	**Fidelity Japanese Growth Fund**	3.00	Foreign
Europe	★	**Fidelity European Growth Fund**	2.83	Foreign
Global Balanced:	■	Fidelity Asset Manager Fund	2.87	Foreign

Fidelity's Boston-based parent company is the largest mutual fund in the world but, so far, the Canadian subsidiary has been surprisingly low-profile. The company rose quickly to $6 billion in assets under John Simpson (now president of Mulvilhill's private-client division) and Joe Canavan (now president of G.T. Global), but momentum stalled when the original management team left. The company is now rebuilding under a team of former Midland Walwyn retail executives led by Kevin Kelly, appointed president and CEO of the Canadian subsidiary in October 1995, and Dan Geraci, formerly chief architect of the Atlas funds' strategy, as executive vice-president, sales.

For investors who want international equity funds, Fidelity has proven product. K.C. Lee's top-performing $1.6-billion Fidelity Far East fund is the largest Asian equity fund in the world. Of the more than 200 funds Fidelity operates worldwide, however, only 20 or so are available in Canada.

Performance of Fidelity's Canadian funds has been mixed, which is why Fidelity stunned the industry in August by raiding AGF for star Canadian equity manager Veronika Hirsch. Several domestic offerings are fourth quartile the past five years, including Fidelity Canadian Bond Fund, Capital Builder and Short-term Asset. Fidelity Canadian Growth Company, on the other hand, run by Alan Radlo (see profile in Chapter 2), returned 31% in 1995, confirming Radlo's belief that export-oriented Canadian small caps offer far better values than their equivalents in the U.S. His search for lesser known companies ignored by investors has also led to a hefty allocation to Quebec stocks.

Most Fidelity Canada funds emerged relatively unscathed from a worldwide shakeup that Fidelity U.S. imposed on its equity managers early in 1996. The chief casualty from a Canadian unitholder's perspective was veteran George Domolky, who was demoted from portfolio manager to research analyst.

Fidelity's image was somewhat tarnished by events in 1995 and 1996. The resignation of manager Jeff Vinik from the world's largest mutual fund, the US$60-billion Magellan Fund, created considerable controversy. Fidelity was also the subject of a book, *Fidelity's World*, that was considered by many to be a "hatchet job" by a former New York Times reporter. (Fidelity has declined to comment on it.) These incidents had little impact on the managers of the funds in Canada, however. Late in 1996, Fidelity plans to bring out its first two "sector specific" funds, likely covering technology and health sciences.

Smart Funds:

Fidelity Far East, Fidelity Canadian Growth Company, Fidelity European, Fidelity Growth America, Fidelity International Portfolio, Fidelity True North.

Noteworthy Funds:

Fidelity Canadian Asset Allocation. Co-managed by Alan Radlo on equities, Ford O'Neil on bonds and Dick Haberman on asset allocation, this fund has benefited from its merger with the Growth & Income fund. This is a conservative choice for nervous investors who want to let the experts do the market timing.

Fidelity Emerging Markets Portfolio. Management talents Richard Hazelwood and Beso Sikharulidze (replacing Patti Sutherwaite) have taken advantage of the global research abilities of Fidelity to keep this fund among the best in its category.

Fidelity Japanese Growth. Managed by Yoko Tilley from Fidelity's Tokyo offices, this fund is one of the best focusing on Japan. Since Fidelity Far East excludes Japan, the two funds are complementary.

Availability:

Only through brokers and dealers.

19. GBC ASSET MANAGEMENT INC.   NO-LOAD

Strengths:	Low fees, high performance		
	Small and medium cap growth		
Weaknesses:	$100,000 minimum		
	Limited menu of funds		
Web Site:	www.gbc.ca	Toll Free:	1-800-668-7383

CANADIAN	Category	Rating	Fund Name	M.E.R.%	RRSP/Foreign
Money Market:		■	GBC Money Market Fund	0.75	RRSP
Fixed Income:	Long-term	★	GBC Canadian Bond Fund	1.19	RRSP
Equity:	Small- to med-cap	▲	GBC Canadian Growth Fund	1.89	RRSP

FOREIGN	Category	Rating	Fund Name	M.E.R.%	RRSP/Foreign
Global Equity:	EAFE	■	GBC International Growth Fund	1.88	Foreign
Regional Equity:	NAFTA/NA	▲	GBC North American Growth Fund	1.86	Foreign

For GBC, high performance hasn't translated into high profile. It's a low-fee, top-performing fund company like Phillips, Hager & North Ltd., but makes itself even more exclusive by requiring a $100,000 minimum investment.

GBC originally stood for Great Britain and Canada Corp., a closed-end fund established 70 years ago for British investors wishing to invest in North America. The company limits itself to just five funds. Like PH&N, it tends to be a core family offering high-net-worth investors a solid base, low M.E.Rs and growth-oriented management. All this makes this family appealing to sophisticated investors.

GBC focuses on small and medium-cap equities. Three of its funds concentrate on Canada, North America and EAFE (Europe, Australia and the Far East). A good complement, therefore, would be a fund family with strong regional equity and fixed-income funds outside North America.

As with any small fund group, there are plenty of gaps in the GBC family: there are no specialty funds such as gold or technology, no regional equity funds, no funds that beat the foreign content limit, nor any global bond funds.

As we noted last year, GBC changed managers on its lacklustre GBC International Growth Fund. Under the previous manager, Ivory & Sime PLC, the fund was fourth quartile for the five years to May 31, 1996. A year later, however, the new manager, Babson Stewart Ivory International, has sold most of the 67 holdings it inherited and its one-year return to May 31, 1996 was 9.8%.

Otherwise, GBC's managers remain the same with Greydanus, Boeckh & Associates Inc. running its money market and bond fund, and Montreal-based Pembroke Management Ltd. the Canadian and North American equity funds. There was, however, one significant departure from Pembroke: in the spring, GBC announced that Ann Thompson, a 10-year GBC veteran, would be leaving the investment business as soon as a replacement could be found.

Smart Funds:

GBC Canadian Bond Fund.

Noteworthy Funds:

GBC Canadian Growth. This was on the Smart Funds' short list last year, having amassed an impressive 18.8% five-year compounded annual growth rate to May 31, 1996, twelfth in a field of 127 domestic equity funds. Technology and communications make up almost 30% of the fund.

GBC North American Growth. This has had consistent above-average performance since inception. Over five years, this small- to medium-cap equity fund has slightly underperformed the Canadian version by about 1.5%. Almost half the portfolio is in technology, communications, drugs and health care.

Availability:

Direct from GBC on a no-load basis in Ontario and Quebec, and through broker and dealers. Clients must invest a minimum of $100,000.

20. GLOBAL STRATEGY FINANCIAL INC.   LOAD

Strengths:	MultiManager global equity funds
	100% RRSP eligible "Diversified" funds
Weaknesses:	Challenge of handling many external advisors
	MERs high but coming down
Web Site: None	**Toll Free:** 1-800-387-1229

CANADIAN	Category	Rating	Fund Name	M.E.R.%	RRSP/Foreign
Money Market:		■	Global Strategy T-Bill Savings Fund	0.85	RRSP
Fixed Income:	Short-term	■	Global Strategy Bond Fund	1.50	RRSP
Equity:	Mid- to Large-cap	■	Global Strategy Canada Growth Fund	2.65	RRSP
	Small-cap	▲	**Global Strategy Cdn. Small Cap Fund**	2.65	RRSP
	Gold/Precious Metal	★	**Global Strategy Gold Plus Fund**	2.95	RRSP
Multi-asset:	Balanced	★	**Global Strategy Income Plus Fund**	2.64	RRSP

FOREIGN	Category	Rating	Fund Name	M.E.R.%	RRSP/Foreign
Fixed Income:		▲	**Global Strategy Diversified Bond Fund**	2.29	RRSP
		■	Global Strategy Div'd. Foreign Bond Fund	2.29	RRSP
		▲	**Global Strategy World Bond Fund**	2.27	Foreign
Global Equity:	All-global	★	**Global Strategy World Equity**	2.95	Foreign
		★	**Global Strategy World Em. Companies Fund**	2.95	Foreign
		■	Global Strategy Diversified World Equity	2.50	RRSP
Regional Equity:	US	■	Global Strategy U.S. Equity Fund	2.70	Foreign
	Latin American	■	Global Strategy Latin America Fund	2.95	Foreign
		■	Global Strategy Div'd. Latin Am. Fund	2.70	RRSP
	Far East	▲	**Global Strategy Asia Fund**	2.95	Foreign
		■	Global Strategy Diversified Asia Fund	2.70	RRSP
	Japan	▲	**Global Strategy Japan Fund**	2.95	Foreign
		▲	**Global Strategy Div'd. Japan Plus Fund**	2.62	RRSP
	Europe	★	**Global Strategy Europe Plus Fund**	2.95	Foreign
		■	Global Strategy Diversified Europe Fund	2.68	RRSP
Global Balanced:		■	Global Strategy World Balanced Fund	2.58	Foreign

Over the past two years, Global Strategy has been the load company many brokers love to hate. A combination of poor performance in its international bond and Canadian equity funds, alleged service problems and high management expense ratios have chased brokers away.

A year ago, we suggested Global Strategy had addressed many of its problems, notably through its Multi-Adviser funds that provide three different management styles in such regional equity markets as Asia, Europe, Japan, Latin America and the United States. Indeed, some of these funds did perform well in their debut year – not necessarily at the top, but certainly not at the bottom of the field.

One of Global Strategy's original strengths remains: funds that invest internationally but remain 100% RRSP eligible. Those funds – identified by their prefix "Diversified" – continue to be managed by Rothschild, Global Strategy's part owner.

Early in 1996, Global Strategy thinned out its fund ranks, winnowing out about six of its twenty-nine funds that had minimal assets or duplicated more popular offerings. One positive result was that expenses were cut 10% to 20% on seventeen of the surviving funds.

An investor particularly nervous about the Canadian market could create a portfolio of all-international funds within the confines of an RRSP or RRIF using Global Strategy funds: Multi-Adviser funds could fill the 20% foreign content, then Diversified funds the balance. The effects of such a strategy on asset allocation, and the increased risk exposure of foreign currency fluctuations, should be discussed with your financial planner.

The company has two respected Canadian managers in Tony Massie and John Sartz.

Smart Funds:

Global Strategy Europe Plus, Global Strategy Gold Plus, Global Strategy Income Plus, Global Strategy World Emerging Companies, Global Strategy World Equity.

Noteworthy Funds:

Global Strategy Asia. A multi-manager fund featuring Jardine Fleming, Schroders, and Rothschild, it does not invest in Japan.

Global Strategy Japan. A multi-manager fund featuring Prospect, Gartmore and Rothschild. While the fund's primary focus is on Japan (92% of the portfolio at time of writing), it can also invest in other Asian and Australasian countries.

Global Strategy Diversified Japan Plus. The only 100% RRSP-eligible Japan fund in Canada.

Global Strategy Canadian Small Cap. A Smart Fund in 1996, but an eclectic management style left the fund in the fourth quartile for the year to May 31, 1996. Manager John Sartz didn't ride either the gold or tech stock waves but continues to stick to the style that has made him one of the country's better small-cap managers over the long term. It has been coming on strong in recent months.

Global Strategy World Bond and Diversified Bond. These funds attracted huge amounts of assets and had a rough '94. However, investors who stayed with them are now above water. While still useful for diversification, the attractiveness of this asset class is much lower than it was three years ago.

Availability:

Only through brokers and dealers.

21. GT GLOBAL CANADA INC.

LOAD

Strengths: Unique foreign sector funds
Inhouse management by giant GT Global
Weaknesses: Few Canadian content funds
High management expense ratios
Web Site: None **Toll Free:** 1-800-588-5684

CANADIAN	Category	Rating	Fund Name	M.E.R.%	RRSP/Foreign
Equity:	Mid- to Large-cap	★	GT Canada Growth Class	2.95	RRSP
Tax-advantaged:	Dividend	★	GT Canada Income Class	(new)	RRSP
Multi-asset:	Balanced	■	GT Global Growth & Income Fund	2.95	RRSP

FOREIGN	Category	Rating	Fund Name	M.E.R.%	RRSP/Foreign
Money Market:		■	GT Short-Term Income Fund	1.75-2.25	Foreign
Fixed Income:		■	GT World Bond Fund	2.45	Foreign
Global Equity:	Specialty	★	GT Global Infrastructure Class	2.95	Foreign
		■	GT Global Natural Resources Class	2.95	Foreign
		★	GT Global Telecommunications Class	2.95	Foreign
		▲	GT Global Health Sciences Class	2.95	Foreign
Regional Equity:	US	▲	GT America Growth Class	2.95	Foreign
	Latin American	★	GT Global Latin America Growth Class	2.95	Foreign
	Far East	▲	GT Global Pacific Growth Class	2.95	Foreign

One of the hottest investment styles in the '90s has been "theme investing" – buying stocks in an industry expected to do well because of demographics, global power shifts or other external factors. Predicting trends is a risky business, however, and few retail investors can afford to take the chance of being wrong. G.T. Global funds make theme investing accessible to small investors, by providing a diversified portfolio of stocks in four areas: Global Infrastructure, Natural Resources, Telecommunications and Health Sciences. The latter was one of the top-selling funds in the country during the summer of 1996, with more than $164 million at time of writing.

Indeed, just two years after entering the Canadian market on Oct. 4, 1994, G.T. Global Canada Inc. had passed the $950-million mark in assets under management. While the attraction of the theme funds undoubtedly helped, a good deal of the credit has to go to company president Joe Canavan and his team, whose tireless work ethic and focus on the markets is doing for G.T. what it did for Fidelity in 1993.

G.T. Canada's funds were derived from a menu of more than 100 worldwide mutual funds offered by the parent company – giant Liechtenstein Global Trust (LGT). Established in London in 1969, LGT manages more than US$60 billion worldwide. G.T. Global Canada Inc.

is an affiliate of LGT Asset Management Inc. of San Francisco.

G.T. Canada's approach is two-fold: the funds allow investors to maximize foreign content in an RRSP and minimize capital gains liabilities incurred from frequent switching of foreign equity funds.

It accomplishes the latter by setting up its global equity product as a single incorporated mutual fund, G.T. Global Fund Inc., with seven share classes: the four theme classes and three regional classes: America Growth, Latin America Growth and Pacific Growth. Switching between these classes does not trigger a deemed disposition. Capital gains are realized only upon redemption from G.T. Global Fund Inc.

To maximize foreign content, the 100% eligible Canadian equity fund, Canada Growth Class (formerly Worldwide RSP Class) uses the permitted 20% foreign content and then chooses for its 80% Canadian content local companies that have a global focus. An RRSP composed 80% of this fund and 20% of GT's 20% RRSP-eligible equity funds would effectively have 36% foreign content, plus globally oriented Canadian companies in the balance.

Last May, G.T. Canada added the new Canada Income Class to complement Canada Growth. Like Global Fund Inc., the two funds minimize tax consequences – in this case, of non-RRSP domestic portfolios. The Income Class spins off a combination of dividends, interest and capital gains, plus some return of capital if necessary, to yield 8%. In this respect, it resembles Mackenzie's Industrial Income fund, with the added benefit that investors can switch between the Growth and Income fund without triggering deemed dispositions.

All in all, the G.T. Funds nicely complement fund families like Templeton, Fidelity and C.I. The family will appeal to international equity-oriented investors who see the world in terms of particular industries rather than geographic areas.

Smart Funds:

GT Canada Growth Class, GT Canada Income Class, GT Global Infrastructure, GT Global Latin America Growth, GT Global Telecommunications.

Noteworthy Funds:

GT Global Pacific Growth. The managers make asset allocation first on a country basis, and then a bottom-up stock selection process is used. This fund, which also invests in Japan, is one to watch and a potential Smart Fund in years to come.

GT Global Health Sciences Class. This fund, the second open-ended fund specializing in this sector, has all the potential of the telecom and infrastructure sectors. The only reason it's not a Smart Fund is because it's too new.

GT America Growth Class. The strength of this fund (a 1996 Smart Fund pick) originally was its manager, Kevin Wenck, and his disciplined and systematic stock selection process. But Wenck left G.T. in the early summer of '96, and Derek Webb, the manager of the Canada Growth Class was named his successor. It remains to be seen if Derek can fill Kevin's shoes.

Availability:

Only through brokers and dealers.

22. GUARDIAN GROUP OF FUNDS LIMITED LOAD

Strengths:	Mid-cap growth funds
	100% RRSP eligible global funds
Weaknesses:	Lack of mind share
Web Site:	None

Toll Free: 1-800-668-7327

CANADIAN	Category	Rating	Fund Name	M.E.R.%	RRSP/Foreign
Money Market:		■	Guardian Cdn. Money Market Fund	0.89-1.50	RRSP
Fixed Income:	Short-term	■	Guardian Canadian Income Fund	1.24-1.85	RRSP
Equity:	Mid- to Large-cap	▲	**Guardian Growth Equity Fund**	2.15-2.91	RRSP
	Small-cap	★	**Guardian Enterprise Fund**	2.14-2.95	RRSP
Tax-advantaged:	Dividend	★	**Guardian Monthly Dividend Fund**	1.25-1.87	RRSP
Multi-asset:	Balanced	★	**Guardian Canadian Balanced Fund**	1.61-2.53	RRSP

FOREIGN	Category	Rating	Fund Name	M.E.R.%	RRSP/Foreign
Money Market:		■	Guardian US Money Market Fund	0.89-1.53	RRSP
Fixed Income:		★	**Guardian International Income Fund**	1.96-2.66	RRSP
		■	Guardian Foreign Income Fund	1.96-2.66	RRSP
Global Equity:	All-global	▲	**Guardian Global Equity Fund**	2.21-2.93	Foreign
Regional Equity:	US	▲	**Guardian American Equity Fund**	2.30-2.95	Foreign
	Emerging Market	★	**Guardian Emerging Markets Fund**	1.53-2.98	Foreign
	Far East	■	Guardian Asia Pacific Fund	1.90-2.99	Foreign
Global Balanced:		★	**Guardian International Balanced Fund**	2.40-2.99	RRSP

The Guardian Group's reputation as a conservative investor has deterred aggressive investors in the past. They should look again, particularly at the recently revamped small-cap Enterprise Fund (a Smart Fund this year.) Even further out on the risk/reward spectrum are the group's new Asia Pacific and Emerging Markets funds.

Guardian is a low-profile fund family often overlooked by investors but well known and regarded in the broker/dealer community. Guardian retail mutual funds passed the $1-billion mark in assets in 1995, but remain secondary to Guardian's core business of managing money for pension funds and high-net-worth individuals through the pooled funds of Guardian Capital Advisers. The retail mutual fund investors benefit from the same seasoned investment in-house investment team: John Priestman on Canadian equities, and Larry Kennedy on fixed income. Outside Canada, Guardian has two long-standing joint ventures: Guardian Dietche Field Inc. of New York, which manages the Guardian American Equity Fund; and Kleinwort Guardian Overseas Ltd. of London, which manages the overseas funds.

In October 1995, Guardian unitholders approved a restructuring of the family's 14 funds into two classes: A units (with a front load) and B units (rear load). This eliminated a 0.625% financing fee formerly applied on the rear-load units.

RRSP or RRIF investors who want to maximize foreign content have three funds from which to choose: the 100% RRSP-eligible Guardian International Balanced, International Income and Foreign Income funds. The firm's reputation for managing money very conservatively shows in the low volatility, relative to the competition, of many of the funds.

Smart Funds:

Guardian Canadian Balanced, Guardian Emerging Markets, Guardian Enterprise, Guardian International Balanced, Guardian International Income, Guardian Monthly Dividend.

Noteworthy Funds:

Guardian Global Equity. Formerly an EAFE (Europe, Australia, Far East) fund, this has been modified to accommodate a global mandate that now includes North American investments. The fund's five-year and ten-year record has been unimpressive but it's been in the first quartile for three years now.

Guardian Growth Equity. Manager John Priestman focuses this fund on about 30 mid- to large-cap Canadian growth stocks. Return is in the first quartile over five years.

Guardian American Equity. Managed by Guardian Dietche Field Inc. in New York, this fund has a top-quartile ranking over three and five years but has slipped of late. Their bottom-up, stock picking style means the managers must shoulder the responsibility for the lagging performance. This was a Smart Fund in 1996 and is still considered a hold for the long term.

Availability:

Only through brokers and dealers.

23. HONGKONG BANK SECURITIES INC.   NO-LOAD

Strengths: Far East equities
Weaknesses: No 100% RRSP eligible global funds
Web Site: None   Toll Free: 1-800-830-8888

CANADIAN	Category	Rating	Fund Name	M.E.R.%	RRSP/Foreign
Money Market:		■	HKB Money Market Fund	0.97	RRSP
Fixed Income:	Long-term	■	HKB Canadian Bond Fund	1.69	RRSP
	Mortgage	★	**HKB Mortgage Fund**	1.76	RRSP
Equity:	Mid- to Large-cap	■	HKB Equity Fund	2.15	RRSP
	Small-cap	▲	**HKB Small-Cap Growth Fund**	3.08	RRSP
Tax-advantaged:	Dividend	▲	**HKB Dividend Income Fund**	2.73	RRSP
Multi-asset:	Balanced	■	HKB Balanced Fund	2.08	RRSP

FOREIGN	Category	Rating	Fund Name	M.E.R.%	RRSP/Foreign
Fixed Income:		■	HKB Global Bond Fund	2.37	Foreign
Regional Equity:	NAFTA/NA	■	HKB Americas Fund	2.84	Foreign
	Emerging Market	■	HKB Emerging Markets Fund	3.11	Foreign
	Far East	★	**HKB Asian Growth Fund**	2.46	Foreign
	Europe	■	HKB European Growth Fund	2.71	Foreign
Global Balanced:		■	Guardian International Balanced Fund	2.40-2.99	RRSP

This Vancouver based no-load group has built on the strength of its Far East fund (obviously a natural for it, and a Smart Fund in 1996) with several new global funds launched late in 1994. In January 1995, it added Canadian Bond, Dividend Income and Small-Cap Growth, bringing the fund stable to twelve.

The firm's origins go back to 1989, when Lloyds Bank of Canada had three basic mutual funds: Balanced, Money Market and Equity Index. In May 1990, Hongkong Bank of Canada purchased Lloyds Bank Canada from Lloyds Bank PLC in Britain, along with the funds. They were renamed by adding the prefix Hongkong Bank and became administered by Hongkong Bank Securities Inc. The bank bought M.K. Wong & Associates Ltd., named them managers of several funds, and recast the index fund as an equity fund. A mortgage fund was added a few months later.

Truly international funds had to wait until November 1993, when the Asian Growth Fund was launched with HSBC Asset Management Ltd. of Hong Kong as the fund manager. The global lineup was rounded out late in 1994 with emerging markets, global bonds, European growth and an Americas fund, all managed by local versions of HSBC Asset Management.

The fund managers generally take a top-down approach, analysing economic conditions before they pick individual securities.

While no-load, Hongkong Bank does pay trailer (service) fees to dealers that carry the funds. The simplified prospectus, by the way, is one of the best in terms of simplicity of disclosure. Particularly noteworthy is the section on risks and the symbols that identify security risks, market risks, foreign market risk, interest rate risk and derivative use.

Smart Funds:

Hongkong Bank Asian Growth, Hongkong Bank Mortgage.

Noteworthy Funds:

Hongkong Bank Small-Cap Growth. Launched in January 1995 and employing M.K. Wong's Greg Bay, this fund was second quartile in the year ended May 31st, 1996.

Hongkong Bank Dividend Income. Also launched in January 1995 and managed by Greg Bay and Robert Dehart of M.K. Wong, this fund was top quartile as at May 31, 1996. The fund is heavily weighted to common equity and pays distributions quarterly.

Availability:

Hongkong Bank branches, their discount brokerage office, James Capel Canada Inc., TD Green Line Discount Trading Inc., Action Direct and Investor's Edge.

24. INVESTORS GROUP

Strengths: Conservative, long-term approach
Now extensive choice globally
Weaknesses: Hard to mix with other fund families
Complexity of 5 in-house families
Web Site: www.investorsgroup.com   **Toll Free:** 1-800-644-7707

CANADIAN	Category	Rating	Fund Name	M.E.R.%	RRSP/Foreign
Money Market:		■	Investors Money Market Fund	1.07	RRSP
Fixed Income:	Long-term	■	Investors Government Bond Fund	1.89	RRSP
		■	Investors Corporate Bond Fund	1.90	RRSP
	Mortgage	■	Investors Mortgage Fund	1.89	RRSP
Equity:	Mid- to Large-cap	▲	**Investors Canadian Equity Fund**	2.40	RRSP
		▲	**Investors Retirement Mutual Fund**	2.38	RRSP
		■	Merrill Lynch Canadian Equity Fund	2.25	RRSP
		▲	**Rothschild Select GS Cdn. Equity Fund**	2.65	RRSP
	Other	■	Investors Summa Fund	2.44	RRSP
Tax-advantaged:	Dividend	■	Investors Dividend Fund	2.33	RRSP
	Real Estate	■	Investors Real Property Fund	2.36	RRSP
Multi-asset:	Balanced	■	Investors Mutual Fund	2.35	RRSP
		★	**Rothschild Canadian Balanced Fund**	2.64	RRSP
	Asset Allocation	▲	**Investors Asset Allocation Fund**	2.65	RRSP
	Portfolio of Funds*	▲	**Investors Growth Portfolio**	0.18	Foreign
		▲	**Investors Growth Plus Portfolio**	0.18	Foreign
		■	Investors Income Portfolio	0.17	RRSP
		■	Investors Income Plus Portfolio	0.17	RRSP
		■	Investors World Growth Portfolio	0.19	Foreign
		■	Investors Retirement Plus Portfolio	0.18	RRSP
		■	Investors Retirement Growth Portfolio	0.20	RRSP

FOREIGN	Category	Rating	Fund Name	M.E.R.%	RRSP/Foreign
Fixed Income:		■	Investors Global Bond Fund	2.18	Foreign
		■	Merrill Lynch World Bond Fund	1.90	RRSP
		■	Rothschild Select GS International Bond	2.29	RRSP
Global Equity:	All-global	■	Investors Global Fund	2.43	Foreign
		■	Rothschild Select GS Int'l. Equity Fund	2.95	Foreign
Regional Equity:	US	▲	**Investors U.S. Growth Fund**	2.37	Foreign
		■	Rothschild Select GS American Equity	2.70	Foreign
	NAFTA/NA	■	Investors North American Growth Fund	2.38	Foreign
	NA small-cap	■	Investors Special Fund	2.38	Foreign
	Emerging Market	▲	**Merrill Lynch Emerging Markets**	2.25	Foreign
	Far East	★	**Investors Pacific International Fund**	2.53	Foreign
	Japan	★	**Investors Japanese Growth Fund**	2.42	Foreign
	Europe	■	Investors European Growth Fund	2.44	Foreign
Global Balanced:		★	**Merrill Lynch World Allocation**	2.25	Foreign
	U.S. Balanced	■	Merrill Lynch Capital Asset Fund	2.25	Foreign

* plus MERs of underlying funds

Investors Group Inc. of Winnipeg is the largest, as well as one of the oldest, mutual fund firms in Canada. Its services go well beyond mutual funds, encompassing all aspects of financial planning. The company was founded in 1894 as Investors Diversified Services and the first Canadian sales operation was launched in 1926. A separate company, Investors Syndicate Ltd., was created in 1940, and in 1950 Investors Group's first mutual fund was introduced: Investors Mutual of Canada.

1995 was a watershed year for Investors Group, as president Sandy Riley and other senior executives were forced to meet increasing demands by its customers and 3,200 captive sales reps to "open up its shelf" to funds other than just its in-house proprietary products.

Despite speculation that such brand names as Mackenzie or Trimark might be included, Investors ultimately opted to hedge its bets. It picked two Canadian firms better known in the pension business: Beutel Goodman and Sceptre Investment Counsel, and two international giants: Merrill Lynch Asset Management of New York and Rothschilds of Britain, represented in Canada by Global Strategy Financial Inc.

Investors had always been a self-contained fund family. Its in-house sales reps sold only Investors products, which other brokers and dealers are unable to market. Now, with four additional fund families, Investors Group believes it is the definitive "all you need is us" family of funds. The only rival that comes close in its scope of funds is the combined AGF-20/20.

Mind you, there are quite a number of redundant funds, as the fund matrix shows. No investor would ever want to invest in all the 40 or so funds the combined families provide. Even so, there are still a few gaps in product offerings: there are no gold, global small cap, technology or 100% RRSP-eligible global equity funds. This last omission is curious, given that Rothschilds is expert at creating 100% RRSP-eligible global products for Global Strategy Financial Inc. (see Global Strategy Investment Funds).

The initial Investors version of the Rothschild funds, "Rothschild Select," became available in March 1996. These include a 100% RRSP global bond fund, as well as Canadian equity and Canadian balanced funds run by Tony Massie, an American equity run by Mark Tavel, and an international equity fund run by Rupert Robinson. Note that none of these Rothschild Select funds is equivalent to Global Strategy's "MultiAdvisor" funds, which each feature three distinct managers. So Investors Group is really not availing itself of the two main strengths of the Global Strategy family. Still, all the Rothschild funds were in the top two quartiles in their first month.

The Merrill Lynch funds caused the most excitement when the affiliations were announced late in 1995. Merrill Lynch Asset

Management, created in 1976, is one of the world's largest money managers, with more than US$170 billion under management. The Merrill Lynch products were also the first of the new funds to be available, in January 1996, although none was in the first quartile at the end of its first quarter. Three of the five funds available through Investors are balanced or asset allocation funds: Merrill Lynch Capital Asset Fund invests in U.S. stocks and bonds but can also invest 25% globally. The Merrill Lynch World Allocation Fund is theoretically the only fund you need to buy, since it invests in equities, and short- and long-term bonds around the globe. The Merrill Lynch World Bond Fund duplicates Rothschild Select in being 100% RRSP eligible. Perhaps the most exciting of the new funds, though, is the Merrill Lynch Emerging Markets Fund. The Merrill Lynch Canadian Equity Fund is the fourth Canadian equity fund available to Investors Group clients. Its "value" style may appeal to those who like the objectivity of a foreigner picking Canadian stocks.

Smart Funds:

Merrill Lynch World Allocation, Rothschild Select GS Canadian Balanced, Investors Japanese Growth, Investors Pacific International.

Noteworthy Funds:

Investors Growth Portfolio Fund and Investors Growth Plus Portfolio. These are both "fund of funds" offerings made up of underlying Investors funds. Growth is a global equity fund and Growth Plus is an international balanced fund. Judged strictly on performance, these pools may seem average. However, on a risk-adjusted basis over three and five years, they have done very well.

Investors Canadian Equity. While you're never going to go wrong investing with manager Scott Penman, this fund dropped out of the Smart Fund category this year as the competition got a bit stiffer. In addition, Scott, like some of his competitors, is now faced with the difficulties of investing a much bigger fund.

Investors Asset Allocation. A newer Canadian balanced fund run by the veteran Bob Darling, this fund will try to maximize foreign content.

Merrill Lynch Emerging Markets. An interesting fund, based on Merrill Lynch's involvement. It appears the bias of the fund is toward South America.

Investors Retirement Mutual. Another Penman-run fund with a slightly more conservative bent than the Canadian Equity fund.

Rothschild Select GS Canadian Equity. While this fund will be run in a more conservative manner than the very successful Sceptre Equity, if Sceptre Equity fund manager Allan Jacobs has any involvement with the fund, it is likely to do well.

Investors U.S. Growth. Again, a Smart Fund from last year that has lost ground in a competitive field. Nonetheless, we would recommend this fund over the new Rothschild fund as the results produced by the manager of the latter, Mark Tavel, have been a disappointment.

Availability:

Exclusively from Investors reps.

25. JONES HEWARD GROUP OF FUNDS   LOAD

Strengths: Half a century pension experience
Primarily Canadian family
Weaknesses: Global funds
Relatively high M.E.R.s
Web Site: no (but see www.fcfunds.bomil.ca)   **Toll Free:** 1-800-361-1392

CANADIAN	Category	Rating	Fund Name	M.E.R.%	RRSP/Foreign
Money Market:		■	Jones Heward Money Market Fund	1.00	RRSP
Fixed Income:	Long-term	■	Jones Heward Bond Fund	1.75	RRSP
Equity:	Small-cap	▲	**Jones Heward Fund Ltd.**	2.50	RRSP
Multi-asset:	Balanced	■	Jones Heward Canadian Balanced Fund	2.40	RRSP

FOREIGN	Category	Rating	Fund Name	M.E.R.%	RRSP/Foreign
Regional Equity:	US	▲	**Jones Heward American Fund**	2.50	Foreign

Given its lacklustre performance, high management fees and limited choice, the fund management team at Jones Heward has its work cut out for it trying to lure investors from other fund families in today's competitive marketplace.

Although Jones Heward established its first mutual fund – a closed-end trust – in 1939, it was not until 1983 that a second fund, the American fund, was added. The firm merged with Burns Fry Investment Management in 1990, at which time the former Burns Fry bond fund became the Jones Heward Bond fund and the Canadian

Balanced fund was created. The money market fund was added in 1994.

In 1994, Burns Fry was purchased by Bank of Montreal and merged with Nesbitt Thomson to form Nesbitt Burns. Bank of Montreal Investment Management (BOMIC) was at the same time merged with Jones Heward. The Jones Heward name was maintained.

Despite their investment management pedigree, the retail funds have been something less than award winners. The money market fund has been the only one consistently in the top two quartiles. Jones Heward American Fund has been a dismal fourth-quartile performer for ten years. Recognizing this underperformance, Jones Heward hired Harris Bretall Sullivan & Smith of San Francisco to manage the fund, effective May 1, 1995.

The five funds are regular load funds, with an optional front load negotiable to 9% and rear load of 5%, declining to nil after seven years. They are the sort of lineup you might have expected several years ago from the big banks or life insurance segregated funds.

Noteworthy Funds:

Jones Heward Fund Ltd. This is one of the oldest mutual funds in Canada, established in 1939 as Group Investment Ltd., and becoming the Jones Heward Fund Ltd. in 1969. It had first-quartile performance over five years to May 31, 1996, but fell off a while. This year it is back in first-quartile territory. Formerly invested in small emerging growth stocks, many of them high-tech issues, its mandate has been changed to all market cap sizes, but particularly those above $100 million.

Jones Heward American. Now managed for Jones Heward by Harris Bretall Sullivan & Smith (HBSS), this fund should see a pickup in performance. HBSS is a growth manager who invests in large-cap stocks, many of which would be recognizable to most investors. Its track record in the U.S. is outstanding, and we think this will be a fund to watch in future years.

Availability:

Through brokers and dealers, primarily Nesbitt Burns.

26. LAURENTIAN FUNDS MANAGEMENT INC. LOAD

Strengths:		Long, conservative track record			
		Broad domestic and global offerings			
Weaknesses:		Performance on several funds sub-par			
		MERs on high side			
Web Site:		none		**Phone:**	(416) 324-1617

CANADIAN	Category	Rating	Fund Name	M.E.R.%	RRSP/Foreign
Money Market:		■	Laurentian Money Market Fund	1.10	RRSP
Fixed Income:	Long-term	■	Laurentian Income Fund	2.14	RRSP
	Short-term	■	Laurentian Government Bond Fund	2.14	RRSP
Equity:	Mid- to Large-cap	■	Laurentian Canadian Equity Fund	2.66	RRSP
	Small-cap	■	Laurentian Special Equity Fund	2.65	RRSP
Tax-advantaged:	Dividend	▲	**Laurentian Dividend Fund**	2.65	RRSP
Multi-asset:	Balanced	■	Laurentian Canadian Balanced Fund	2.65	RRSP

FOREIGN	Category	Rating	Fund Name	M.E.R.%	RRSP/Foreign
Global Equity:	All-global	■	Laurentian International Fund	2.70	Foreign
Regional Equity:	US	■	Laurentian American Equity Fund	2.65	Foreign
	Emerging Market	■	Laurentian Emerging Market Fund	2.95	Foreign
	Far East	■	Laurentian Asia Pacific Fund	2.70	Foreign
	Europe	■	Laurentian Europe Fund	2.70	Foreign
Global Balanced:		■	Laurentian Global Balanced Fund	2.70	Foreign
		▲	**Laurentian Commonwealth Fund**	2.70	Foreign

Few Canadian mutual fund companies can trace their funds as far back as Laurentian. The company's marketing material includes a graph of the performance of the Commonwealth Fund relative to the consumer price index, back to April 1932. It shows that $10,000 invested in the fund then had grown to more than $4.7 million by December 1995 – a period during which the CPI increased just more than ten-fold, to $129,305.

That fund is still available today, along with thirteen other domestic and international offerings. The visibility and availability of the group is not as extensive, however, as some of the larger load fund companies normally found at brokers and dealers. No new funds were launched in the past year.

Investors pay a front load of 3% for purchases under $50,000, declining to 2% for purchases of more than $100,000, or a rear load of 5.5%, declining to nil after five years.

Laurentian Funds Management Inc. describes its investment approach as "mainly conservative," that is, protecting capital while pursuing some growth opportunities. Most of the domestic funds are managed by Canagex Associates, a pension manager with a reputation for solid, conservative investing. But aggressive investors may be disappointed by some of the equity funds: a few Laurentian funds, such as Laurentian Canadian Equity Fund and even the balanced fund, have been consistently in the fourth quartile for ten years.

The fund family features other old-time offerings too, such as American Equity Fund, launched in 1949, and a more aggressive International Fund, which was launched in 1968. Three global equity funds launched in January 1995 have had unspectacular beginnings. The Laurentian Emerging Markets, Asia Pacific and Europe funds are all in the bottom half of their respective fields.

Management expense ratios tend to be on the high side: 2.70% for most of the global equity funds, and 2.14% for the bond funds.

Noteworthy Funds:

Laurentian Commonwealth. A Smart Fund in 1996, Laurentian's largest fund, with more than $320 million in assets, provides a deliberately conservative approach for investors who want international equity exposure with lower-than-average volatility. While mostly invested in global equities, it has about 10% in bonds and another 10% in preferred shares. The fund's performance is second quartile over ten years, but has been lagging in more recent years. Also available is the Laurentian Global Balanced Fund, with 40% in bonds. International stock picking is provided by Guiness Flight Global Asset Management.

Laurentian Dividend. Given Laurentian's conservative style, it should excel at a blue-chip dividend fund. This fund, which is heavy on big banks and utilities, has a 7.6% average ten-year compound annual growth rate to the end of May 1996 – about average – and an attractive after-tax yield outside an RRSP. It is second quartile over ten years, but has slipped more recently.

Availability:

Limited to certain brokers. Also at Laurentian Financial Centres, located at certain Eaton's stores across Canada and through Laurentian Bank and Laurentian Trust branches.

27. MACKENZIE FINANCIAL CORP. LOAD

Strengths: Three solid fund families
STAR asset allocation service
Three RRSP eligible global funds
Weaknesses: Giant funds may slow down
Web Site: through fundlib.com   **Toll Free** 1-800-387-0614

CANADIAN	Category	Rating	Fund Name	M.E.R.%	RRSP/Foreign
Money Market:		■	Industrial Cash Management Fund	0.50	RRSP
		■	Industrial Short Term Fund	1.39	RRSP
Fixed Income:	Long-term	■	Industrial Bond Fund	2.14	RRSP
	Mortgage	★	**Industrial Mortgage Securities Fund**	1.88	RRSP
		■	Ivy Mortgage Fund	1.90	RRSP
Equity:	Mid- to Large-cap	▲	**Industrial Growth Fund**	2.39	RRSP
		▲	**Industrial Horizon Fund**	2.39	RRSP
		★	**Ivy Canadian Fund**	2.42	RRSP
		▲	**Universal Canadian Growth Fund**	2.43	RRSP
	Small-cap	■	Industrial Equity Fund	2.42	RRSP
		■	Ivy Enterprise Fund	2.39	RRSP
	Gold/Precious Metal	▲	**Universal World Precious Metals Fund**	2.56	RRSP
	Resource	★	**Universal Canadian Resource Fund**	2.43	RRSP
	Technology	★	**Industrial Future**	2.41	RRSP
Tax-advantaged:	Dividend	▲	**Industrial Dividend Fund Ltd.**	2.41	RRSP
Multi-asset:	Balanced	■	Industrial Balanced Fund	2.39	RRSP
		■	Industrial Income Fund	1.89	RRSP
		■	Industrial Pension Fund	2.47	RRSP
		▲	**Ivy Growth & Income Fund**	2.59	RRSP
	Asset Allocation	▲	**STAR service**	2.47	RRSP & F

FOREIGN	Category	Rating	Fund Name	M.E.R.%	RRSP/Foreign
Money Market:		■	Universal U.S. Money Market Fund	1.25	Foreign
Fixed Income:		■	Universal World Income RRSP Fund	2.21	RRSP
		■	Universal World Tactical Bond Fund	2.48	Foreign
Global Equity:	All-global	■	Universal Growth Fund	2.35	Foreign
		★	**Universal World Equity Fund**	2.46	Foreign
		★	**Universal World Growth RRSP Fund**	2.46	RRSP
		■	Ivy Foreign Equity Fund	2.50	Foreign
Regional Equity:					
	US Large-cap	■	Industrial American Fund	2.39	Foreign
	US Small-cap	★	**Universal U.S. Emerging Growth Fund**	2.46	Foreign
	NAFTA/NA	■	Universal Americas Fund	2.45	Foreign
	Emerging Market	■	Universal World Emerging Growth Fund	2.55	Foreign
	Far East	■	Universal Far East Fund	2.56	Foreign
	Japan	■	Universal Japan Fund	2.58	Foreign
	Europe	★	**Universal European Opportunities Fund**	2.58	Foreign
Global Balanced:		■	Universal World Asset Allocation	2.45	Foreign
		★	**Universal World Balanced RRSP**	2.43	RRSP

Mackenzie marketing people love to show off the 25-year charts of Industrial Growth Fund, still run by founder and chairman Alex Christ. It's almost the Canadian equivalent of the 40-year mountain chart of Templeton Management Ltd. However, as the fund matrix shows, Mackenzie offers much more: it has a fund in almost every major category and, in some categories, three or four alternatives.

Indeed, Mackenzie's recent resurgence has little to do with the Industrial family, and a lot to do with its newer Ivy and Universal groups, and an innovative service that ties them all together: the STAR strategic asset allocation service. (See profile of Gordon Garmaise in Chapter 2.) More than 50,000 Mackenzie unitholders, with more than $1 billion in fund assets, now use STAR. We believe that within two to three years, all major fund companies and many distributors, especially the banks, will offer a similar product. Many have them already, although none as sophisticated as STAR. And if, as rumored, the STAR program is broadened to include other major fund families, this service will be even more enticing.

While the volatility in both the Growth and Horizon funds (see Noteworthy Funds below) has plagued the Industrial group, the repositioning of the Industrial Future fund to incorporate 50% Industrial Group investment ideas and 50% technology stocks has been well received. The bottom-up value style of Gerry Coleman and Jerry Javasky, the two managers behind the Ivy Group, has produced above-average performance. These two investment industry veterans have now attracted $1.75 billion to their funds.

The Universal Group of Funds includes international and specialty funds. Unlike the Industrial and Ivy families, which are managed in-house, the Universal family engages primarily outside managers, each with a distinctly different style. These include British-based Henderson Administration Group PLC, who are top-down investors; Thornton Management (Asia) Ltd., which has local managers in Japan and the Far East; and Paris-based Cursitor-Eaton Asset Management. Cursitor-Eaton uses top-down economic research to produce tactical asset allocation calls used in the Universal World Asset Allocation and Universal World Tactical Bond funds. The Universal funds also avail themselves of Mackenzie's Boca Raton-based U.S. subsidiary, Mackenzie Investment Management Inc. (MIMI). The managers there include Jim Broadfoot, manager of the red-hot Universal U.S. Emerging Growth Fund, and Leslie Ferris and Barbara Trebbi, who manage the 100% RRSP-eligible global funds.

Many of the Universal funds have been top-quartile

performers. There are three funds in the group that, while investing in foreign markets, are 100% RRSP eligible. The domestic specialty funds within the group – wide ranging alternatives to the core funds of Industrial and Ivy – are also doing well. And, of course, Bill Kanko and Dina DeGeer, both former Trimark fund managers, are managing the Universal Growth and Universal Canadian Growth funds. Mackenzie unitholders who like the Trimark "buy businesses and hold for the long term" or "bottom-up growth" approach may find the funds a good complement to the Industrial family's traditional "top-down value" style.

Mackenzie is one of the few fund families in this book (along with AGF and Investors Group Inc.) within which an investor could construct an entire fund portfolio.

Smart Funds:

Industrial Future, Industrial Mortgage Securities, Ivy Canadian, Universal Canadian Resource, Universal European Opportunities, Universal U.S. Emerging Growth, Universal World Balanced RRSP, Universal World Equity, Universal World Growth RRSP.

Noteworthy Funds:

Industrial Dividend Fund Ltd. Made up predominantly of common equity, this has been a solid performer and is appropriate for those requiring a tax-favourable income stream or a conservative Canadian equity fund.

Industrial Growth/Horizon. Horizon was a Smart Fund last year. These funds have proven to be more volatile than we like, however. The group's managers are trying to lessen the volatility.

Ivy Growth & Income. This is a tactical balanced fund, which can be 100% in or out of an asset class, that has proven to be a steady performer. It should be considered by a conservative investor seeking a low-volatility growth fund.

Universal Canadian Growth. Dina DeGeer inherited the former Universal Canadian Equity Fund, so it will take time to transform the fund into the equivalent of the three big Trimark Canadian funds. For now, the smaller size is an advantage.

Universal World Precious Metals. Managed by Industrial team member Fred Sturm since inception, this fund has been a solid contender in its category. The fund holds significant positions in bullion and a conservative mix of senior and intermediate producers, and some junior exploration companies.

STAR. This is the most sophisticated asset allocation service on the market, and provides portfolios for both RRSP and non-RRSP accounts. While it currently uses only the Mackenzie fund groups (Industrial, Ivy and Universal), it may be expanded to include funds from other major families.

Availability:

Through brokers and dealers.

28. MANULIFE CABOT FUNDS

NO-LOAD

Strengths:	Altamira as adviser
	Canadian equities
Weaknesses:	Foreign line-up
Web Site:	none

Toll Free 1-800-265-7401

CANADIAN	Category	Rating	Fund Name	M.E.R.%	RRSP/Foreign
Money Market:		■	Manulife Cabot Money Market Fund	1.25	RRSP
Fixed Income:	Long-term	■	Manulife Cabot Diversified Bond Fund	2.00	RRSP
Equity:	Mid- to Large-cap	▲	**Manulife Cabot Canadian Equity Fund**	2.50	RRSP
		▲	**Manulife Cabot Blue Chip Fund**	2.50	RRSP
	Small-cap	■	Manulife Cabot Canadian Growth Fund	2.50	RRSP
		■	Manulife Cabot Emerging Growth Fund	2.50	RRSP

FOREIGN	Category	Rating	Fund Name	M.E.R.%	RRSP/Foreign
Global Equity:	All-global	■	Manulife Cabot Global Equity Fund	2.50	Foreign

Manulife Securities International Ltd., a unit of Manulife Financial Co., is the sleeping giant of the Canadian mutual fund industry. Since Manulife's merger with North American Life (forming Canada's largest life insurance company), its empire includes Altamira Investment Services Inc. and Elliott & Page as investment advisers, and both life insurance companies' segregated funds and regular mutual funds.

John Vivash, president and CEO of Manulife Securities (formerly the first president of Fidelity Investments Canada Ltd. and then chairman of CIBC Securities Inc.) is exploiting the combined expertise to its fullest. Several of the new Manulife Cabot Funds, a group of seven no-load funds launched in February 1994, are managed by Altamira. This family is predominantly Canadian equity, with one pure global fund, Global Equity. Because Altamira seldom maximizes the foreign content in its Canadian equity funds, Manulife Cabot offers a "fund-on-fund" strategy on two of its domestic funds for investors who wish to maximize foreign content. Manulife International Fund Management Ltd., a Manulife subsidiary based in Britain, picks the foreign stocks. Thus, the Cabot Blue Chip Fund invests its 80% domestic component in the large-cap Cabot Canadian Equity Fund and 20% in global blue chips, while the Cabot Emerging Growth Fund is invested 80% in the small-cap Canadian Growth Fund and 20% in emerging countries. Both funds are 100% RRSP eligible.

Noteworthy Funds:

Manulife Cabot Blue Chip Fund: This is 80% invested in Canadian blue chips, with most of the balance invested in the U.S., Japan, Britain and Germany. It achieved first-quartile performance for its first two years, to May 31, 1996.

Manulife Cabot Canadian Equity: This is 100% Canadian content, mostly large-cap Canadian blue chips from major economic sectors. First quartile for its first two years to May 31, 1996.

Availability:

Through Manulife agents.

29. MAWER INVESTMENT MANAGEMENT   NO-LOAD

Strengths:	Low MERs	
	Mawer New Canada Fund	
Weaknesses:	Limited distribution	
	Low profile	
Web Site:	none	**Toll Free** 1-800-889-6248

CANADIAN	Category	Rating	Fund Name	M.E.R.%	RRSP/Foreign
Money Market:		■	Mawer Canadian Money Market Fund	0.63	RRSP
Fixed Income:	Long-term	▲	**Mawer Canadian Bond Fund**	0.92	RRSP
	Short-term	■	Mawer Canadian Income Fund	0.96	Not RRSP eligible
	Corporate	■	Mawer High Yield Bond Fund	1.00+	RRSP
Equity:	Mid- to Large-cap	■	Mawer Canadian Equity Fund	1.34	RRSP
	Small-cap	▲	**Mawer New Canada Fund**	1.29	RRSP

| Multi-asset: | Balanced | ■ | Mawer Canadian Balanced Retirement Savings Fund | 0.90 | RRSP |
| | | ■ | Mawer Canadian Diversified Investment Fund | 1.01 | Not RRSP eligible |

FOREIGN	Category	Rating	Fund Name	M.E.R.%	RRSP/Foreign
Global Equity:	EAFE	■	Mawer World Investment Fund	1.33	Foreign
Regional Equity:	US	▲	**Mawer U.S. Equity Fund**	1.33	Foreign

This small Calgary-based no-load firm, like its fellow Albertan competitor Bissett, does minimal marketing and passes the savings along via very low management expense ratios on its ten funds. MERs on both its Canadian and global equity funds are at the very low end of their category averages. There are no switching charges.

The firm was founded in 1974 as a high-net-worth investment counsellor, expanded into pensions and in 1987 into mutual funds. It does not subcontract subadvisors, even in its international funds (which also helps keep fees down). Its seven in-house investment managers together have more than 130 years experience. Like Bissett's, its Canadian funds tend to have strong western Canada representation, particularly in oil and gas and other natural resources. That may make it attractive to investors concerned about possible Quebec separation.

Mawer's newest fund is the High Yield Bond Fund, launched in April 1996 and managed by Gary Feltham. It invests in bonds and debentures of lower-rated or non-rated Canadian companies.

Most Mawer funds have been second-quartile performers. About the only real disappointment has been the Mawer Canadian Equity Fund, a large-cap fund that has languished in the fourth quartile the last three years.

Asset allocation is handled by partner Don Ferris, a 19-year veteran who manages the Canadian Balanced Retirement Savings Fund and Canadian Diversified Investment Fund.

Noteworthy Funds:

Mawer New Canada Fund. Originally the North American Shares Fund, the name was changed to the New Canada Fund in 1993 to reflect its concentration on Canadian small-cap securities. The fund has been consistently second quartile for five years. Manager Leigh Pullen seeks under-researched stocks with a market capitalization of less than $350 million. With $61 million in assets, the M.E.R. is a parsimonious 1.27%.

Mawer Canadian Bond Fund. A second-quartile performer over three years. Gary Feltham employs interest rate anticipation strategies, but the fund's volatility is low to average and the M.E.R. a slim 0.92%.

Mawer U.S. Equity Fund. Another consistent second-quartile performer in the past three years. Manager Darrell Anderson invests in forty to fifty U.S. stocks of mixed market capitalization. The M.E.R. of 1.33% is one of the lowest for American equity funds sold in Canada.

Availability:

Directly from Mawer. Minimum initial investment is $25,000.

30. MAXXUM GROUP OF FUNDS (formerly Prudential)   LOAD

Strengths:	Canadian equities
	Natural resources and precious metals
Weaknesses:	Marketing
Web Site:	none **Toll Free** 1-800-463-6778

CANADIAN	Category	Rating	Fund Name	M.E.R.%	RRSP/Foreign
Money Market:		■	Maxxum Money Market of Canada	0.65	RRSP
Fixed Income:	Long-term	■	Maxxum Income Fund of Canada	1.50	RRSP
Equity:	Mid- to Large-cap	★	**Maxxum Growth Fund of Canada**	1.75	RRSP
	Gold/Precious Metal	★	**Maxxum Precious Metals Fund**	1.76	RRSP
	Resource	★	**Maxxum Natural Resource Fund**	1.75	RRSP
Tax-advantaged:	Dividend	★	**Maxxum Dividend Fund of Canada**	1.50	RRSP
Multi-asset:	Balanced	■	Maxxum Diversified Investment Fund	1.50	RRSP

FOREIGN	Category	Rating	Fund Name	M.E.R.%	RRSP/Foreign
Global Equity:	All-global	▲	**Maxxum Global Equity Fund**	2.51	Foreign
Regional Equity:	US	▲	**Maxxum American Equity Fund**	2.26	Foreign

MAXXUM (formerly Prudential) is somewhat of an undiscovered gem. Its marketing is minimal and low-key, which means its MERs are low. Performance to date is superior – six of nine funds are first quartile over the five-year period ended May 31, 1996.

New owners London Life are expected to leave most of the mutual fund operation alone. Still, it's impossible to know what individual investment managers may do in response to new management.

Contrary to what one might think, the former Prudential Group of Funds were not life insurance segregated funds, but regular load mutual funds, sold with front-load sales charges that started at 5% and dropped after $100,000 had been invested and again after $200,000. Prudential agents receive trailer fees of no more than 0.4% a year. Investors can make four switches a year at no charge; after that, it's $25 a switch.

All four funds remained in the first quartile as of May 31, 1996. Jackee Pratt, who replaced former manager Veronika Hirsch in September 1995 on the natural resources fund, Prudential Growth Fund and part of the Dividend Fund, has 23 years experience, most recently with CIBC Securities Inc.'s T.A.L. Investment Counsel Ltd. The precious metals fund was taken over by Martin Anstee, a 27-year investment industry veteran who was Hirsch's boss at Prudential.

This is primarily a domestic fund family, and one with lower-than-average management expense ratios. After the flagship Growth Fund was launched in 1970, a bond fund was added in 1974. But it wasn't until 1986 that Prudential started to create a full fund family. Dividend and Money Market funds came in 1986, and the balanced Diversified Fund, Natural Resource and Precious Metals were added in 1988.

Maxxum/Prudential has been tardy in introducing global funds. It launched its American Equity and Global Equity funds in January, 1995. Both are managed by U.S. affiliate Prudential Mutual Fund Investment Management, and have impressive debut performance numbers (see below).

Smart Funds

Maxxum Growth, Maxxum Precious Metals, Maxxum Natural Resource, Maxxum Dividend.

Noteworthy Funds:

Maxxum American Equity Fund. Manager Kim Goodwin racked up an impressive 42.2% in the fund's debut year ended March 31, 1996, the second best of all U.S. equity funds in the period. Goodwin left in April, and was replaced by Greg Goldberg, who has eleven years in the business.

Maxxum Global Equity Fund. Manager Dan Duane, a top-down investor, had a top-quartile fund at May 31, 1996. At that time his country mix was 35% U.S., 14% Japan, and the rest in Europe, Hong Kong and other Asian countries.

Availability:

Mainly through Prudential Insurance Co. of America and Nesbitt Burns Inc.

31. McDONALD FINANCIAL CORP.   LOAD

Strengths:	Global equities
	Performance-tied funds
Weaknesses:	Lack of Canadian funds
	Very stiff MERs on some funds
Web Site:	none Phone (416) 594-1979

CANADIAN	Category	Rating	Fund Name	M.E.R.%	RRSP/Foreign
Multi-asset:	Balanced	■	McDonald Canada Plus Fund	2.71	RRSP

FOREIGN	Category	Rating	Fund Name	M.E.R.%	RRSP/Foreign
Fixed Income:		▲	**McDonald Enhanced Global Bond Fund**	4.62	RRSP
Global Equity:	All-global	▲	**McDonald Global Fund**	(new)	RRSP
Regional Equity:	US	■	McDonald U.S. New Economy Fund	4.96	Foreign
	Emerging Market	■	McDonald Emerging Economies Fund	3.00	Foreign
	Far East	■	McDonald Asia Plus Fund	3.10	Foreign
	Japan	■	McDonald Japan New Economy Fund	4.93	Foreign
	Europe	■	McDonald Euro Plus Fund	2.50	Foreign

McDonald Financial Corp. is located in Toronto but its investment reach extends around the world. The fund managers, who do their own international equity investing, rely heavily on country allocation – that is, being in the right market at the right time. Investors can pick from several regional equity funds – including Europe, Asia, Japan, the U.S., and Emerging Markets – or one global "fund of funds" through the Ambassador Service. In this newly introduced service, the portfolio managers make country-mix decisions for individual investors, relying on a questionnaire-driven international equity allocation service made possible by McDonald's proprietary WORLDMIX model. This program, like Mackenzie's

STAR, automatically rebalances clients' portfolios twice a year to realign it with their original strategic mix. The family also has a 100% RRSP-eligible global fund, the McDonald Global Fund.

The McDonald funds debuted in 1995, but they received little attention compared with higher-profile outfits launched the same year, such as Scudder Canada or O'Donnell Funds. While retail mutual funds are new for McDonald, it does have a seven-year track record providing international portfolio management services to pension funds and high-net-worth individuals. John McDonald, who has served with the International Monetary Fund and the United Nations, set up the firm to offer international expertise and take advantage of the interest in global equities generated by the loosened foreign content rules for pension funds and RRSPs.

The funds feature declining fee schedules based on assets, and performance-based fees. To encourage longer term commitments, only two switches a year are allowed, after which a 3% fee is charged.

Initially these were no-load funds, and still are if purchased directly from the company. Management fees are cut in half for investors committing to five years or more. Part of that fee is paid to the manager, but only if certain above-average performance targets are met. Recently, as it started to build distribution through traditional broker channels, McDonald introduced acquisition and redemption sales charges.

Noteworthy Funds:

McDonald Enhanced Global Bond. This emphasizes short-term debt instruments around the world and is 100% RRSP eligible.

McDonald Global Fund. It uses derivatives and money market instruments to achieve 100% RRSP eligibility.

Availability:

Directly from McDonald Financial Corp., but third-party distribution is pending. Registered only in Ontario, but will be available in other provinces in late 1996 or early 1997. Minimum investment $1,000.

32. McLEAN BUDDEN LTD. NO-LOAD

Strengths: Half a century's pension experience
Balanced Fund
Weaknesses: Only one global fund
Profile & marketing
Web Site: none   **Phone** (416) 862-9800

CANADIAN	Category	Rating	Fund Name	M.E.R.%	RRSP/Foreign
Money Market:		■	McLean Budden Money Market Fund	0.75	RRSP
Fixed Income:	Long-term	▲	**McLean Budden Fixed Income Fund**	1.00	RRSP
Equity:	Mid- to Large-cap	▣	McLean Budden Equity Growth Fund	1.75	RRSP
Multi-asset:	Balanced	▲	**McLean Budden Balanced Fund**	1.75	RRSP

FOREIGN	Category	Rating	Fund Name	M.E.R.%	RRSP/Foreign
Regional Equity:	US	■	McLean Budden American Growth Fund	1.75	Foreign

McLean Budden Investment Management has been a pension manager and counsellor to high-net-worth private clients since 1947. It runs five pooled funds for these clients, and in 1988 created a similar lineup of no-load retail mutual funds.

The mutual funds so far, however, account for less than $50 million of some $3 billion under management. In addition, their performance tends to lag by 1% or 2% of the equivalent pooled funds – no doubt because of higher management fees. (The management fees are nevertheless relatively low compared with other mutual funds.)

Interestingly, while the pooled funds are first-quartile performers in Canadian and American equities and fixed income, the mutual funds tend to be second quartile. Since quartile rankings are, by definition, relative to the competition, it appears McLean Budden has tougher rivals in retail mutual funds than in pension management.

The group's investment management expertise – the managers each have an average 20 years in the investment industry – is also available through the Green Line Balanced Growth Fund.

If you like McLean Budden's investment style and are affluent enough, you might be better served as one of their private clients. Otherwise, there are plenty of more extensive and aggressive fund families out there that can help you become affluent enough that you can one day be a McLean Budden private client.

Noteworthy Funds:

McLean Budden Balanced Fund. A first-quartile fund over the past five years, this strategic allocation fund varies its bond equity mix largely within a 60/40 band.

McLean Budden Fixed Income Fund. A conservative, spread-trading style has kept this fund in the top of its category since its inception in January '89, while exposing investors to very little volatility.

Availability:

Direct from the company.

33. MD MANAGEMENT LTD.   NO-LOAD

Strengths:	Performance with low fees				
	Strong sub-advisors				
Weaknesses:	Not available to general public				
Web Site:	None			**Toll Free:**	1-800-267-4022

CANADIAN	Category	Rating	Fund Name	M.E.R.%	RRSP/Foreign
Money Market:		■	MD Money Fund	0.53	RSSP
Fixed Income:	Long-term	▲	**MD Bond Fund**	1.05	RSSP
	Short-term	■	MD Income Fund*		RSSP
	Mortgage	■	MD Bond and Mortgage Fund	1.17	RSSP
Equity:	Mid- to Large-cap	▲	**MD Equity Fund**	1.03	RSSP
	Small-cap	■	MD Select Fund	1.08	RSSP
Tax-advantaged:	Dividend	■	MD Dividend Fund	1.09	RRSP
	Real Estate	■	MD Realty Fund	1.50	RRSP
Multi-asset:	Balanced	▲	**MD Balanced Fund**	1.04	RRSP

FOREIGN	Category	Rating	Fund Name	M.E.R.%	RRSP/Foreign
Fixed Income:		■	MD Global Bond Fund	1.24	Foreign
Global Equity:	All-global	★	**MD Growth Fund**	1.04	Foreign
Regional Equity:	US	■	MD U.S. Equity Fund	1.06	Foreign
	Emerging Market	★	**MD Emerging Markets Fund**	2.54	Foreign
Global Balanced:					

* not a fund but a deferred group annuity contract

If you've ever wondered where your family doctor invests, it may well be in this exclusive fund family. MD Management Ltd. is a subsidiary of the Canadian Medical Association, and its funds are sold only to CMA members and their families.

MD Management sells a broad package of services, including GICs, financial planning and medical-practice management services, and has been doing so for more than twenty-five years. In fact, in the early 50s the CMA was an early advocate of government-endorsed retirement savings plans, which were introduced in 1957 as RRSPs.

In 1969, the CMA established Lancet Management Ltd., a wholly owned financial subsidiary offering three funds. It was renamed MD Management Ltd. in 1971. Some funds were renamed and more added, and now MD has almost $6 billion in assets under management.

At least six of the funds are first quartile, which is not surprising as they are managed by some of the best load fund enterprises in the business: Guardian Capital, Mackenzie, T.A.L. Investment Counsel and Templeton. Even better, for those investors who qualify for this exclusive club, the management fees are much lower than the equivalent load funds.

The only underperformers have been the notorious real estate funds, MD Realty Fund A and B, which were temporarily closed to new subscriptions early in 1996.

If there is a weakness, it's the lack of 100% RRSP-eligible foreign funds. If that's desired, you could supplement this family with 20/20, Mackenzie, C.I., Global Strategy or Canada Trust.

Smart Funds:

MD Emerging Markets, MD Growth.

Noteworthy Funds:

MD Equity. This fund has done well for long-term investors under the stewardship of Mackenzie's Fred Sturm. In June '96, it was announced that Mackenzie would no longer be managing the fund. Instead, management has been divided among O'Donnell Investment Management (mid-cap focus), McLean Budden (large-cap growth) and J.R. Senecal & Associates (large-cap sector rotators). This may well breathe some life back into the fund's performance, since, at almost $1.5 billion, it will be easier to manage in pieces than as a whole.

MD Balanced. Managed by Connor, Clark & Lunn, with WorldInvest on the foreign portion, it's been first quartile consistently the last three years. The M.E.R. is 1.04%, one of the lowest for balanced funds.

MD Bond. It's been first quartile consistently the past five years and is managed by T.A.L. Investment Counsel's John Braive, one of the country's best fixed-income managers.

Availability:

Available only to members of Canadian Medical Association and their immediate families, and sold through MD Management Financial Consultants.

34. MUTUAL GROUP OF FUNDS   LOAD

Strengths:	Several second quartile no-load funds
	Balanced funds
Weaknesses:	Confusion of old and newer families
	No 100% RRSP eligible global funds
Web Site: None	**Phone:** (519) 888-3900

CANADIAN	Category	Rating	Fund Name	M.E.R.%	RRSP/Foreign
Money Market:		■	Mutual Money Market Fund	1.03	RRSP
Fixed Income:	Long-term	■	Mutual Premier Bond Fund	1.90	RRSP
	Short-term	■	Mutual Bond Fund	1.85	RRSP
	Mortgage	■	Mutual Premier Mortgage Fund	1.58	RRSP
Equity:	Mid- to Large-cap	■	Mutual Equifund	1.80	RRSP
		■	Mutual Premier Blue Chip Fund	2.30	RRSP
	Small-cap	▲	**Mutual Premier Growth Fund**	2.29	RRSP
Multi-asset:	Balanced	■	Mutual Diversifund 40	1.78	RRSP
		▲	**Mutual Premier Diversified Fund**	2.36	RRSP

FOREIGN	Category	Rating	Fund Name	M.E.R.%	RRSP/Foreign
Global Equity:	EAFE	■	Mutual Premier International Fund	2.37	Foreign
Regional Equity:	US	■	Mutual Premier American Fund	2.09	Foreign
	Emerging Market	■	Mutual Premier Emerging Markets Fund	3.83	Foreign

The Mutual Group is unlikely to appeal to aggressive investors seeking "shoot the lights out" performance. But it may appeal to investors who want to do better than guaranteed savings vehicles and are looking for conservative management.

There are two groups of mutual funds offered by the Mutual Group of Companies: some long-established funds that carry a front load of 3.75%, and a three-year-old no-load group known as Mutual Premier. (Mutual Money Market Fund is also no-load.)

While these fund families are managed by subsidiaries of life insurance company Mutual Life of Canada, they are not segregated funds[1]. Mutual Asset Management Ltd. took over management of the funds in 1993. The distributor is Mutual Investco Inc.

One drawback of the group is the confusion generated by the merging of old and new fund families. In December 1995, the eight Strata Funds of Prudential of England were merged into the Mutual Group. The assets of the basic Strata fixed-income funds were merged into similar Mutual Group funds while four other funds – StrataFund 40, StrataFund 60, Mutual Diversifund 25 and Mutual Diversifund 55 – were merged into Mutual Diversifund 40, a balanced fund with a poor long-term track record that has moved up to the first and second quartile the past two years. Two Strata Canadian equity funds became part of the comparable Mutual Premier funds, and Strata Growth Fund and Mutual Canadian Index fund became part of Mutual Equifund – a bit of a loss, as there are only a handful of index funds available in Canada.

The result is a family of thirteen funds, including the recent introduction of the Mutual Premier Emerging Markets Fund. That fund is the first to use an external adviser: Morgan Grenfell Investment Services Ltd. of Britain (which has been managing the Bullock Asian Dynasty Fund since 1993).

Performance has been less than spectacular on the older load funds – most are in the fourth quartile over either five or ten years. The newer Mutual Premier funds now have three-year track records and appear more promising: Mutual Premier Blue Chip and Mutual Premier Growth are both second quartile for the three years to May 31, 1996, while Mutual Premier Diversified is first quartile for the past year.

Noteworthy Funds:

Mutual Premier Growth. A Smart Fund last year, this small-cap fund has not disappointed its unitholders in absolute terms, although it has given way somewhat to competition in the category.

Mutual Premier Diversified Fund. Two years old as of June '96, this balanced fund has produced above-average returns. At the time of writing, the fund was almost 70% equity.

Availability:

Distributed through agents licensed by Mutual Investco Inc., one of the Mutual Group of Companies.

---

[1] Segregated funds are similar to mutual funds, but with a life insurance component that guarantees 75% or more of the capital contributed. They are sold only by insurance companies.

35. NATIONAL BANK SECURITIES INC.   NO-LOAD

Strengths: Quebec's big bank no-load group
Fixed income funds
Weaknesses: North American equities
No 100% RRSP eligible global equity funds
Web Site: None   **Toll Free:** 1-800-280-3088

CANADIAN	Category	Rating	Fund Name	M.E.R.%	RRSP/Foreign
Money Market:		▨	InvesNat Treasury Bill Fund	0.79	RRSP
		▣	InvesNat Money Market Fund	1.05	RRSP
		■	InvesNat Corp. Cash Management Fund	0.58	RRSP
		■	General Trust Money Market Fund	1.07	RRSP
Fixed Income:	Long-term	■	InvesNat Canadian Bond Fund	1.52	RRSP
		■	General Trust Bond Fund	1.56	RRSP
	Short-term	■	InvesNat Short-term Gov't. Bond Fund	1.43	RRSP
	Mortgage	▲	**InvesNat Mortgage Fund**	1.53	RRSP
		▣	General Trust Mortgage Fund	1.56	RRSP
Equity:	Mid- to Large-cap	■	InvesNat Canadian Equity Fund	2.13	RRSP
		■	General Trust Canadian Equity Fund	2.13	RRSP
	Small-cap	■	General Trust Growth Fund	2.08	RRSP
Tax-advantaged:	Dividend	■	InvesNat Dividend Fund	1.78	RRSP
Multi-asset:	Balanced	■	InvesNat Retirement Balanced Fund	2.11	RRSP
		■	General Trust Balanced Fund	2.01	RSP

FOREIGN	Category	Rating	Fund Name	M.E.R.%	RRSP/Foreign
Money Market:		■	InvesNat U.S. Money Market Fund	1.12	Foreign
Fixed Income:		■	InvesNat International RSP Bond Fund	2.22	RRSP
Global Equity:	All-global	■	General Trust International Fund	2.13	Foreign
Regional Equity:	US	■	InvesNat Blue Chip American Equity Fund	3.03	Foreign
		▲	**General Trust U.S. Equity Fund**	2.15	Foreign
	Far East	▲	**InvesNat Far East Equity Fund**	2.47	Foreign
	Japan	■	InvesNat Japanese Equity Fund	2.51	Foreign
	Europe	■	InvesNat European Equity Fund	2.21	Foreign

Quebec-based National Bank has put its no-load fund family through some changes in recent years. Previously, National Bank offered twelve InvesNat funds for average investors, as well as its exclusive ($50,000 minimum) NatCan group of five funds for well-heeled investors. But the exclusive strategy did not provide equivalent performance. Effective August 1995, the NatCan funds were integrated under the InvesNat umbrella. The high minimum investment has been dropped and the lower management fees are being raised on some of the former NatCan funds.

In July 1993, National Bank acquired General Trust of Canada, another Quebec group of eight basic no-load funds. General Trust and the NatCan families cover almost identical ground, though. The InvesNat family offers the most global diversification, offering a 100% RRSP global bond fund and regional funds in the Far East, Japan and Europe.

About the only InvesNat funds to generate first-quartile performance are money market products and the mortgage fund. The Canadian equity funds have been particular underperformers, with both InvesNat Canadian Equity and General Trust Canadian Equity lagging the competition. The portfolios do reflect higher than normal levels of Quebec-based equities and bonds, and political uncertainties have likely hindered these funds' performance.

While General Trust funds have a longer track record, they also have disappointing returns, with the exception of the more aggressive General Trust Growth Fund.

Noteworthy Funds:

InvesNat Far East Equity. Baillie Gifford Overseas Ltd. advises this new Asian fund (as well as the new Japanese fund). It has been a top-quartile fund since inception.

InvesNat Mortgage Fund. First quartile for three years to May 31, 1996, it was the third-best mortgage fund in the first three months of 1996. In addition, it was one of the rare mortgage funds that didn't lose money as interest rates rose in 1994.

General Trust U.S. Equity. Managed by Framlington Investment Management, this is one of the more promising General Trust funds, with a solid 10.4% average compound annual growth rate for the ten years to May 31, 1996. That's slightly above average for U.S. equity funds and considerably better than the anemic numbers posted by the newer InvesNat Blue Chip American Equity fund.

Availability:

Only in National Bank branches and through Levesque Beaubien brokers.

36. NATIONAL TRUST COMPANY NO-LOAD

Strengths: Fixed income
Conservative approach to equities
Weaknesses: North American equities
Web Site: None   **Toll Free:** 1-800-563-4683

CANADIAN	Category	Rating	Fund Name	M.E.R.%	RRSP/Foreign
Money Market:		■	National Trust Money Market Fund	1.17	RRSP
Fixed Income:	Long-term	■	National Trust Canadian Bond Fund	1.34	RRSP
	Mortgage	▲	**National Trust Mortgage Fund**	1.53	RRSP
Equity:	Mid- to Large-cap	■	National Trust Canadian Equity Fund	1.60	RRSP
	Small-cap	■	National Trust Special Equity Fund	2.46	RRSP
Tax-advantaged:	Dividend	■	National Trust Dividend Fund	1.87	RRSP
Multi-asset:	Balanced	■	National Trust Balanced Fund	1.83	RRSP

FOREIGN	Category	Rating	Fund Name	M.E.R.%	RRSP/Foreign
Fixed Income:		■	National Trust Int'l. RSP Bond Fund	2.10	RRSP
Global Equity:	EAFE	▲	**National Trust Int'l. Equity Fund**	2.79	Foreign
Regional Equity:	US	■	National Trust American Equity Fund	2.81	Foreign
	Emerging Market	■	National Trust Emerging Markets Fund	3.10	Foreign

National Trust prides itself on being a conservative money manager so, not surprisingly, its fund performance has been decidedly average. It's unlikely to appeal to more aggressive investors willing to stomach a little volatility in order to generate better returns. No National Trust fund has been consistently first quartile. A major disappointment has been the large-cap National Trust Canadian Equity fund, which has been fourth quartile most of the last ten years.

But with all the gunslinger-style fund families out there, there's probably a place for National Trust. Its funds may appeal to Canadians who feel comfortable with GICs and government bonds but want to venture a little farther afield.

National Trust was one of the first major Canadian financial institutions to offer mutual funds. Its basic Canadian bond and equity funds go back to 1957, but it didn't start building its current group of eleven no-load funds until 1990.

Most are managed and distributed internally by Natrusco Investment Funds. In 1994, it set up its first foreign subadvisor, New York-based Brown Brothers Harriman & Co., which manages the new International Equity (an EAFE fund) and Emerging Markets funds.

Three new global equity offerings complement the older U.S. equity fund, while the International RSP Bond Fund, launched in 1994, is 100% RRSP eligible.

In 1995, an Auto Balancing service was introduced to ensure foreign content in an RRSP or RRIF would not exceed 20%. National Trust is also putting more emphasis on a wider financial-planning context for fund selection. Early in 1996, it launched its Financial Fitness Planner, a four-step questionnaire that matches investors' risk tolerance and investment objectives to the appropriate mix of mutual funds.

Noteworthy Funds:

National Trust Mortgage. Launched late in 1992, this fund ranked in the top ten in the first quarter of 1996. It avoids the weak commercial real estate market, investing only in residential first mortgages.

National Trust International Equity. A promising start, as its 18% one-year return to May 31, 1996, put it in the second quartile for the category.

Availability:

National Trust branches.

37. O'DONNELL INVESTMENT MANAGEMENT CORP. LOAD

Strengths:	Former Mackenzie ace Jim O'Donnell
	Aggressive small-mid cap growth funds
Weaknesses:	Lack of EAFE (non North American) global products
	MERs a tad high
Web Site: None	**Toll Free:** 1-800-292-5658

CANADIAN	Category	Rating	Fund Name	M.E.R.%	RRSP/Foreign
Money Market:		■	O'Donnell Money Market Fund	1.00	RRSP
		■	O'Donnell Short Term Fund	1.35	RRSP
Fixed Income:	Short-term	★	**O'Donnell High Income Fund**	2.00	RRSP
Equity:	Medium-cap	▲	**O'Donnell Growth Fund**	2.55	RRSP
	Small-cap	★	**O'Donnell Canadian Emerging Growth Fund**	2.55	RRSP

FOREIGN	Category	Rating	Fund Name	M.E.R.%	RRSP/Foreign
Regional Equity:	US Mid-cap	▲	**O'Donnell U.S. Mid-Cap Fund**	2.65	Foreign
	US Small-cap	▲	**O'Donnell American Sector Growth Fund**	2.65	Foreign

One of the most successful of the new fund company startups of 1995-1996 was the O'Donnell Group, launched officially on Dec. 21, 1995. Many see this as a tribute to founder James (Jim) F. O'Donnell and his broker/dealer relationships that go back a quarter-century to the marketing heyday of Mackenzie Financial Corp.[2] But it's also a recognition of the big-name investment talent he's snared to run his funds.

By the spring of '96, the seven new O'Donnell Funds were bringing in more than $4 million a day. The funds include small- and medium-cap versions of Canadian and American equity funds, with three fixed-income funds.

More than 75% of the cash flow was being directed to the O'Donnell Canadian Emerging Growth Fund, run by Wayne Deans (see profile Chapter 2). But Deans' fund is by no means the only arrow in O'Donnell's quiver.

Less well known but almost matching Deans on the performance front is the medium-cap O'Donnell Growth Fund, run by Jim Goar – the only in-house manager, who also manages O'Donnell's money market and short-term funds.

O'Donnell also landed two big U.S. investment names. New York-based Mario Gabelli, who is managing the O'Donnell U.S. Mid-Cap Fund, has a reputation for capitalizing on mega-mergers in the media and telecommunications worlds. The fund invests in companies with a market capitalization of US$500 million to US$1 billion. The other big-name American fund manager is Elaine Garzarelli, an oft-quoted market timer whose main claim to fame is bailing out investments one week before the crash of 1987.

For the first few years, the O'Donnell funds will have the advantage of being smaller and less constrained by the need to invest in the highly liquid, large-cap issues that form the backbone of so many established funds. Although some advisors recommend waiting three years before buying a new fund, investors who do so will miss out on the main advantages this family has to offer. In fact, O'Donnell has stated publicly the funds may be closed if it appears too much popularity – and cash – will curb performance for the early investors.

The O'Donnell Funds don't cover all bases but they certainly can complement a more conservative, large-cap-oriented "get rich slowly" family.

---

[2] Industry sales practices are currently being revamped following OSC Commissioner Glorianne Stromberg's report on the mutual fund industry last year, which criticized sales incentives and certain other marketing practices, many of which were pioneered by O'Donnell during his years at Mackenzie.

Smart Funds:

O'Donnell Canadian Emerging Growth, O'Donnell High Income.

Noteworthy Funds:

O'Donnell Growth. This is the only in-house managed fund in the family. Manager Jim Goar worked previously at Mu-Cana Investment Management. Despite his relatively obscurity, he has fared well in the mid-cap market. Goar was one of four managers named to replace Mackenzie on the MD Equity fund in mid-'96.

O'Donnell American Sector Growth. Elaine Garzarelli earned a reputation as an economist when she predicted the '87 crash. Her credentials as a manager are less convincing. This fund invests in S&P500 companies using an econometrics model that identifies well-valued sectors. If the model calls for being out of the market, the fund goes to 100% cash.

O'Donnell U.S. Mid-Cap. As mentioned, O'Donnell attracted Mario Gabelli to manage this fund. Gabelli, with a specialty in telecommunications, has earned a reputation as a good manager and a better marketer. He manages with a well-defined value discipline.

Availability:

Through brokers and dealers.

38. PHILLIPS, HAGER & NORTH LTD. NO-LOAD

Strengths:	Performance with low MERs		
Weaknesses:	Marketing		
	$25,000 Minimum		
Web Site:	None	**Toll Free:**	1-800-661-6141

CANADIAN	Category	Rating	Fund Name	M.E.R.%	RRSP/Foreign
Money Market:		■	PH&N Canadian Money Market Fund	0.51	RRSP
Fixed Income:	Long-term	★	PH&N Bond Fund	0.60	RRSP
	Short-term	■	PH&N Short Term Bond & Mortgage Fund	0.67	RRSP
Equity:	Mid- to Large-cap	★	PH&N Canadian Equity Fund	1.13	RRSP
		■	PH&N RSP/RIF Equity Fund	1.21	RRSP
	Small-cap	▲	PH&N Vintage Fund*	1.75	RRSP
Tax-advantaged:	Dividend	★	PH&N Dividend Income Fund	1.19	RRSP
Multi-asset:	Balanced	★	PH&N Balanced Fund	0.92	RRSP

FOREIGN	Category	Rating	Fund Name	M.E.R.%	RRSP/Foreign
Money Market:		■	PH&N $U.S. Money Market Fund	0.53	RRSP
Global Equity:	EAFE	▲	PH&N International Equity Fund	1.49	Foreign
Regional Equity:	US	★	PH&N U.S. Equity Fund	1.12	Foreign
	NAFTA/NA	■	PH&N North American Equity Fund	1.12	Foreign

* closed to new investors

Vancouver-based Phillips, Hager & North Ltd. is one of the best-kept secrets in no-load investing. That's because the firm does no advertising and relies on minimal marketing. PH&N's core business is pension investing and running segregated management or pooled funds for high-net-worth individuals. Due, in part, to the funds' low MERs, even its wealthy clients use the same family of no-load funds. (PH&N mutual fund MERs are among the industry's lowest.)

PH&N's investment style is focused on finding good North American companies, based on specific criteria, such as a consistently above average rate of return on shareholder equity, and companies that are industry leaders and in the growth phase of their life cycles.

PH&N's senior investment professionals have considerable experience. Since its founding 31 years ago by Art Phillips, Bob Hager and Rudy North, the firm has not lost a senior investment manager.

Nevertheless, PH&N may not be for everybody. An Altamira investor, for example, may happily pay slightly higher MERs for a package of services PH&N does not provide, such as extensive seminars, educational material, an Internet web site, and so on.

The PH&N eleven-fund family is ideal for building a low-cost, above-average core holding in North American stocks and bonds. But if you want to beat RRSP or RRIF foreign content limitations, or want regional equity funds in such exotic locales as the Far East, Europe or single countries, PH&N is not the place to be.

Smart Funds:

PH&N Balanced, PH&N Bond, PH&N Canadian Equity, PH&N Dividend Income, PH&N U.S. Equity.

Noteworthy Funds:

PH&N Vintage. This is PH&N's small-cap fund. The fund has a top-quartile ranking, but back in 1993, when the fund reached $60 million, it was closed (and remains closed) to new investors.

PH&N International Equity Fund. This is the only PH&N fund that invests outside North America. It focuses on the twenty countries in the EAFE (Europe, Australia and Far East) index. The expense ratio is low because PH&N concentrates its research primarily on country selection. Once the managers have what they feel is the correct country mix, they simply buy that country's market index, a strategy they refer to as "active country allocation/ passive stock selection." This is the only PH&N fund to use derivatives and, to date, the results have been sub-par.

Availability:

Direct from PH&N, subject to a $25,000 minimum investment, $3,500 for an RRSP.

39. ROYAL MUTUAL FUNDS INC.   NO-LOAD

Strengths:	Specialty and global equity funds
	Huge distribution through branch network
	John Embry's Royal Precious Metals
Weaknesses:	Billion-dollar funds
Web Site:	www.royalbank.com **Toll Free:** 1-800-463-3863

CANADIAN	Category	Rating	Fund Name	M.E.R.%	RRSP/Foreign
Money Market:		■	RoyFund Canaadian T-Bill Fund	0.86	RRSP
		■	Royal Trust Canadian T-Bill Fund	1.56	RRSP
Fixed Income:	Long-term	■	RoyFund Bond Fund	1.53	RRSP
		■	Royal Trust Bond Fund	1.34	RRSP
	Mortgage	■	RoyFund Mortgage Fund	1.78	RRSP
		■	Royal Trust Mortgage Fund	1.83	RRSP
Equity:	Mid- to Large-cap	■	RoyFund Canadian Equity	2.10	RRSP
		■	Royal Trust Canadian Stock Fund	1.81	RRSP
	Small-cap	■	Royal Canadian Growth Fund	2.26	RRSP
		■	Royal Canadian small Cap Fund	2.12	RRSP
	Gold/Precious Metal	★	**Royal Precious Metals Fund**	2.27	RRSP
	Resource	■	Royal Energy Fund	2.22	RRSP
Tax-advantaged:	Dividend	▲	**RoyFund Dividend Fund**	1.83	RRSP
		▲	**Royal Trust Growth & Income Fund**	2.22	RRSP
Multi-asset:	Balanced	■	Royal Balanced Fund	2.30	RRSP
		■	Royal Trust Advantage Income	1.54	RRSP
		■	Royal Trust Advantage Balanced	1.59	RRSP
		■	Royal Trust Advantage Growth	1.73	RRSP

FOREIGN	Category	Rating	Fund Name	M.E.R.%	RRSP/Foreign
Money Market:		■	RoyFund U.S. Money Market Fund	1.18	RRSP
		■	Royal Trust U.S. Money Market Fund	1.08	Foreign
Fixed Income:		■	RoyFund International Income Fund	2.00	RRSP
		▲	**Royal Trust International Bond Fund**	1.72	RRSP
Global Equity:	EAFE	■	Royal International Equity Fund	2.51	Foreign
	Specialty	▲	**Royal Life Science & Technology Fund**	2.53	Foreign
Regional Equity:					
	US Large-cap	▲	**Royfund U.S. Equity Fund**	2.24	Foreign
		■	Royal Trust American Stock Fund	1.92	Foreign
	US Small-cap	▲	**Zweig Strategic Growth Fund**	2.52	Foreign
	Latin American	■	Royal Latin American Fund	3.86	Foreign
	Far East	▲	**Royal Asian Growth Fund**	3.01	Foreign
	Japan	■	Royal Japanese Stock Fund	2.53	Foreign
	Europe	■	Royal European Growth Fund	2.41	Foreign
Global Balanced:		■	Zweig Global Managed Assets Fund	3.40	Foreign

Canada's largest no-load group of mutual funds led all banks in fund sales in the 1996 RRSP season. That could be a mixed blessing – some investors believe performance falls when a fund gets too big.

The company continues the consolidation work of integrating the Royal Trust and RoyFund families, including making more of each available through the combined branch network. Royal Mutual believes these mergers will result in better economies, which presumably will further reduce its already reasonable management expense ratios. But the mergers also create larger funds. The group now has four billion-dollar funds: the $1-billion Canadian Equity, $2-billion Balanced, $1-billion Mortgage and $2-billion Canadian T-Bill. While size is a positive in fixed-income funds, the equity managers may be more constrained.

It's interesting to note that in Royal's own performance review to investors for the year ended Dec. 31, 1995, many of their flagship funds merely matched or slightly underperformed the relevant index benchmarks. For example, RoyFund Canadian Equity returned 13.2% to the TSE 300's 14.5%; Royfund U.S. Equity 30.6% to the S&P 500's 33.8%; Royal Asian Growth 3.1% to the Far East ex-Japan's 5.8%; and Royal European Growth returned 8.9% to the 18.3% of the Morgan Stanley Europe Index. The obvious question is whether investors should pay 2% or higher annual management fees to get index-like performance, when an index fund could achieve the same end for less. Royal does not offer index funds; they are available from Bank of Montreal's First

Canadian Funds, Canada Trust's Everest Funds, CIBC Securities Inc., and T.D.'s Green Line funds.

John Embry's Royal Precious Metals Fund beat the indexes in dramatic fashion, however. The fund returned 63.8% in 1995, far exceeding the 1% rise in the price of gold. The fund beat all other gold or precious metals funds and most other funds as well. Embry also runs the large-cap Canadian Equity Fund and the small- to mid-cap Canadian Growth Fund, whose returns were less spectacular. At the other extreme, Royal Japanese Stock has been a fourth-quartile performer for five straight years.

Royal Mutual introduced three new funds in the summer of 1995: Royal Latin American Fund, Zweig Global Managed Assets, and Royal Life Science & Technology. The most interesting of these is the latter, run by Jim Young, who also manages the U.S. equity fund. The fact that CIBC, Altamira, and now even Trimark have introduced similar funds indicates the acceptance technology stocks have achieved within the mutual fund industry. Royal's view is that "technology is going to be the building block of the 21st century, in much the same way as oil, gas and metals have been the economic cornerstone of the past 100 years."

Most of Royal's Canadian and some U.S. funds are managed internally by Royal Bank Investment Management. RBIM also has a Global Investment Group, so the international funds are managed partly through its internal resources and partly through six externally contracted subadvisors. These include Delaware International Advisers Ltd. of Britain for the International Equity Fund; Bankers Trust Co. of the U.S. for European Growth, Nikko International Capital Management Co. Ltd. of Tokyo for Japanese Stock, RBC Investment Management (Asia) Ltd. for Asian Growth and Latinvest Investment Management Ltd. for the Latin American Fund.

Early in 1996, Royal scrapped an asset allocation service that automatically rebalanced the Canadian Stock and Canadian Small Cap funds, the Bond Fund and Canadian money market fund.

Smart Funds:

Royal Precious Metals.

Noteworthy Funds:

RoyFund Dividend and Royal Trust Growth & Income: Predominantly blue-chip, high-yielding common equity funds, their performance is virtually identical. Because a high percentage of the distributions on the fund will be dividends, these funds are most appropriate for non-registered accounts. Royfund Dividend was a Smart Fund in 1996.

RoyFund U.S. Equity. Manager Jim Young's top-down growth style served this fund well over the mid-term, but it did get off to a poor first half in '96.

Royal Life Science & Technology. This Jim Young-managed fund is focused on sectors that have tremendous growth potential. However, the growth will be accompanied by a good deal of volatility.

Royal Asian Growth: This ex-Japan fund is managed by Andrew Buchanan using a top-down (by country) growth style. Its performance has been steady.

Royal Trust International Bond: Managed by RBIM's senior fixed-income strategist Barry Edwards, this fund has a history of above-average performance, although it struggled in the first half of '96. However, on a relative risk-return basis, this fund has done well since inception and will likely remain competitive.

Zweig Strategic Growth Fund: Investors worried that the inflated U.S. stock market might drop may find the Zweig Strategic Growth Fund attractive, since – like the O'Donnell American Sector Fund managed by Elaine Garzarelli – this fund will move 100% to cash if deemed advisable. In 1995, the Zweig fund was 40% out of the market, but it still generated a 21% return from its exposure to U.S. small companies. By March 31, 1996 the fund was also 7% hedged with S&P 500 futures contracts. The new Zweig Global Managed Assets expands this concept globally and across asset classes. As of March 31, 1996, it was 43% in equities, 44% in cash and 13% in bonds.

Availability:

Royal Bank and Royal Trust branches; RBC Dominion Securities.

40. SAGIT INVESTMENT MANAGEMENT LTD. LOAD

Strengths: Small- and medium-cap growth
Asia and China funds
Weaknesses: Volatility
High MERs
Web Site: none   **Toll Free:** 1-800-663-1003

CANADIAN	Category	Rating	Fund Name	M.E.R.%	RRSP/Foreign
Money Market:		■	Trans-Canada Money Market	0.56	RRSP
Fixed Income:	Long-term	■	Trans-Canada Bond	2.49	RRSP
Equity:	Mid- to Large-cap	■	Trans-Canada Value Fund	3.00	RRSP
		■	Trans-Canada Pension	3.00	RRSP
	Small-cap	▲	**Cambridge Growth**	3.00	RRSP
		▲	**Cambridge Special Equity**	3.00	RRSP
	Gold/Precious Metal	■	Cambridge Precious metals	3.00	RRSP
	Resource	▲	**Cambridge Resource**	3.00	RRSP
Tax-advantaged:	Dividend	■	Trans-Canada Dividend		RRSP
Multi-asset:	Balanced	■	Cambridge Balanced	3.00	RRSP

FOREIGN	Category	Rating	Fund Name	M.E.R.%	RRSP/Foreign
Global Equity:	All-global	■	Cambridge Global	3.00	Foreign
Regional Equity:	US	■	Cambridge American Growth	3.00	Foreign
	NAFTA/NA	■	Cambridge Americas	3.00	Foreign
	Far East	■	Cambridge Pacific	3.00	Foreign
	Other	▲	**Cambridge China**	3.00	Foreign

If you're looking for highly aggressive growth equity funds and can stomach the volatility that comes with them, the nine funds in Sagit's Cambridge family could be for you.

There are essentially three types of Sagit growth funds: small- to medium-cap equity funds, sector funds specializing in resources or precious metals, and regional equity funds investing in such high-economic-growth parts of the world as the Far East and China. Some of the latter are double bets on both small caps and high-growth regions.

Vancouver-based Sagit also runs the more conservative Trans-Canada family of funds, with five funds covering the money market, fixed income, large-cap Canadian equity and dividend categories. Their performance is hardly comparable to the Cambridge funds, however, with most at fourth quartile over five and ten years.

While some Sagit funds sport spectacular numbers, keep in mind that some of the longer-term track records belonged to Tony Massie, who has since moved on to the Global Strategy fund group. The main two in-house managers are Raoul Tsakok, chief investment officer, and Ted Ohashi, senior vice president, both 20-year-plus investment industry veterans. They favour a bottom-up stock picking style, searching out stocks with low price/earnings ratios, selling at a discount to book value, with high return on equity and above-average growth prospects.

Cambridge Americas Fund changed its name from Cambridge American Fund to reflect the inclusion of Latin American investments. So far, though, it's still in the fourth quartile it's inhabited most of the past five years.

Generally, this fund family would complement some of the better known families that have large billion-dollar funds invested mostly in large-cap stocks. Sagit could be used to beef up the small-cap portion of growth portfolios.

Growth oriented, risk-tolerant investors who choose Sagit as their core family should buffer the pure equity funds with the Cambridge Balanced Fund and some of the Trans-Canada offerings.

Noteworthy Funds:

Cambridge Growth: This is a relatively conservative Canadian equity fund within the Cambridge family. Nonetheless, it displays more volatility than the average small- to mid-cap Canadian equity fund. As with all Cambridge funds, the key to success appears to be sticking with them over a long period and, ideally, using dollar-cost averaging.

Cambridge Special Equity: If you can stomach the ride, climb aboard. This small-cap Canadian equity fund lost money in three of the past five years, twice falling 20% but in 1993 it returned 147%.

Cambridge China Fund: This is one of only three or four China-specific funds available in Canada. Launched in May 1994, it got off to a good start. The fund can be defensive: it recently had 40% in cash and another 20% invested in Canadian companies that get most of their revenue from doing business in China.

Cambridge Resource. A first-quartile fund through most of the past ten years when viewed on a compound annual return basis, this fund can have spectacular performance. However, most investors can't stomach the huge swings in performance.

Availability :

Through brokers and dealers.

41. SAXON FUNDS NO-LOAD

Strengths: No frills, low fees
Flexible from small asset size
Weaknesses: Limited range of funds
Profile & marketing
E-mail: saxon@saxonfunds.com   **Toll Free:** 1-888-AT-SAXON

CANADIAN	Category	Rating	Fund Name	M.E.R.%	RRSP/Foreign
Equity:	Mid- to Large-cap	▲	**Saxon Stock Fund**	1.75	RRSP
	Small-cap	■	Saxon Small Cap	1.75	RRSP
Multi-asset:	Balanced	★	**Saxon Balanced Fund**	1.75	RRSP

FOREIGN	Category	Rating	Fund Name	M.E.R.%	RRSP/Foreign
Global Equity:	All-global	★	**Saxon World Growth**	1.75	Foreign

Saxon Funds is a small, no-frills, no-load company with just four funds in its stable, but as word spread on this family in 1995, the number of investors and assets more than doubled.

The investment firm that runs the funds, Toronto-based Howson Tattersall Investment Counsel Ltd., manages $300 million in assets, including pension funds and private-client investment portfolios. Bob Tattersall has been a Saxon principal since the company's inception ten years ago, and Richard Howson has been on board seven years. Each has about twenty-five years of investment industry experience and, as sole owners, can be expected to stick around.

Both men employ a value approach (Tattersall more so than Howson), insisting that stocks be statistically cheap. Similar in approach to Trimark, they view themselves as investors in companies, not traders in shares.

Ironically, while Howson Tattersall is known in the pension world as a small-cap manager, the Saxon Small Cap Fund has lagged its competitors. Billed as "the original small-cap mutual fund," Saxon notes that its value approach dictates investing in the less glamorous stocks that are temporarily out of favour with investors during the current small-cap mania. Still, the fund is fourth quartile over both five and ten years.

Management fees for all funds is 1.75%, which is also the MER, since the managers absorb all other expenses.

Smart Funds:

Saxon Balanced, Saxon World Growth.

Noteworthy Funds:

Saxon Stock: Managed by Richard Howson, this fund mixes some small caps with some large caps. As mentioned, although Howson's value discipline is less stringent than his partner's, it has kept the fund out of some of the higher performing small-cap stocks.

Availability:

Direct from Saxon and some brokers. The funds are available only in Ontario, British Columbia and Alberta. There is a $5,000 minimum initial purchase.

42. SCEPTRE INVESTMENT COUNSEL LTD. NO-LOAD

Strengths:	High performance with low MERs
	No frills marketing
Weaknesses:	No specialty funds
	Low profile
Web Site:	none **Toll Free:** 1-800-265-1888

CANADIAN	Category	Rating	Fund Name	M.E.R.%	RRSP/Foreign
Money Market:		■	Sceptre Money Market Fund		RRSP
Fixed Income:	Short-term	■	Sceptre Bond Fund	1.25	RRSP
Equity:	Small-cap	★	**Sceptre Equity Fund**	1.68	RRSP
Multi-asset:	Balanced	★	**Sceptre Balanced Fund**	1.57	RRSP

FOREIGN	Category	Rating	Fund Name	M.E.R.%	RRSP/Foreign
Global Equity:	All-global	★	**Sceptre International Fund**	2.10	Foreign
Regional Equity:	Far East	▲	**Sceptre Asian Growth Fund**	2.40	Foreign

Well known in the pension fund world, Sceptre Investment Counsel is still a well-kept secret to most mutual fund investors. This no-nonsense, no-fuss, no-load, low-MER family is, admittedly, a small one. But if you're looking for a firm with definite investment opinions and the courage to stick with them, Sceptre's six funds should fit the bill.

Take, for example, its limited international menu. There are two choices: an all-global equity fund, Sceptre International, which is currently overweighted in Asia and Japan and holds only a token position in Latin America; and Asian Growth Fund. There are no separate Europe, Latin America or emerging markets funds. Lennox McNeely – part of the management team, all of which works out of Toronto – believes in overweighting areas with promising long-term economic growth, and sees little point in exposing the portfolio to positions in such variable performers as Latin America.

But perhaps the best news about Sceptre is its Canadian funds. Under manager Allan Jacobs, Sceptre Equity, a small- to mid-cap Canadian equity fund, returned 53% in the year ended March 31, 1996, and boasts a 30.6% average three-year compound annual growth rate. It's been a first-quartile performer since Jacobs took over in 1993. If you're a believer in the theory that larger funds are hard pressed to outperform, you'll like this $110-million fund, as well as its MER of 1.68%.

There were no fund launches in 1995-1996. The Sceptre Bond Fund, which has slightly underperformed the ScotiaMcLeod bond index for most of its ten-year history, got a new manager in March in Ian Lee. His influence remains to be seen. The fund is about the only third-quartile Sceptre fund.

Sceptre Balanced, managed by Lyle Stein since 1993, returned 24.6% in the year to March 31, 1996. It has been a consistent first-quartile fund for ten years and has an MER of just 1.57%.

Smart Funds:

Sceptre Balanced, Sceptre Equity, Sceptre International.

Noteworthy Funds:

Sceptre Asian Growth: This fund has been managed by Tariq Ahmad since July of '95. Ahmad came to Sceptre with an extensive background in Asian investing. As the fund includes Japan, it's a good way to play the whole region.

Availability:

Ontario residents can purchase direct from Sceptre. Others must buy through brokers or dealers, at a maximum 2% acquisition charge. Minimum $5,000 investment required.

43. SCOTIA EXCELSIOR FUNDS NO-LOAD

Strengths: Balanced funds
100% RRSP eligible global funds
Weaknesses: Some global funds still finding their way
Few small-cap offerings
Web Site: www.Scotiabank.ca   **Toll Free:** 1-800-268-9269

CANADIAN	Category	Rating	Fund Name	M.E.R.%	RRSP/Foreign
Money Market:		■	Scotia Excelsior T-Bill Fund	1.00	RRSP
		■	Scotia Excelsior Premium T-Bill Fund	0.52	RRSP
		■	Scotia Excelsior Money Market Fund	1.00	RRSP
Fixed Income:	Long-term	■	Scotia Excelsior Income Fund	1.37	RRSP
	Short-term	■	Scotia Excelsior Defensive Income Fund	1.37	RRSP
	Mortgage	▲	**Scotia Excelsior Mortgage Fund**	1.56	RRSP
Equity:	Mid- to Large-cap	■	Scotia Excelsior Canadian Blue Chip Fund	2.05	RRSP
		★	**Scotia Excelsior Canadian Growth Fund**	2.11	RRSP
	Gold/Precious Metal	■	Scotia Excelsior Precious Metals Fund	2.19	RRSP
Tax-advantaged:	Dividend	★	**Scotia Excelsior Dividend Fund**	1.07	RRSP
Multi-asset:	Balanced	▲	**Scotia Excelsior Total Return Fund**	2.32	RRSP
		■	Scotia Excelsior Balanced Fund	2.01	RRSP
	Asset Allocation	■	Autopilot service		

FOREIGN	Category	Rating	Fund Name	M.E.R.%	RRSP/Foreign
Fixed Income:		■	Scotia CanAm Income Fund	1.60	RRSP
		■	Scotia Excelsior Global Bond Fund	1.82	Foreign
Global Equity:	All-global	■	Scotia Excelsior International Fund	2.24	Foreign
Regional Equity:	US	■	Scotia CanAm Growth Fund	1.34	RRSP
		■	Scotia Excelsior Am. Equity Growth Fund	2.19	Foreign
	Latin American	▲	**Scotia Excelsior Latin American Fund**	2.11	Foreign
	Far East	■	Scotia Excelsior Pacific Rim Fund	2.12	Foreign

Fund industry observers have been surprised by the recent strength of the Scotia fund group, which certainly qualifies as "most improved" among bank fund families.

That's been particularly true since the Oct. 1, 1995 merger of the 16 Scotia Mutual Funds with Montreal Trust's eight Excelsior funds. After redundant funds were eliminated or consolidated, the group was left with 19 Scotia Excelsior funds, roughly split between domestic and global offerings, 13 of which racked up double-digit returns in 1995. The only weakness is Scotia Excelsior International Fund, which is fourth quartile over ten years and third the past five years.

No new funds were launched in 1995, but additions to the line-up may occur in 1996-1997. Scotia Investment Management Ltd. (SIML) is adviser to most of the domestic fixed-income funds, the Canadian Blue Chip Fund, and the regional equity funds. Montrusco Associates Inc.

handles the Dividend, Balanced, International and Total Return funds.

In addition to improved performance, Scotia Excelsior is also matching the initiative of CIBC Securities Inc. to make management expense ratios lower. Scotia started by cutting the management fee on the Balanced Fund to 1.75% from 2.25%, while the former M.T. Excelsior Mortgage and Income funds have dropped management fees to 1.25% from 1.5%. Scotia's average managed fees are now 1.75% for its equity, balanced and global bond funds, 1.95% for global equity funds and a relatively attractive 1.31% on domestic bond funds.

Scotia Excelsior is ahead of most of its bank competitors in having both a 100% RRSP-eligible U.S. Equity fund (CanAm Growth) and a 100% RRSP-eligible global bond fund (Can Am Income). And, in order to help clients track other foreign fund holdings, Scotia has a free foreign content monitoring service for RRSP customers. Accounts are monitored monthly, and automatically adjusted to make sure the 20% foreign limit is not exceeded.

Given that asset allocation programs are becoming an almost obligatory value-added service for bank funds, it's worth noting that Scotia was relatively early with its Autopilot Service, which was introduced in 1993.

Smart Funds:

Scotia Excelsior Canadian Growth, Scotia Excelsior Dividend.

Noteworthy Funds:

Scotia Excelsior Total Return: A Smart Fund last year, it's fallen from its former glory. After being a top-quartile fund for years, its more recent performance has been below average.

Scotia Excelsior Mortgage Fund: Banks are the best place for mortgage funds, and this one has been a steady above-average performer.

Scotia Excelsior Latin American: Scotiabank has taken a large equity position in a prominent Mexican Bank and the fund's manager, Tony Genua, is a frequent visitor to the region and fluent in the language and customs. Much of the fund's relative performance, however, is a result of the fact that when the Mexican currency crisis hit, this fund was still new, largely in cash, and thus relatively unaffected.

Availability:

Through branches of Bank of Nova Scotia, Scotiabank and Scotia Trust, Montreal Trust, Scotia Discount Brokerage and ScotiaMcLeod.

44. SCUDDER FUNDS OF CANADA NO-LOAD

Strengths: Global equities
No-load and low expense ratios
Weaknesses: Sparse Canadian funds
Few fixed income funds
Web Site: www.scudder.ca   **Toll Free:** 1-800-850-FUND

CANADIAN	Category	Rating	Fund Name	M.E.R.%	RRSP/Foreign
Fixed Income:	Short-term	■	Scudder Canadian Short Term Bond Fund	0.50	RRSP
Equity:	Mid- to Large-cap	■	Scudder Canadian Equity Fund	1.25	RRSP

FOREIGN	Category	Rating	Fund Name	M.E.R.%	RRSP/Foreign
Global Equity:	All-global	★	**Scudder Global Fund**	1.75	Foreign
Regional Equity:					
	Emerging Market	▲	**Scudder Emerging Markets Fund**	2.00	Foreign
	Far East	▲	**Scudder Pacific Fund**	1.75	Foreign
	Europe	▲	**Scudder Greater Europe Fund**	1.75	Foreign

Scudder, the first foreign no-load global giant to enter Canada, promises to shake up the big banks and no-load powerhouse Altamira with its lower management expense ratios. So far, though, while its global offerings are interesting, its Canadian fund choices are still fairly sparse.

The family numbers just six funds, with the emphasis being the four global equity funds: a basic global equity fund, a European equity fund for more conservative investors, and Far East and Emerging Markets funds for more aggressive investors seeking long-term growth. Initially at least, there are no 100% RRSP-eligible global funds, no U.S., no balanced and no Latin American funds.

Several of the funds have considerably different country allocations than their competitive counterparts. The Greater Europe Fund, for example, has a relatively low 13% weighting in Britain. The Pacific Fund has a similarly low 11% allocation to Hong Kong, with a big 37% bet on Japan.

The most interesting is Scudder Global Fund, which does not invest in specific countries or economic sectors but in "themes," including aging population/health care, life insurers, infrastructure, corporate restructurings and companies with large customer bases that are technological standard setters.

While Scudder Stevens & Clark of New York has a 75-year pedigree in the U.S., the Canadian fund group was set up only in October, 1995.

It remains to be seen how strong it will be at picking

Canadian stocks. As with its foreign funds, its domestic offering has a slightly unusual mandate: It calls for investments in companies that are "a little smaller and more profitable than the typical TSE 300 company, while having less exposure to the U.S. economy." Some less obvious top ten picks include Bombardier Inc., Extendicare, Pan Canadian Petroleum and Canam Manac Group Inc. Scudder uses a bottom-up computerized model and started the year overweighted in paper and forests, financials and oil and gas.

With no loads, low management expense ratios (for now, at least), a 75-year history of strong fiduciary responsibility to investors, and a think-for-yourself approach to portfolio creation, Scudder Canada deserves to be on the short list for no-load global fund portfolios.

Smart Funds:

Scudder Global.

Noteworthy Funds:

Scudder's International Funds: Scudder U.S. has built its fund company around international investment expertise. On a relative basis, its funds have been only average performers. However, the funds follow a value style of investing (and, in the case of the Pacific and European funds, have the same manager as their U.S. equivalent). This conservative style is likely to provide acceptable returns with relatively low volatility.

Availability:

Direct from Scudder Canada.

45. SPECTRUM UNITED MUTUAL FUNDS INC.   LOAD

Strengths:	Small-cap funds in U.S., Canada and Europe
	United Canadian equity funds
Weaknesses:	Duplication and confusion from merger
	Spectrum funds sub-par
Web Site:	none **Toll Free:** 1-800-263-1851

CANADIAN	Category	Rating	Fund Name	M.E.R.%	RRSP/Foreign
Money Market:		■	Spectrum Cash Reserve Fund	1.12	RRSP
		■	Spectrum Savings Fund	0.99	RRSP
		■	United Canadian Interest Fund	1.39	RRSP

Fixed Income:	Long-term	■	United Canadian Bond Fund	1.92	RRSP
		■	Spectrum Government Bond Fund	1.50-2.00	RRSP
	Medium-term	■	Spectrum Interest Fund	1.44-1.94	RRSP
	Mortgage	■	United Canadian Mortgage Fund	1.88	RRSP
Equity:	Mid- to Large-cap	■	Spectrum Canadian Equity Fund	2.08-2.57	RRSP
		★	**United Canadian Equity Fund**	2.34	RRSP
		■	Canadian Investment Fund, Ltd.	2.28	RRSP
	Small-cap	▲	**United Canadian Growth Fund**	2.46	RRSP
Tax-advantaged:	Dividend	■	Spectrum Dividend Fund	1.46-1.96	RRSP
Multi-asset:	Balanced	■	Spectrum Diversified Fund	1.82-2.33	RRSP
	Asset Allocation	▦	Bullock Asset Strategy Fund	2.32-2.82	RRSP
	Portfolio of Funds	★	**United Portfolio of Funds**	1.17	RRSP

FOREIGN	Category	Rating	Fund Name	M.E.R.%	RRSP/Foreign
Money Market:		■	United U.S. Dollar Money Market Fund	0.77	Foreign
Fixed Income:		■	Bullock Global Bond Fund	2.03-2.53	Foreign
		■	Spectrum International Bond Fund	1.79-2.28	RRSP
Global Equity:	All-global	▲	**United Global Equity Fund**	2.74	Foreign
		▲	**Spectrum International Equity Fund**	2.32-2.83	Foreign
	Small-cap	■	United Global Growth Fund Ltd.	2.53	Foreign
	Specialty	▲	**United Global Telecommunications Fund**	2.80	Foreign
Regional Equity:					
	US Large-cap	★	**United American Equity Fund Ltd.**		Foreign
		▦	Bullock Optimax USA Fund	2.33-2.83	Foreign
	US Small-mid-cap	■	United American Growth Fund Ltd.	2.23	Foreign
		▲	**Bullock American Fund**	2.31-2.82	Foreign
	Emerging Market	★	**Bullock Emerging Markets Fund**	2.33-2.83	Foreign
	Far East	▲	**Bullock Asian Dynasty Fund**	2.33-2.83	Foreign
	Europe	★	**Bullock European Enterprise Fund**	2.30-2.80	Foreign
Global Balanced:					
	Portfolio of Funds	▦	United Global Portfolio of Funds	0.78	Foreign

The second-biggest fund company merger of 1995 (after that of AGF and 20/20) was Spectrum Bullock with United Financial Inc. United is one of Canada's pioneering mutual fund firms – its Canadian Investment Fund was founded in 1932.

The merged entity is the seventh largest in the broker-sold or "load" sales channel. Nevertheless, with 31 funds, the choice is so broad that many investors will have difficulty narrowing it down.

There are, for example, three money market funds, two domestic bond funds and one mortgage fund, two global bond funds, six Canadian equity or dividend funds, four U.S. equity funds, three broad-based global equity funds, two balanced funds and two "portfolios" or funds of funds.

Some of these can easily be eliminated on the basis of performance. Many of the Spectrum funds (Spectrum is a unit of Sun Life Assurance Co. of Canada) have been third- and fourth-quartile performers the past ten years. But the addition of the United funds and, in an earlier merger, Bullock funds, has strengthened the lineup.

With this many funds there are bound to be some winners and, indeed, the group had fourteen top-quartile one-year performers to the end of 1995, and nine with top-quartile numbers over five years.

The firm provides the complementary strengths of three money management companies, and ten external fund managers around the world. United's focus has always been North American equities. Spectrum funds tend to be value-oriented and strong in fixed income, while Bullock's forte is growth equity, particularly in small caps.

The home-run hitter in the local Canadian market is Kiki Delaney of Toronto-based Delaney Capital Management. (Spectrum president Allen Marple refused to close the deal to acquire United Financial Corp. until Delaney signed a five-year management contract.) Both Delaney and Lynn Miller, her colleague on the small mid-cap fund, have proven very successful.

The best-known Bullock fund – Bullock American, a Smart Fund this year – has had a change of manager, to MFS Asset Management of Boston, a sister company of Sun Life, Spectrum United's owner, and one of the most successful mutual fund operations in the U.S.

Spectrum's only new fund launch in 1995 was Bullock European Enterprise fund, a small-cap European equity fund that just might mimic the performance of Bullock American.

While it will take time for the company to adjust to the latest merger, once the fund families are fully integrated, Spectrum United should emerge as one of the stronger fund families in Canada.

Smart Funds:

United American Equity, United Canadian Equity, United Canadian Portfolio of Funds, Bullock Emerging Markets, Bullock European Enterprise.

Noteworthy Funds:

Spectrum International Equity/ United Global Equity. By the time this book hits the shelves, these funds will have been combined into Spectrum United Global Equity. The new fund will be managed by Morgan Grenfell (Asian Dynasty). This is a highly disciplined investment firm that should keep this fund very competitive.

Bullock Asian Dynasty, managed by Morgan Grenfell, is an Asian fund that also invests in Japan, unlike some of the funds in this category. Performance has been above average since inception. (Although Japan is picking up lately, participation in its market over the past two years has had a negative effect on many Asian portfolios.)

United Canadian Growth Fund. A Smart Fund in 1996, Lynn Miller's growth fund was the largest domestic small-cap fund in Canada – for good reason. Its performance was outstanding. In April, Spectrum United announced it was closing the fund to new investors and merging it with Bullock Growth fund. While performance has slipped over the year to date, Miller is one of the better managers in his class.

United Global Telecommunications. A Smart Fund in 1996, it's been second quartile over two years. Roughly half the portfolio is in U.S. technology and communications stocks. Piper Capital Management of Minneapolis picks the U.S. stocks, and determines the overall geographic allocation. Edinburgh Fund Managers of Scotland handles stock selection outside the U.S. This fund was demoted from Smart Fund status because GT Global is clearly the premier choice in this sector.

Availability:

Through brokers, dealers and Sun Life agents.

46. TALVEST FUND MANAGEMENT   LOAD

Strengths:	Fixed income and asset allocation
	Hyperion regional equity funds
Weaknesses:	Large-cap Canadian equities
Web Site:	None (but see CIBC Securities Inc.)
Toll Free:	1-800-465-165

CANADIAN	Category	Rating	Fund Name	M.E.R.%	RRSP/Foreign
Money Market:		■	Talvest Money Fund	0.85	RRSP
Fixed Income:	Long-term	▲	**Talvest Bond Fund**	1.99	RRSP
		■	Hyperion Fixed Income Fund	2.10	RRSP
	Short-term	★	**Talvest Income Fund**	1.50	RRSP
Equity:	Mid- to Large-cap	■	Talvest Growth Fund	2.40	RRSP
	Small-cap	■	Hyperion Aurora Fund	2.54	RRSP
	Other	▲	**Talvest New Economy Fund**	2.50	RRSP
Tax-advantaged:					
	Labour-sponsored	▲	**Canadian Medical Discoveries Fund**	5.00	RRSP
Multi-asset:	Dividend	▲	**Talvest Dividend**	1.99	RRSP
	Balanced	■	Talvest Diversified Fund	2.42	RRSP

FOREIGN	Category	Rating	Fund Name	M.E.R.%	RRSP/Foreign
Fixed Income:		★	**Talvest Foreign Pay Cdn. Bond Fund**	2.15	RRSP

Global Equity:	All-global	■	Talvest Global RRSP Fund	2.50	RRSP
Regional Equity:	US	■	Talvest U.S. Growth Fund Inc.	2.25	Foreign
	NAFTA/NA	▲	**Hyperion Value Line Equity Fund**	3.01	Foreign
	Far East	★	**Talvest Hyperion Asian Fund**	3.26	Foreign
	Europe	■	Hyperion European Fund	3.03	Foreign
Global Balanced:		■	Talvest U.S. Diversified Fund	2.27	Foreign
		■	Talvest Global Diversified Fund	2.75	Foreign

The "Tal" in Talvest stands for T.A.L. Investment Counsel Ltd., Talvest Fund Management's parent company. T.A.L. was founded in Montreal in 1972 and today manages $20 billion, much of it in pension funds.

The company decided to leverage its pension expertise to mutual funds and launched Talvest in 1985. In 1994, T.A.L. was acquired by Canadian Imperial Bank of Commerce, but TAL's operating shareholders retain management control.

The Hyperion funds transferred from CIBC Securities Inc. to Talvest in May 1995 are now fully integrated as part of the Talvest family. The minimum initial investment of $2,500 at CIBC has been dropped to $500, as with most Talvest funds, but the Hyperion name still appears. The more equity-oriented Hyperion funds are managed by experienced external advisors around the globe. However, they tend to carry higher than average management expense ratios.

While Talvest funds are broker-sold load funds (front load 5%, rear 5.5% declining to nil after seven years), many of the T.A.L. portfolio managers also manage similar funds for CIBC's no-load funds.

Talvest's regular funds are especially strong in fixed income. Talvest Bond has been consistently in the second quartile the past ten years, while Talvest Income was in the first quartile for the two years to April 30, 1996. The money market fund, Talvest Money, is first quartile over five years.

Talvest also uses derivatives that allow RRSP investors to maximize foreign content: it has both a 100% RRSP-eligible global bond fund as well as the less common 100% RRSP-eligible Global Equity fund.

It's worth noting that Talvest brokers have an interesting asset allocation software program called Asset Allocation Analyst, one of the better such programs available for Windows-based personal computers. Brokers can plug in both Talvest and competitive funds to develop a strategic approach to asset allocation that can be tactically tweaked, based on TAL's recommendations, as market conditions change.

Smart Funds:

Talvest Foreign Pay Canadian Bond, Talvest Hyperion Asian, Talvest Income.

Noteworthy Funds:

Canadian Medical Discoveries Fund. This labor-sponsored fund is one of the most promising of the tax-driven field of venture capital funds. Talvest markets and distributes it, but it's jointly managed by Medical Discovery Management Corp. and MDS Health Ventures. Note that the high MER of 5% is actually less than the category average of 5.09%. Much of the formerly generous tax incentives of labour-sponsored funds has been eliminated in recent budgets, however, so be sure to consider this strictly on its investment merits.

Talvest Bond. Under manager John Braive, this core bond fund has been consistently in the second quartile over the past ten years. Braive is considered one of the county's most astute fixed-income managers. His style of spread trading is less aggressive than that of those who try to anticipate interest rate moves.

Talvest New Economy: With new manager Pierre Bernard, Talvest New Economy is now in the first quartile for the year ended April 30, 1996, and second quartile over two years. Strategic input comes from Canadian economist and author Nuala Beck. As with Trimark's new Discovery Fund, the idea is that there are many more knowledge-based industries than just high technology. Unlike Trimark's, this one is 100% RRSP eligible.

Hyperion Value Line Equity Fund: This is managed by Value Line Inc., a well-respected research firm that ranks more than 1,700 U.S. growth stocks.

Talvest Dividend: Invested in large-cap, high-yield stocks, this would suit a conservative investor, or a growth-oriented investor looking for a tax-favourable income stream outside a registered account.

Availability:

Brokers and dealers across Canada.

47. TD GREEN LINE FUNDS

Strengths: Global equity funds
First bank to sell rival loads at branches
Education & support
Weaknesses: No 100% RRSP eligible global equity funds
Web Site: www.tdbank.ca/tdbank   **Toll Free:** 1-800-268-8166

CANADIAN	Category	Rating	Fund Name	M.E.R.%	RRSP/Foreign
Money Market:		■	Green Line Canadian Money Market Fund	0.78	RRSP
		■	Green Line Canadian T-Bill Fund	0.78	RRSP
Fixed Income:	Long-term	★	**Green Line Canadian Gov't. Bond Fund**	0.98	RRSP
		■	Green Line Real Return Bond Fund	1.70	RRSP
	Short-term	■	Green Line Short Term Income Fund	1.27	RRSP
	Mortgage	■	Green Line Mortgage Fund	1.61	RRSP
		■	Green Line Mortgage Backed Fund	1.67	RRSP
Equity:	Mid- to Large-cap	▲	**Green Line Blue Chip Equity Fund**	2.28	RRSP
	Mixed cap	■	Green Line Canadian Equity Fund	2.13	RRSP
		■	Green Line Canadian Value Fund	0.78	RRSP
	Index	▲	**Green Line Canadian Index Fund**	1.13	RRSP
	Gold/Precious Metal	▲	**Green Line Precious Metals Fund**	2.29	RRSP
	Resource	■	Green Line Resource Fund	2.25	RRSP
	Other	■	Green Line Energy Fund	2.29	RRSP
Tax-advantaged:	Dividend	■	Green Line Canadian Dividend Fund	2.02	RRSP
Multi-asset:	Balanced	■	Green Line Balanced Growth Fund	2.29	RRSP
		★	**Green Line Balanced Income Fund**	2.27	RRSP

FOREIGN	Category	Rating	Fund Name	M.E.R.%	RRSP/Foreign
Money Market:		■	Green Line U.S. Money Market Fund	1.30	RRSP
Fixed Income:		▲	**Green Line Global Gov't. Bond Fund**	2.11	Foreign
		■	Green Line Global RSP Bond	2.07	RRSP
Global Equity:	All-global	★	**Green Line Global Select Fund**	2.39	Foreign
	EAFE	■	Green Line International Equity Fund	2.35	Foreign
	Specialty	★	**Green Line Science & Technology Fund**	2.71	Foreign
Regional Equity:	US	▲	**Green Line U.S. Index Fund**	0.78	Foreign
	NAFTA/NA	★	**Green Line North American Growth Fund**	2.41	Foreign
	Latin American	■	Green Line Latin American Growth Fund	2.70	Foreign
	Emerging Market	★	**Green Line Emerging Markets Fund**	2.60	Foreign
	Far East	▲	**Green Line Asian Growth Fund**	2.61	Foreign
	Japan	■	Green Line Japanese Growth Fund	2.73	Foreign
	Europe	■	Green Line European Growth Fund	2.73	Foreign

The case for making TD Green Line your core no-load fund family is a compelling one: it offers 31 in-house funds plus some brand-name funds from outside families, the convenience of branch access, and an account service that allows you to mix and match other investments with your mutual funds in one portfolio. Not only that, but TD Green Line had more Smart Funds in the 1996 edition of this guide than does any other bank.

TD was among the first to recognize that the quickest way to build competent foreign funds is to set up a number of outside sub-advisers. It now has eleven external advisers around the world, including such respected firms as Sceptre Investment Counsel of Toronto, Morgan Stanley Asset Management Inc. of New York (a pioneer in emerging markets); T. Rowe Price Associates Inc. of Baltimore (manager of the top-performing Green Line Science & Technology Fund); Schroder Capital Management International, and Perpetual Portfolio Management of Britain, an award-winning investment shop that has also improved the performance of Global Strategy Group's hot World Emerging Companies fund.

Early in 1996, TD was the first major bank to allow its branches to sell outside funds – initially, five brand-name load funds including Templeton Growth and Trimark Canadian, all with a 2% front-end load.

TD also announced a related service, the TD Asset Accumulator Account, which allows clients to consolidate all money market, fixed-income and mutual fund investments: mixing and matching various funds from multiple companies along with direct investments in stocks, bonds, GICs and other products.

The bank also boasts one of the industry's more sophisticated staff-education programs, which includes an annual exam that all TD representatives must pass, and some innovative work on asset allocation. TD is also one of the few companies that offer low-cost index funds, both Canada and U.S. It also has the only indexed bond fund in Canada – the Canadian Government Bond Fund.

TD is making it easier to adjust portfolios too, with detailed quarterly statements and a free rebalancing service. TD even took a leaf from Trimark's "Appreciating Your Worth" campaign with its "Women in the Know II" program offering 600 investment seminars a year for women.

Smart Funds:

Green Line Balanced Income, Green Line Canadian Government Bond, Green Line Emerging Markets, Green Line Global Select, Green Line North American Growth, Green Line Science & Technology.

Noteworthy Funds:

Green Line Canadian Index Fund and Green Line U.S. Index Fund. With only a handful of managers beating the index on a consistent basis, a growing group of investors are turning to funds that simply

promise to match it. The funds' MERs are 1.11% and .78%, respectively.

Green Line Blue Chip Equity. This fund is managed by Sceptre Investment Counsel, a highly regarded equity manager. Expect consistent above-average performance and relatively low volatility.

Green Line Global Government Bond. A Smart Fund in 1996, this is managed by J.P. Morgan, which is internationally recognized for global fixed-income management. The J.P. Morgan Global Government Bond Index is one of the two most commonly quoted international bond indexes.

Green Line Asian Growth. Managed by Gartmore Capital Management in Britain, this fund (which excludes Japan) has delivered above-average returns since its inception in late '93. It was a Smart Fund in 1996.

Green Line Precious Metals. Like most metals funds, this fund has enjoyed the ride in gold stocks. Managed in-house by TD Asset Management.

Availability:

TD Bank branches; many dealers and brokers.

48. TEMPLETON MANAGEMENT LIMITED   LOAD

Strengths:	All-global equities		
	Bargain hunting value style		
Weaknesses:	Canadian funds		
	No 100% RRSP eligible global funds		
Web Site:	www.templeton.ca	Toll Free:	1-800-387-0830

CANADIAN	Category	Rating	Fund Name	M.E.R.%	RRSP/Foreign
Money Market:		■	Templeton Treasury Bill Fund	0.75	RRSP
Fixed Income:	Long-term	■	Templeton Canadian Bond Fund	1.65	RRSP
Equity:	Mid- to Large-cap	■	Templeton Canadian Stock Fund	1.65	RRSP
Multi-asset:	Balanced	■	Templeton Balanced Fund	2.45	RRSP
	Asset Allocation	■	Templeton Cdn. Asset Allocation Fund	2.15	RRSP

FOREIGN	Category	Rating	Fund Name	M.E.R.%	RRSP/Foreign
Fixed Income:		■	Templeton Global Bond Fund	2.25	Foreign
Global Equity:	All-global	★	**Templeton Growth Fund Ltd.**	2.00	Foreign
	EAFE	★	**Templeton International Stock Fund**	2.55	Foreign
	Small-cap	★	**Templeton Global Smaller Companies Fund**	2.62	Foreign

Regional Equity:				
	Emerging Market	★ **Templeton Emerging Markets Fund**	3.28	Foreign
Global Balanced:		■ Templeton International Balanced Fund	2.55	Foreign
		■ Templeton Global Balanced Fund	2.55	Foreign

When it comes to international equity investing, Templeton is an obvious and easy decision. As good as many of the newcomers are, it's hard to make a case why the average investor shouldn't buy Templeton Growth, and maybe a dash of Templeton Emerging Markets or Templeton Smaller Companies, and avoid frustrating regional equity decisions. The famous Templeton Growth mountain chart keeps on soaring into the clouds: $10,000 invested in 1954 was, as of Jan. 31, 1996, worth $3.6 million, a compound annual growth rate of 15.4%.

Unlike many of its rivals, Templeton doesn't pick Asia over Latin America, or Europe over North America. It doesn't make such "top-down" decisions at all: rather, it goes wherever in the world there are bargain-priced stocks. The four "laws of Templeton" are: hunt for bargains on a worldwide basis; buy low, sell high; all investments are risky; and, don't follow the crowd.

Nevertheless, some people like to make regional or top-down decisions, and if you're one of them, you'll likely be happier with C.I., Fidelity, Mackenzie Universal, and other fund families that offer more control. Templeton, at this point, offers no 100% RRSP-eligible global equity funds that help beat foreign content limitations. It makes no attempt to hedge foreign currencies. And, while it is increasing its bond and balanced fund emphasis, Templeton is still primarily a global equities specialist.

The firm doesn't jump in on various new fund fads. It views U.S.-based tech stocks as overvalued, for instance, and has for many years considered the Japanese stock market overvalued.

As a result, Templeton's twelve funds make an excellent core international equity fund family for Canadian investors, but should be supplemented with another Canadian equity family.

The four core funds are Growth, International Stock, Emerging Markets and Global Smaller Companies – all Smart Funds. Most investors put the lion's share in Growth, spicing the mix with Smaller Companies and/or Emerging Markets according to their risk/return objectives. International Stock, with its non-North American mandate, is used by those who already have a sizable exposure in Canada and the United States.

In late June of 1996, Franklin Resources, Templeton's

parent company, announced it was acquiring Michael Price and Heine Securities Corp., advisors to the top-ranked Mutual Series funds in the U.S. So far, this has not affected Templeton's Canadian operations, but it has expanded the selection of funds for U.S. investors. However, it is possible the Canadian subsidiary will introduce a Michael Price-run fund for Canadian investors. Such a fund would be focused on the U.S. market and hence complementary to the existing global products.

Smart Funds:

Templeton Emerging Markets, Templeton Global Small Companies, Templeton Growth, Templeton International Stock.

Noteworthy Funds:

The U.S. Templeton organization offers a wider selection of funds than the Toronto-based Templeton Management Ltd. Some of these are closed-end regional and single-country funds, traded on the New York Stock Exchange and thus available to Canadians.

Availability:

Brokers and planners, Municipal Trust, Bayshore Trust and TD Bank.

49. TRIMARK INVESTMENT MANAGEMENT INC. LOAD

Strengths:	North American equities
	Low MERs bond funds
	Service & education
Weaknesses:	No 100% RRSP eligible global funds
Web Site:	www.Trimark.com **Toll Free:** 1-800-387-9841

CANADIAN	Category	Rating	Fund Name	M.E.R.%	RRSP/Foreign
Money Market:		■	Trimark Interest Fund	0.75	RRSP
Fixed Income:	Long-term	★	**Trimark Canadian Bond Fund**	1.25	RRSP
		■	Trimark Advantage Bond Fund	1.25	RRSP
	Short-term	■	Trimark Government Income Fund	1.25	RRSP
Equity:	Mid- to Large-cap	★	**Trimark Canadian Fund**	1.54	RRSP
		▲	**Trimark RSP Equity Fund**	2.00	RRSP
		▲	**Trimark Select Canadian Growth Fund**	2.30	RRSP
Multi-asset:	Balanced	★	**Trimark Income Growth Fund**	1.73	RRSP
		▲	**Trimark Select Balanced Fund**	2.21	RRSP

FOREIGN	Category	Rating	Fund Name	M.E.R.%	RRSP/Foreign
Global Equity:	All-global	★	**Trimark Fund**	1.53	Foreign
		▲	**Trimark Select Growth Fund**	2.25	Foreign
	Specialty	▲	**Trimark Discovery Fund**	(new)	Foreign
Regional Equity:	NAFTA/NA	■	The Americas Fund	2.52	Foreign
	Far East	★	**Trimark Indo-Pacific Fund**	2.74	Foreign

A million Canadian investors and 22,000 financial planners and dealers would agree that Trimark richly deserves its solid reputation. This family delivers consistent performance as well as excellent customer service and reporting. It's so popular, in fact, that investors would have been better off buying Trimark's own stock in 1994-1995 – while the funds did well, the stock soared more than 600%.

As a fund family, Trimark does have its limits. It is essentially a specialist in North American stocks, which makes it vulnerable to any major setback in the U.S. stock market. In Canada, its sheer popularity has made the flagship fund, under lead manager Robert Krembil, so large (more than $5 billion) that it's increasingly difficult to outperform the market. (See the profile of Vito Maida in Chapter 2.)

Trimark's latest three funds, Indo Pacific, Trimark Americas and the new high-tech-plus Trimark Discovery, offer only limited scope for avoiding the North American focus. The Americas fund is half invested in large companies in Latin America and half in small companies in the U.S. Trimark Discovery is a small- to medium-cap "Trimark Fund Junior" with a focus on science and technology companies, many of them based in the U.S. Indo Pacific is the only Trimark equity fund that escapes the North American bias.

While Trimark is not normally an automatic choice for bonds, its bond funds, run by Patrick Farmer, are among the most competitively priced in the broker-sold channel. This bond expertise also shows up in the giant Trimark Select Balanced and Income Growth funds.

Most brokers and planners sell multiple fund families, and it's a safe bet that one of those families is Trimark. Trimark has several funds that can act as core holdings (notably in the Canadian and global equity category), and would be a reasonable complement to at least one other fund family that fills in the gaps, such as precious metals, dividend fund, global bond, energy, small-caps and other niche categories.

There used to be a saying that no one ever got fired for recommending IBM computers. The same could be said about Trimark in mutual funds. But it shouldn't necessarily be your only fund family. In a diversified fund portfolio, Trimark could provide the core North American funds, complemented by a more globally oriented family.

Smart Funds:

Trimark Canadian, Trimark Canadian Bond, Trimark Fund, Trimark Income Growth, Trimark Indo-Pacific.

Noteworthy Funds:

Trimark RSP Equity and Trimark Select Canadian Growth. These are simply DSC, or declining service charge, versions, with higher MERs, of the Trimark Canadian fund.

Trimark Select Growth. The DSC version, with a higher MER, of the Trimark Fund.

Trimark Select Balanced. The DSC version, with a higher MER, of the Trimark Income Growth Fund.

Trimark Discovery Fund. Trimark came late to the high-tech party with this more aggressive, smaller-cap version of the Trimark Fund. It focuses on science and technology as well as "mature industry innovators." Manager Rick Serafini isn't quite as experienced as some of his high-tech competitors at Altamira, Green Line and Mackenzie, but his mentors Krembil and Richard Whiting are investment industry veterans.

Availability:

Through brokers and dealers.

50. UNIVERSITY AVENUE MANAGEMENT LTD.   NO-LOAD

Strengths:	Canadian equities	
	Small and flexible	
Weaknesses:	Global funds	
	Distribution & profile	
Web Site:	www.fundlib.com	**Toll Free:** 1-800-465-1812

CANADIAN	Category	Rating	Fund Name	M.E.R.%	RRSP/Foreign
Money Market:		■	University Avenue Money Fund	(new)	RRSP
Fixed Income:	Long-term	▲	**University Avenue Bond Fund**	1.93	RRSP

Equity:	Mid- to Large-cap ▲	University Avenue Canadian Fund	2.53	RRSP

One of the smaller no-load families, University Avenue has attracted a disproportionate share of publicity. Among the attention-getters: president Andrew Roblin is president of the No-Load Fund Association; Roblin and vice-president Gordon Bonn made waves when they hired former Dynamic Canadian Growth Fund manager Jonathan Baird to advise the University Avenue Growth Fund; and, while there are only four funds in the stable, some have generated good performance. (The U.S.-oriented University Avenue Growth Fund, however, is fourth quartile over the ten years to May 31, 1996.)

Unlike some of the other no-frills, no-load outfits profiled in this book, management expense ratios at University Avenue are on the high side. Investors receive some assistance, however, including the company's informative yearly brochure, "Taxes and the Mutual Fund Investor."

Noteworthy Funds:

University Avenue Canadian Fund. This is the main reason a no-load investor might gravitate to University Avenue. Even before it snagged top-performing Baird from Dynamic, this fund was in the first quartile for the five years ended April 30, 1996. The previous manager was Richard Long, and Baird, a self-proclaimed "investment pragmatist," has maintained the momentum. Its MER is a high 2.53%. Baird is on board for another year, but has recently become the manager of two new C.I. funds.

University Avenue Bond Fund. Managed by Greg Black of Black Investment Management since its inception in 1993, this fund is in the second quartile for the three years to April 30, 1996. It holds mostly government bonds with a blended maturity structure; the MER is high at 1.93%.

Availability:

Direct from University Avenue; some brokers and dealers.

The 125
Smart Funds

Once an investment strategy is in place, the investor is faced with the difficult task of selecting the individual funds that will make up his or her portfolio. This chapter contains details of the 125 funds that we, along with the selection committee, would feel comfortable recommending to family and friends. We call these Smart Funds.

There are six criteria for selecting a Smart Fund. While performance is a key criterion, it is not the only one. Further, absolute performance is not that important. It is relative performance that is critical. We have represented this by quartile-ranking the Smart Funds against other funds in that asset category. This apples-to-apples comparison allows us to group the more than 1,200 funds sold in Canada into manageable groups. We can then maintain a watch over money managers with similar styles and mandates to determine who emerges the best of the bunch.

A unique feature of the Smart Fund Family is the inclusion of funds with less than three years performance history. In certain instances, this has forced a compromise of the criteria used on the more mature funds. However, we would be remiss if we did not identify some of the extraordinary money management talent that Canadian fund companies have developed or hired in recent years. Securities regulations make it difficult for fund companies to advertise the past track records of managers without reams of disclaimers. This is appropriate because past performance is not a guarantee of future performance, and the investing circumstances surrounding the new fund may be different from the old fund's. Still, we cannot ignore the manager's successful past and we have a bias toward managers who have proven track records.

SELECTION CRITERIA

Quartile ranking is the prime performance measure. Examining performance relative to a fund's category peers, both in compound and annual returns, allows for a more broad-based evaluation than the use of raw return numbers. Consistent, top-quartile performance over several periods is sought. Quartile rankings are determined by ranking the funds by their return numbers and then grouping the top 25% into the first category, or quartile, the next 25% into the second quartile, and so on. A mutual fund that can consistently achieve first- or second-quartile rankings will generate superior long-term returns for its unit-holders.

Management expense ratio (MER) is calculated by dividing the total annual expenses of the fund by the fund's assets. Currently, there is a wide range of MERs, even within the same asset classes. Good quality management must come at a reasonable price. These expenses are always deducted from the fund before returns are calculated.

Standard deviation is a measure of a fund's performance relative to its average return. It is a key measure of the historic variability of a fund's monthly returns. About 95% of the time a fund's returns will fall within two standard deviations of the average return. A fund with an average monthly return of 1% and a standard deviation of 3, should produce monthly returns of between -5% and 7%, 95% of the time. The lower the number, the less likely it is a fund will experience wide performance swings in the future.

Asset size is considered relative to the fund's asset type and its mandate. For example, small bond funds face a price disadvantage against larger bond funds, which, because of their size, can negotiate lower commissions. Likewise, small-cap funds with a large asset pool may find it difficult to move in and out of the stocks they want.

When choosing funds for income-oriented portfolios, distribution of income and capital gains is a key criterion. Monthly distributions are preferred.

The authors conduct interviews with hundreds of money managers a year. These meetings are designed to confirm stated positions on style, explore the reasons behind past success (or lack of it), and ensure adherence to a stated methodology. This qualitative process balances the other more quantitative aspects of fund selection.

SMART FUND LEGEND

There are many different pieces of information that are important to an investor when selecting a fund. We have included only the most important in each Smart Fund overview. Most do not need an explanation but we'd like to touch on a few.

Fund manager: The person or team listed on a page is the principal decision maker on the fund – the individual responsible for achieving the fund's performance. By the nature of the funds being selected, you could call these the Smart Managers. These managers are the best in Canada and should be on anyone's all-star team. The individual named is in-house, unless a sub-adviser is noted.

RRSP eligibility: 100% indicates that the fund is fully eligible; 20% means it can be held in an RRSP or RRIF as part of your foreign content.

Management style: *Equity style can be one of the following:*
- Bottom-up growth. The manager selects stocks based on their growth potential.
- Bottom-up value. The manager selects stocks based on price.
- Top-down growth. The manager selects for the growth potential of an industry, sector or geographic region.
- Sector rotator. The manager moves between industry sectors to capture growth.
- Growth at a reasonable price, or GARP, is a blend of growth and value.

Fixed income managers can adopt one of two styles or a blend of the two:
- Interest rate anticipation. Managers endeavour to predict the direction of interest rates, and structure the fund to take advantage of this movement.
- Spread trading. Managers trade bonds to capture the differences between the interest rates of bonds of different credit qualities.

Risk: While many investors are uncomfortable with a fund that is volatile – one that changes in value frequently and dramatically – it is really the loss of money that is disturbing. Therefore, this year, we have looked at the maximum loss that has been experienced by a fund over a three-month period of time. These quarters are not calendar quarters – they are "rolling" three-month periods – January, February, March would be the first quarter of the year; February, March, April would be the second rolling quarter; March, April, May is the third rolling quarter. There are 10 of these rolling quarters in a year.

We've also used the three-month time period to look at a fund's worst and best performance. The worst three-month performance for an older fund is often the three months ended November 1987. This risk indicator lets you see the fund at its worst and at its best.

Performance: The graph compares the growth of a $1,000 investment in the fund, a benchmark, and Canada Savings Bonds. The dots on the graph represent the fund's quartile performance in each calendar year. Beneath the graph are the fund's annual returns for each of the past nine calendar years and for the six months ending June 30, 1996. We have also calculated the compound returns for the periods ending June 30, 1996.

CANADIAN EQUITY FUNDS

For most Canadians, a significant portion of their core portfolio should be in mid-to large-cap Canadian equity funds. This is not because the Canadian market has outperformed other markets (it has not) but because:

- most Canadian investors are investing ultimately to spend in Canadian dollars,
- there is a familiarity with the companies that are picked for investment, and
- most investors are saving in their RRSPs, which are governed by foreign content rules.

Over the longer term, Canadian equities have outperformed Canadian bonds, so a core equity base is essential for long-term wealth accumulation.

Small-cap stocks are not for the conservative investor, or at least not as a significant portion of a portfolio. While they have a history of outperforming large-cap stocks over the long term, when they move down, they can go down a lot. However, Canada is becoming internationally recognized for our small-cap opportunities. Once dominated by junior oils, the sector is diversifying as our expertise in computer systems and software grows. But small-cap investing is a skill. The managers often rely on their own research, culled from a wide variety of services that help them find that company or niche that is still largely undiscovered. The attraction is the huge growth potential when the manager is right. Mutual funds are a natural vehicle for most investors who want to participate in this area of the market. The stocks are volatile, and owning a diversified portfolio will lessen the impact.

CANADIAN DIVIDEND FUNDS

Generally, dividend funds should be considered only by those investors who need to generate income from their non-RRSP portfolios. This is because of the tax treatment of dividends, which are taxed at 75% of the rate that applies to interest income from bonds and GICs. The major difference between dividend funds is the percentage of dividends coming from preferred stock. Preferred stock is issued with a fixed dividend rate, making it possible for an investor to determine what the return will be. And, there is greater security in preferred stock. A company must first pay its debt (bond) holders, and next in line are the preferred shareholders. Common equity holders are last in this hierarchy. In slower economic times, companies can suspend common equity payments without any obligation to make up these payments in the future. Rarely do they suspend preferred equity payments. If they do, they must pay the preferred dividends in arrears before any payments can be made to common shareholders. The tradeoff is that in good times, you could enjoy capital gains from common equity. The funds with a higher percentage of dividends from preferred stock will underperform in rising markets but they are the choice for those who want a higher degree of income certainty and less price volatility.

SPECIALTY FUNDS

These funds must be considered only in the context of a diversified portfolio. They are volatile, but investing in these funds wisely can have the effect of enhancing performance and reducing risk, since many behave different from broader market funds.

BALANCED FUNDS

Holding balanced funds is convenient. Ideally, investors should make their own decisions about asset mix and then invest with managers who specialize in equity or fixed income. If you do not have the time to do this, put the decision in the hands of those who do it for a living. There are essentially two types of balanced funds. Most are strategic allocation funds. These funds have fixed minimum and maximum percentages of stock and bond holdings. This type of fund is best suited to the more conservative investor. The tactical asset allocation funds can make more extreme bets. Their managers can be 100% in an asset class if they believe strongly enough to make such a decision. This type of balanced fund is clearly for the more risk-tolerant investor. International balanced funds have the same benefits as their domestic counterparts but include the benefit of geographic and currency diversification.

UNITED STATES EQUITY FUNDS

Too often Canadians feel they have to look across an ocean to get international investing exposure. The truth is that Canada has the largest capital market in the world just south of the border. For many, this market should represent a first step into global investing and serve as a significant portion of their international allocation over time.

The U.S. economy, in global terms, is not as big as it once was. However, it still represents approximately 40% of the global economy. Many of the world's largest and most successful companies are headquartered in the U.S. Many are multinational and derive much of their revenue from international activity. By investing in them, managers get international exposure without having to invest in less-regulated markets.

In addition, the U.S. has a fertile small-cap market. The entrepreneurial spirit in the U.S. is such that good ideas and talented people find the money to develop business propositions.

INTERNATIONAL EQUITY FUNDS

Global equity funds should be in almost everyone's portfolio. The Canadian equity market represents only 3% to 4% of world capital markets and it is prudent to look outside Canada when building a properly diversified portfolio. Yet, with the potential for increased return comes the potential for increased risk. Therefore, we favour globally diversified funds rather than regionally specific funds. Investors can enhance their portfolio returns while minimizing their reliance on any one region. Another reason to invest internationally is to diversify away from the Canadian dollar. Many people are concerned about the loonie losing its competitiveness; international investing is one way of protecting against that loss.

Ideally, every growth-oriented portfolio should include some emerging market exposure. However, the volatility that will be experienced by these funds means that anyone who finds such movement unsettling should steer clear of these funds. Broad-based emerging market funds, rather than their region-specific cousins, are the best way to take advantage of the areas around the world that will experience greater economic growth than more mature economies. Political stability and economic crises that exist in these regions will continue to cause short- to mid-term performance to remain uncertain.

While we believe that a true Smart Fund strategy employs global rather than regional funds for core holdings, there is no question that capturing the economic growth potential of the Far East could add significantly to an investment portfolio's performance. A huge population, a keen work ethic, and cultures that emphasize discipline make the Far East the region most likely to lead world growth over the next ten years. However, outside of Japan, this is largely a play on newly industrialized countries and is subject to volatility. Even Japan, now a mature market, has proven it has a volatile stock market. Therefore, the smart funds chosen represent broad-based approaches to the region, with investment weightings that are evenly distributed.

Other than the Far East, there is no region of the world likely to grow at the rates of the countries in Latin America. However, while these economies do not promise a smooth ride, they are going to benefit from the proximity to the North American economy and the many opportunities flowing from the NAFTA agreement. What is critical for investors is the breadth of investments chosen. Our selection again avoids fund managers who make big bets on any one country.

Europe is familiar to most investors; there is a sense of comfort with business practices and cultures there. We believe, however, that Europe represents the most conservative international step outside North America. The Western European markets, like our own, are mature and we do not expect the same growth potential as we do from Latin America or the Far East. However, these countries are not in the same economic cycle at the same time. There is an opportunity to invest during times when the other mature markets are out of cycle and thereby enhance a portfolio's return and lower its risk. Most of the funds in this section have looked at the Eastern European markets and are at various stages of investing in them. However, these countries are considered emerging markets, and the area is still seen as risky.

CANADIAN BOND FUNDS

Most of the excitement and glamour in mutual funds surrounds equity funds. But investing in bonds, mortgage and other fixed-income products can also be lucrative. This was certainly the case as rates came down in the early 1990s. The reverse is also true, as too many found out the hard way in 1994.

Just as there are many different types of equity funds, there are also differences among bond funds. The three key ones are term to maturity, credit quality, and style.

Average term to maturity measures a bond portfolio's

sensitivity to interest rate moves. The longer the bond fund's term to maturity, the more sensitive the fund is to these moves. Most bond fund managers have the flexibility to shorten or lengthen their term. There are a growing number that simply focus on short term (five years and under), and a few that have remained committed to longer term (eight years and more).

The second criteria is credit quality. Credit quality is expressed in terms of As and Bs. The highest quality is AAA. National governments often get this top rating. Most Canadian mutual funds invest across the range of A- to AAA-rated bonds.

And, there is style. There are two main styles in bond management: interest rate anticipation and spread trading. An interest rate anticipator has an opinion on where interest rates are headed. If the manager believes that rates are going up, he or she will shorten the average term to maturity. A spread trade focuses on credit quality and the prices of bonds. The lower the credit rating, the higher the interest rate the issuer pays to compensate the investor for the increased risk.

In looking for a Smart Bond Fund, there are two more criteria – size and price. In fact, price (MER) usually goes down as the size goes up. The debt market is huge. Those who trade bonds make a little on each transaction. Those with bigger amounts to buy and sell can demand better prices. As a rule of thumb, a bond fund under $100 million is going to fund it hard to compete. Ideally, a bond fund should have $500 million or more under management. Bond funds charging more than 2% are not competitive. 1% is ideal.

INTERNATIONAL BOND FUNDS

The criteria reviewed in the Canadian bonds fund section are also applicable to international bond funds. Currency is an important fourth variable. Today's securities markets make it possible to buy bonds issued in German marks or British pounds, without exposure to either of these currencies, through hedging. If, in the opinion of the manager, the currency of the bond is likely to be weak against the unitholder's currency, the international bond fund manager will try to manage the currencies defensively. The benefits of international bond investing are similar to international equity investing. Economic markets around the world are at different stages and hence will have different interest rates than Canada. Global bond managers can take advantage of many more investment opportunities to hedge the return, or reduce the risk, in their portfolios.

MONEY MARKET FUNDS

For most investors, these funds should be used as a temporary parking place for money to be spent or invested in the near-term. Often investors will "sit on the sidelines" waiting for the right time to invest. We believe, and a number of studies in the U.S. confirm the view, that, rather than trying to assess the right time, it is best just to make a move and get into the market. Market timing is a mug's game. Alternatively, for the cautious, a dollar-cost-averaging, automatic investment program could be used to gradually invest cash. If cash is to be spent within two years, a money market fund is a low-risk investment vehicle until the purchase date arrives.

Money market funds generally invest in the highest quality, Government of Canada treasury bills. The net asset value per share (NAVPS) is fixed at $10 and the total return is from the interest earned. Barring a sudden and severe shift in interest rates, the NAVPS should not fluctuate.

There are two things to keep in mind in shopping for a money market fund. If investing on a deferred sales charge (DSC) basis, use that fund family's money market fund to avoid redemption charges.

On the other hand, if you are looking only for a money market fund to hold some money prior to a purchase, shop for the one with the lowest fee, and which is still convenient to purchase. If this is the only investment you are making, you should not pay more than 0.75% in annual fees.

Money market funds can also represent the cash component of a portfolio. Cash plays two important roles in building an investment portfolio. First, cash, or money market, is the safest mutual fund investment and its low volatility will add stability to a portfolio that includes riskier funds. Second, money market funds provide liquidity. Investors can be left unprepared when an event occurs that requires a part of their portfolio to be sold. Money market funds can be sold quickly with no loss of principal, and when other investments may be temporarily down in price. Additionally, they will not generate a taxable capital gain. Without a money market fund, the alternative may be selling a fund with a good unrealized gain, only because of the emergency, leaving the investor exposed to a potential tax bill.

For most investors, the money market fund they use will be determined by the other mutual fund investments they make. Therefore, we do not recommend any money market funds as Smart Funds. However, if you are shopping only for a money market fund, consider them a form of bond fund and pay attention to the size and MER of the fund.

THE TOP SIX FUND FAMILIES

The first section of the book demonstrated the quality and product availability of the major mutual fund families in the Canadian mutual fund marketplace. This section presents what we feel to be the best individual funds available. It is important to recognize the high equality of money management talent available to Canadian investors. In general, when such talent has not been available here at home, Canadian fund companies have been fortunate to attract some of the best money managers from around the world. However, there are six fund companies that stand out from the competition. Within the fund companies that charge a sales load, the companies we feel deserve recognition are AGF-20/20, Guardian, and Mackenzie. Among the no-load families, we select Altamira, Phillips, Hager & North, and TD Green Line.

The choices were based not only on the number of Smart or Noteworthy Funds each company held, although this was a significant factor, but also on the range of funds in all asset classes, the range of management styles, the level of support to clients as determined by outside consultants, the depth of management talent and experience, and the extent of communications with clients and advisers.

All three of the no-load fund families were our choices in last year's edition of this book. The gap between Altamira, Phillips Hager & North and TD Green Line and the rest of their no-load competition remains significant.

AGF has certainly benefited from its acquisition of 20/20. It has increased both the quality and number of funds it offers. Complete integration of the fund families is scheduled for January 1997. This will be a very beneficial step for current and prospective unit holders. At that time, it will join the ranks of Mackenzie as a fully diversified fund family with quality managers, distinguished amongst their peers. Guardian is a fund company that has earned its recognition by seeking out the conservative side of the investment spectrum. Its appeal is not in pure performance, but in risk-adjusted performance. It has few competitors in this niche and even fewer rivals.

Remember, it's time, not timing that is important for all but the most fortunate. Successful investing requires a strategy. A strategy that is developed long before specific products are considered. Once you've determined the strategy, the fund families above, and the Smart Funds which follow, provide quality product choices.

We wish you success with whichever strategy you choose.

ABC FUNDAMENTAL VALUE   NO-LOAD

Primary Objective:	Aggressive Growth
Sponsor:	ABC
Fund Manager:	Irwin Michael, I.A. Michael Investment
Style:	Bottom-up, Value
Size (MMs):	$145.750
RRSP:	100%
Management Expense Ratio:	2.00% (Category Average: 2.32%)

COMMENTS

This is a concentrated portfolio (about 50 companies), which employs a value-investing style. This explains recent under performance, since it's been a growth investor's market of late. But the same style propelled this fund to a 3% gain when the category average was -8.6%. It also helped Michael produce an eye-popping 121.7% return in '93. While Michael has proven himself a great manager, the fund's $150,000 minimum makes him beyond the reach of most investors. Those who want a similar approach to the U.S. equity market should investigate Michael's new ABC American Value Fund.

RISK

The fund lost money in	31 of 87 Months
The fund lost money in	26 of 85 Quarters
Worst 3 Months	-9.28% (1995)
Best 3 Months	40.09% (1993)

ASSET ALLOCATION

Natural resources	31.0%
Industrial products	21.0%
Communications	18.0%
Consumer products/tech.	12.0%
Cash & equivalents	10.0%
Other	8.0%

COMPARISON OF FUND TO INDEXES

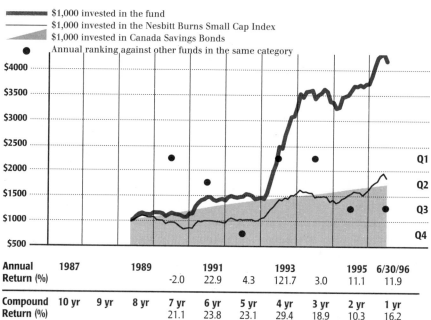

- $1,000 invested in the fund
- $1,000 invested in the Nesbitt Burns Small Cap Index
- $1,000 invested in Canada Savings Bonds
- Annual ranking against other funds in the same category

Annual Return (%)	1987			1989			1991			1993			1995	6/30/96
							-2.0	22.9	4.3	121.7	3.0		11.1	11.9

Compound Return (%)	10 yr	9 yr	8 yr	7 yr	6 yr	5 yr	4 yr	3 yr	2 yr	1 yr
				21.1	23.8	23.1	29.4	18.9	10.3	16.2

AGF GROWTH EQUITY A

Primary Objective:	Growth
Sponsor:	AGF Management
Fund Manager:	Bob Farquharson
Style:	Bottom-up Growth
Size (MMs):	$170.835
RRSP:	100%
Management Expense Ratio:	2.44% (Category Average: 2.32%)

COMMENTS

Because there is no mandate on this fund to be in small- or mid-cap, it is not usually classified as such. (The quartile rankings below are comparative to mid-to large-cap funds.) Farquharson (vice-chairman of AGF), has managed the fund for more than 30 years with a bottom- up growth style, but focuses on the mid-cap market with a leaning to the small-caps. The fund has displayed the characteristics of a small -cap fund, riding high in '93, suffering in '94 and recovering in '95 and early '96.

RISK

The fund lost money in..............49 of 114 Months
The fund lost money in ....40 of 112 Quarters
Worst 3 Months ....-30.23% (1987)
Best 3 Months...................................23.91% (1987)

ASSET ALLOCATION

Industrial Products...................26.0%
Oil & gas 17.0%
Gold & precious metals..........12.0%
Healthcare & biotech 7.0%
Other..38.0%

COMPARISON OF FUND TO INDEXES

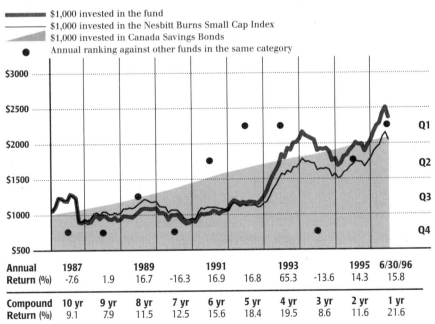

- $1,000 invested in the fund
- $1,000 invested in the Nesbitt Burns Small Cap Index
- $1,000 invested in Canada Savings Bonds
- Annual ranking against other funds in the same category

Annual Return (%)	1987		1989		1991		1993		1995	6/30/96
	-7.6	1.9	16.7	-16.3	16.9	16.8	65.3	-13.6	14.3	15.8

Compound Return (%)	10 yr	9 yr	8 yr	7 yr	6 yr	5 yr	4 yr	3 yr	2 yr	1 yr
	9.1	7.9	11.5	12.5	15.6	18.4	19.5	8.6	11.6	21.6

BPI CANADIAN SMALL COMPANIES LOAD

Primary Objective:	Aggressive Growth
Sponsor:	BPI Capital Management
Fund Manager:	Steven Misener, BPI
Style:	Bottom-up Growth
Size (MMs):	$373.500
RRSP:	100%
Management Expense Ratio:	2.61% (Category Average: 2.32%)

COMMENTS

This fund was one that, in hind-sight, should have made the Smart Funds list last year. However, at the time, Misener was still new to the fund. Misener was equal to the task, moving the fund into the top quartile of the category. A bottom-up value discipline is spiced-up with the addition of some private placements and special warrants, specifically in the high-tech sector. The fund, like many in the category, is attracting assets at a rate that has led BPI to discuss capping it. While no firm number had been announced, it will likely be capped around $450 million.

RISK

The fund lost money in ....40 of 104 Months
The fund lost money in ....38 of 102 Quarters
Worst 3 Months ....-9.38% (1990)
Best 3 Months 31.33% (1996)

ASSET ALLOCATION

Gold & silver.............................23.9%
Cash & equivalents..................16.6%
Technology................................12.4%
Industrial products.................11.1%
Other...36.0%

COMPARISON OF FUND TO INDEXES

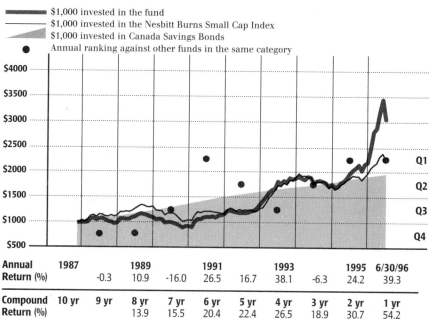

- $1,000 invested in the fund
- $1,000 invested in the Nesbitt Burns Small Cap Index
- $1,000 invested in Canada Savings Bonds
- Annual ranking against other funds in the same category

Annual Return (%)	1987		1989		1991		1993		1995	6/30/96
		-0.3	10.9	-16.0	26.5	16.7	38.1	-6.3	24.2	39.3

Compound Return (%)	10 yr	9 yr	8 yr	7 yr	6 yr	5 yr	4 yr	3 yr	2 yr	1 yr
			13.9	15.5	20.4	22.4	26.5	18.9	30.7	54.2

FIDELITY CANADIAN GROWTH COMPANY LOAD

Primary Objective:	Aggressive Growth
Sponsor:	Fidelity Investments Canada
Fund Manager:	Alan Radlo, Fidelity Management Research
Style:	Bottom-up, Growth
Size (MMs):	$504.991
RRSP:	100%
Management Expense Ratio:	2.64% (Category Average: 2.32%)

COMMENTS

This fund has lived up to the authors' expectations. Radlo, who had managed the Capital Builder fund before former manager, George Domolky, has parlayed Fidelity's unparalleled research ability into solid performance. A bottom-up growth investor, Radlo prefers the technology sector to the mining sector, believing the latter is too speculative in nature. This has both hindered and helped, as the mining sector has produced both huge wins and much volatility. Unlike many of his competitors, Radlo does not currently see fund size as a threat.

RISK

The fund lost money in ....4 of 23 Months
The fund lost money in ....2 of 21 Quarters
Worst 3 Months ....-0.56% (1995)
Best 3 Months......................................9.98% (1996)

ASSET ALLOCATION

Financial services......................3.3%
Communications & media 20.4%
Industrial products.................18.7%
Retail & merchandising 10.7%
Other...46.9%

COMPARISON OF FUND TO INDEXES

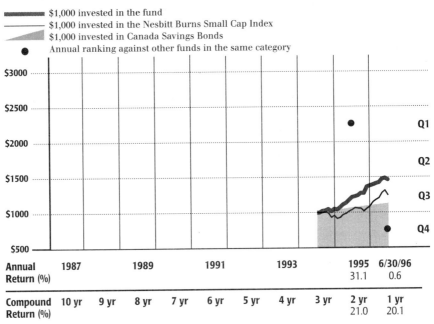

- $1,000 invested in the fund
- $1,000 invested in the Nesbitt Burns Small Cap Index
- $1,000 invested in Canada Savings Bonds
- Annual ranking against other funds in the same category

	1987	1989	1991	1993	1995	6/30/96
Annual Return (%)					31.1	0.6

	10 yr	9 yr	8 yr	7 yr	6 yr	5 yr	4 yr	3 yr	2 yr	1 yr
Compound Return (%)									21.0	20.1

158   SMART FUNDS 1997

GUARDIAN ENTERPRISE A   LOAD

Primary Objective:	Aggressive Growth
Sponsor:	Guardian Group of Funds
Fund Manager:	Gary Chapman, Guardian
Style:	Bottom-up, Growth
Size (MMs):	$18.26
RRSP:	100%
Management Expense Ratio:	2.15% (Category Average: 2.32%)

COMMENTS

Chapman took over the management of this fund in November, 1994 and performance
has dramatically turned around since. Using a bottom-up, stock-picking style, Chapman
tries to identify companies which are undervalued in relation to their earnings growth
rate. In-depth corporate analysis uses a proprietary valuation model and numerous
management contacts. The fund will hold between 40 and 50 companies, diversified
across many industries. If the holdings continue to grow at above-market rates,
Chapman will hold his positions, even if the holding reaches large-cap status.

RISK

The fund lost money in..............42 of 114 Months
The fund lost money in ....36 of 112 Quarters
Worst 3 Months ....-25.33% (1987)
Best 3 Months....................................23.30% (1987)

ASSET ALLOCATION

Cash & equivalents..................21.4%
Oil & gas 20.6%
Industrial products.................15.1%
Consumer products.................12.4%
Other..30.5%

COMPARISON OF FUND TO INDEXES

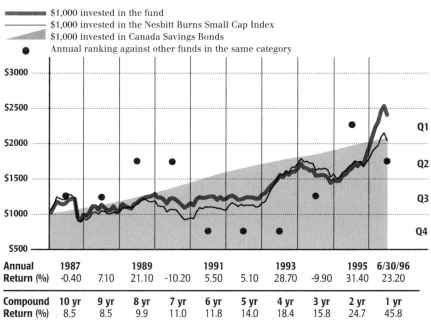

$1,000 invested in the fund
$1,000 invested in the Nesbitt Burns Small Cap Index
$1,000 invested in Canada Savings Bonds
● Annual ranking against other funds in the same category

Annual Return (%)	1987		1989		1991		1993		1995	6/30/96
	-0.40	7.10	21.10	-10.20	5.50	5.10	28.70	-9.90	31.40	23.20

Compound Return (%)	10 yr	9 yr	8 yr	7 yr	6 yr	5 yr	4 yr	3 yr	2 yr	1 yr
	8.5	8.5	9.9	11.0	11.8	14.0	18.4	15.8	24.7	45.8

O'DONNELL CANADIAN EMERGING GROWTH LOAD

Primary Objective:	Aggressive Growth
Sponsor:	O'Donnell Investment Management
Fund Manager:	Wayne Deans, Deans Knight Capital Management
Style:	Bottom-up, Growth
Size (MMs):	$249.150
RRSP:	100%
Management Expense Ratio:	2.55% (Category Average: 2.32%)

COMMENTS

Deans also manages the Marathon Equity Fund, Atlas Canadian Emerging Growth
Fund and Navigator Value Investment Retirement Fund. A bottom-up growth investor,
Deans requires companies to pass 13 growth criteria. Given the firm's location in
Vancouver, Deans is plugged into the mining and exploration sector and the fund will
always have a bias (25%) to that sector of the economy. Another key criterion for
Deans is a strong management team, preferably one with significant ownership in the
company. This fund has propelled the O'Donnell fund family to success in a short
time. It too, will likely be capped before the fund reaches $500 million in assets.

RISK

The fund lost money in .... 1 of 6 Months
The fund lost money in .... 0 of 4 Quarters
Worst 3 Months 7.00% (1996)
Best 3 Months 25.93% (1996)

ASSET ALLOCATION

Industrial products 14.5%
Metals & minerals 13.0%
Gold & silver 10.0%
Other 18.5%
Cash 44.0%

COMPARISON OF FUND TO INDEXES

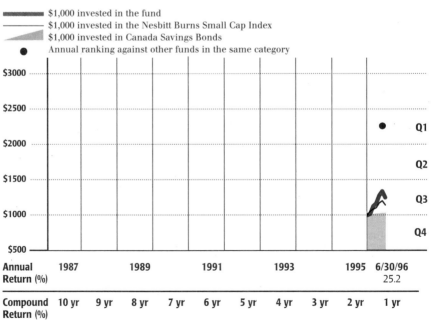

━━━━ $1,000 invested in the fund
──── $1,000 invested in the Nesbitt Burns Small Cap Index
$1,000 invested in Canada Savings Bonds
● Annual ranking against other funds in the same category

Annual Return (%)	1987	1989	1991	1993	1995	6/30/96
						25.2

Compound Return (%)	10 yr	9 yr	8 yr	7 yr	6 yr	5 yr	4 yr	3 yr	2 yr	1 yr

PACIFIC SPECIAL EQUITY

Primary Objective:	Aggressive Growth
Sponsor:	Pacific Capital Management
Fund Manager:	Graham Henderson
Style:	Bottom-up, Growth
Size (MMs):	$8.576
RRSP:	100%
Management Expense Ratio:	2.82% (Category Average: 2.32%)

COMMENTS

Although this is the only fund in the Pacific Capital family, Henderson must be recognized as a highly capable small-cap manager. Henderson's strategy is trend based. After identifying what he feels to be a significant trend (for example, lowering the cost of health care), he looks to industries and then companies that will benefit from this trend. At the company level, research focuses on earnings, growth potential and price relative to the first two. The fund will be concentrated (less than 50 stocks) with a minimum weight of 2% and a maximum weight of 8% to produce the best mix of risk control and performance. Further, it will never hold speculative resource stocks, preferring producing companies with proven expertise.

RISK

The fund lost money in	12 of 36 Months
The fund lost money in	12 of 34 Quarters
Worst 3 Months	-12.50% (1994)
Best 3 Months	40.57% (1993)

ASSET ALLOCATION

Biotech	28.0%
Gold & silver	17.0%
Industrial products	15.0%
Oil & gas	6.0%
Other	34.0%

COMPARISON OF FUND TO INDEXES

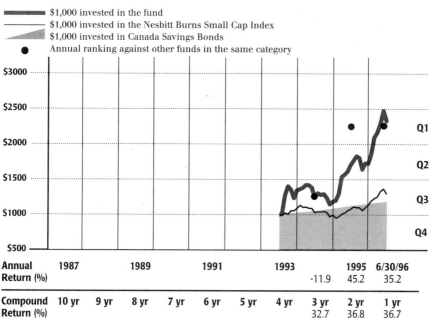

$1,000 invested in the fund
$1,000 invested in the Nesbitt Burns Small Cap Index
$1,000 invested in Canada Savings Bonds
● Annual ranking against other funds in the same category

Annual Return (%)	1987		1989		1991		1993		1995	6/30/96
								-11.9	45.2	35.2

Compound Return (%)	10 yr	9 yr	8 yr	7 yr	6 yr	5 yr	4 yr	3 yr	2 yr	1 yr
								32.7	36.8	36.7

SCEPTRE EQUITY GROWTH

NO-LOAD

Primary Objective:	Aggressive Growth
Sponsor:	Sceptre Investment Counsel
Fund Manager:	Allan Jacobs
Style:	Bottom-up, Growth
Size (MMs):	$118.598
RRSP:	100%
Management Expense Ratio:	1.68% (Category Average: 2.32%)

COMMENTS

This fund should have been a Smart Fund last year. We missed it. Jacobs has been an analyst and manager in small caps for more than 12 years. He joined Sceptre in 1993 and his value-based stock picking style has served this fund's unit holders well. While it has its share of small-cap names, this is predominantly a mid-cap fund. Jacobs is looking for small caps that will become large caps. His search for value finds him actively involved in the IPO markets as well as the Alberta and Vancouver exchanges. Jacobs uses other Sceptre funds for foreign content.

RISK

The fund lost money in..............38 of 114 Months
The fund lost money in ....36 of 112 Quarters
Worst 3 Months ....-19.26% (1987)
Best 3 Months.....................................21.60% (1987)

ASSET ALLOCATION

Industrial products..................22.8%
Financial services....................11.6%
Oil & gas 10.5%
Gold & silver.............................10.1%
Other..45.0%

COMPARISON OF FUND TO INDEXES

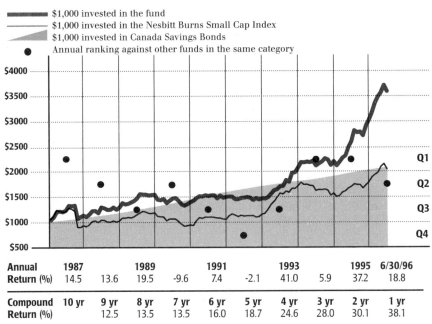

- $1,000 invested in the fund
- $1,000 invested in the Nesbitt Burns Small Cap Index
- $1,000 invested in Canada Savings Bonds
- Annual ranking against other funds in the same category

Annual Return (%)	1987		1989		1991		1993		1995	6/30/96
	14.5	13.6	19.5	-9.6	7.4	-2.1	41.0	5.9	37.2	18.8

Compound Return (%)	10 yr	9 yr	8 yr	7 yr	6 yr	5 yr	4 yr	3 yr	2 yr	1 yr
		12.5	13.5	13.5	16.0	18.7	24.6	28.0	30.1	38.1

AIC DIVERSIFIED CANADA

LOAD

Primary Objective: Growth
Sponsor: AIC Group of Funds
Fund Manager: Jonathan Wellum
Style: Bottom-up, Value
Size (MMs): $64.068
RRSP: 100%
Management Expense Ratio: 2.75% (Category Average: 2.08%)

COMMENTS

Wellum has made a name for himself (*Investment Executive* Fund Manager of the Year in 1995) and AIC by investing in the financial services sector, particularly other mutual fund companies. This fund complements this focus with exposure to a broader range of business sectors within the Canadian economy. Many of the fund's holdings are household names. But it is also Wellum's discipline that makes him stand out. Emulating the bottom-up buy-and-hold strategies of Berkshire Hathaway (headed by Warren Buffett) and Trimark, both of which Wellum has a stake in, he buys companies and will hold them for long periods of time. Turnover is low, as are distributions, making this fund particularly attractive for non-RRSP accounts.

RISK

The fund lost money in .... 4 of 18 Months
The fund lost money in .... 1 of 16 Quarters
Worst 3 Months .... -0.17% (1995)
Best 3 Months 15.69% (1996)

ASSET ALLOCATION

Financial services 50.4%
Consumer products 13.9%
Gold & precious metals 10.3%
Communication & media 9.4%
Other 16.0%

COMPARISON OF FUND TO INDEXES

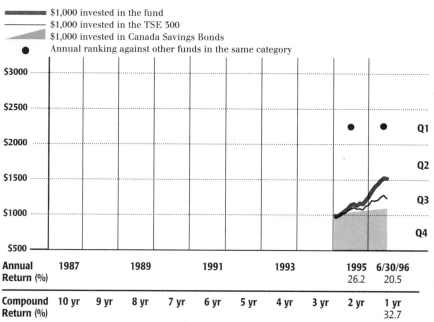

- $1,000 invested in the fund
- $1,000 invested in the TSE 300
- $1,000 invested in Canada Savings Bonds
- Annual ranking against other funds in the same category

Annual Return (%)	1987	1989	1991	1993	1995	6/30/96
					26.2	20.5

Compound Return (%)	10 yr	9 yr	8 yr	7 yr	6 yr	5 yr	4 yr	3 yr	2 yr	1 yr
										32.7

ALTAMIRA EQUITY

NO-LOAD

Primary Objective:	Growth
Sponsor:	Altamira Investment Management
Fund Manager:	Frank Mersch
Style:	Sector Over-weighting
Size (MMs):	$2,472.226
RRSP:	100%
Management Expense Ratio:	2.31% (Category Average: 2.08%)

COMMENTS

This is considered Altamira's flagship fund. Frank Mersch's following is justified, given how wealthy he has made his long-term unit holders. The fund is essentially a large-cap fund (forced there by its size, but it will at times invest in mid- and small-cap names.) Mersch combines growth-oriented stock picks with a thematic approach to market- sector selection. His quick trading style can lead to high turnover in the portfolio. This is in part the reason why the fund's MER remains above the average. As importantly, this fund will generate more realized, therefore taxable, capital gains. Therefore, it is best held in an RRSP.

RISK

The fund lost money in ....28 of 101 Months
The fund lost money in ....17 of 99 Quarters
Worst 3 Months ....-8.36% (1990)
Best 3 Months...................................23.74% (1993)

ASSET ALLOCATION

Gold & precious metals..........19.3%
Oil & gas 15.0%
Metals & minerals..................14.0%
Industrial products.................13.5%
Other...38.2%

COMPARISON OF FUND TO INDEXES

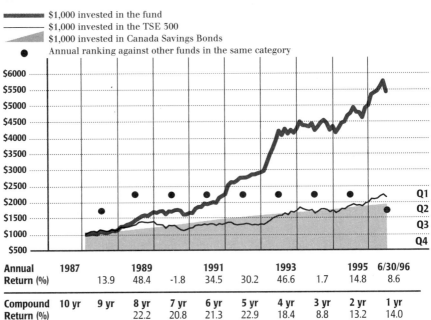

- $1,000 invested in the fund
- $1,000 invested in the TSE 300
- $1,000 invested in Canada Savings Bonds
- Annual ranking against other funds in the same category

Annual Return (%)	1987		1989		1991		1993		1995	6/30/96
		13.9	48.4	-1.8	34.5	30.2	46.6	1.7	14.8	8.6

Compound Return (%)	10 yr	9 yr	8 yr	7 yr	6 yr	5 yr	4 yr	3 yr	2 yr	1 yr
			22.2	20.8	21.3	22.9	18.4	8.8	13.2	14.0

BISSETT CANADIAN EQUITY

NO-LOAD

Primary Objective:	Growth
Sponsor:	Bissett & Associates
Fund Manager:	Michael Quinn, Fred Pynn, Bissett & Associates
Style:	Bottom-up Growth
Size (MMs):	$22.286
RRSP:	100%
Management Expense Ratio:	1.35% (Category Average: 2.08%)

COMMENTS

Quinn and Pynn have been managing this fund for more than ten years and have been giving their boss, David Bissett, a noted small-cap expert, a run for his money. They are bottom-up growth investors who try to manage portfolio volatility by maintaining a broad- based sector representation in the portfolio. The fund's MER of 1.35% makes it one of the least expensive in the category. In '96, the Bissett funds expanded their availability outside Alberta to Ontario and B.C. as well.

RISK

The fund lost money in	43 of 114 Months
The fund lost money in	31 of 112 Quarters
Worst 3 Months	-25.33% (1987)
Best 3 Months	18.03% (1987)

ASSET ALLOCATION

Industrial products	23.5%
Financial services	15.0%
Oil & gas	11.3%
Consumer products	7.3%
Other	42.9%

COMPARISON OF FUND TO INDEXES

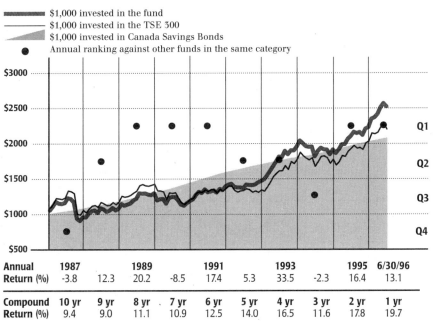

- $1,000 invested in the fund
- $1,000 invested in the TSE 300
- $1,000 invested in Canada Savings Bonds
- Annual ranking against other funds in the same category

Annual	1987		1989		1991		1993		1995	6/30/96
Return (%)	-3.8	12.3	20.2	-8.5	17.4	5.3	33.5	-2.3	16.4	13.1

Compound	10 yr	9 yr	8 yr	7 yr	6 yr	5 yr	4 yr	3 yr	2 yr	1 yr
Return (%)	9.4	9.0	11.1	10.9	12.5	14.0	16.5	11.6	17.8	19.7

ELLIOTT & PAGE EQUITY

LOAD

Primary Objective:	Growth
Sponsor:	Elliott & Page Mutual Funds
Fund Manager:	Nereo Piticco, PCJ Investment Counsel
Style:	Sector Rotation
Size (MMs):	$402.439
RRSP:	100%
Management Expense Ratio:	1.95% (Category Average: 2.08%)

COMMENTS

Managers move amongst the fourteen components, or sectors, that make up the TSE 300. They will target the sectors they anticipate to outperform the TSE 300. The fund will typically be invested in 10 sectors with a maximum commitment to a single sector of 30%. Stock selection within each sector is concentrated on highly liquid, blue-chip companies. On July 17th, 1996, three of the four E&P equity team members (Piticco, Jackson and Campbell) left the firm to form PCJ Investments. However, the separation was amicable, and PCJ retained E&P as their first client managing over $800mm in Canadian pension and mutual fund equities.

RISK

The fund lost money in ....37 of 97 Months
The fund lost money in ....30 of 95 Quarters
Worst 3 Months ....-11.39% (1990)
Best 3 Months 16.83% (1993)

ASSET ALLOCATION

Oil & gas 17.3%
Industrial products.................14.1%
Metals & minerals 13.1%
Communications & media.....10.1%
Other...45.4%

COMPARISON OF FUND TO INDEXES

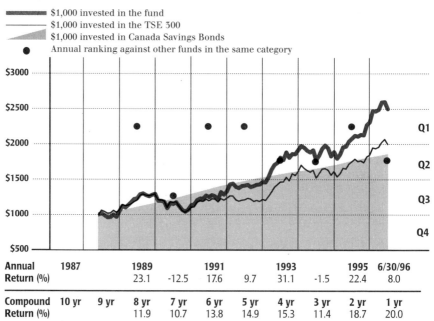

- $1,000 invested in the fund
- $1,000 invested in the TSE 300
- $1,000 invested in Canada Savings Bonds
- Annual ranking against other funds in the same category

Annual Return (%)	1987		1989		1991		1993		1995	6/30/96
			23.1	-12.5	17.6	9.7	31.1	-1.5	22.4	8.0

Compound Return (%)	10 yr	9 yr	8 yr	7 yr	6 yr	5 yr	4 yr	3 yr	2 yr	1 yr
			11.9	10.7	13.8	14.9	15.3	11.4	18.7	20.0

CANADIAN EQUITY

FIDELITY TRUE NORTH

Primary Objective:	Growth
Sponsor:	Fidelity Investments
Fund Manager:	Veronika Hirsch
Style:	
Size (MMs):	(New fund)
RRSP:	
Management Expense Ratio:	(Category Average: 2.08%)

COMMENTS

This fund is chosen strictly because of the manager. It was not in existence at the time of writing. However, the funds that she managed at AGF were to be Smart Funds solely based on her involvement. We feel she will continue as a top quartile manager. Her style is a blend of sector rotation and bottom up stock picking. She is heavily biased towards companies with an export focus, feeling that our economy is not sufficient to support growth focused companies. Given that she spent many years as a mining analyst, she is knowledgeable and well connected in the mining and exploration sectors. She was early on both Diamond Fields and Bre-X, two names which had big positives effects on her portfolios in '96.

RISK

The fund lost money in ....N/A
The fund lost money in ....N/A
Worst 3 Months ....N/A
Best 3 Months ....N/A

ASSET ALLOCATION

COMPARISON OF FUND TO INDEXES

▬▬▬ $1,000 invested in the fund
───── $1,000 invested in the TSE 300
▰▰▰▰ $1,000 invested in Canada Savings Bonds
● Annual ranking against other funds in the same category

(No data: new fund)

Annual Return (%)	1987		1989		1991		1993		1995	6/30/96
Compound Return (%)	10 yr	9 yr	8 yr	7 yr	6 yr	5 yr	4 yr	3 yr	2 yr	1 yr

GT GLOBAL CANADA GROWTH CLASS LOAD

Primary Objective:	Growth
Sponsor:	GT Global Canada
Fund Manager:	Derek Webb, LGT Management
Style:	Bottom-up, Growth
Size (MMs):	$179.207
RRSP:	100%
Management Expense Ratio:	2.95% (Category Average: 2.08%)

COMMENTS

This fund uses a disciplined security selection process that focuses on corporate growth. Incorporated in Webb's analysis are corporate growth projections, analyst expectations and price momentum. Negative moves in any of these areas often leads to a holding being sold. The model has been back tested with favourable results. A fund mandate is to have a minimum 15% foreign content and often closer to the maximum 20%.

RISK

The fund lost money in .... 4 of 18 Months
The fund lost money in .... 2 of 16 Quarters
Worst 3 Months .... -2.14% (1995)
Best 3 Months 17.61% (1996)

ASSET ALLOCATION

Metals & minerals 38.4%
Consumer products 20.6%
Industrial products 12.4%
Cash 11.6%
Other 17.0%

COMPARISON OF FUND TO INDEXES

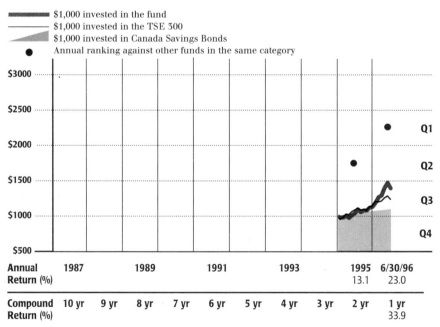

- $1,000 invested in the fund
- $1,000 invested in the TSE 300
- $1,000 invested in Canada Savings Bonds
- Annual ranking against other funds in the same category

Annual Return (%)	1987	1989	1991	1993	1995	6/30/96
					13.1	23.0

Compound Return (%)	10 yr	9 yr	8 yr	7 yr	6 yr	5 yr	4 yr	3 yr	2 yr	1 yr
										33.9

IVY CANADIAN

Primary Objective:	Growth
Sponsor:	Mackenzie Financial
Fund Manager:	Gerry Coleman
Style:	Bottom-up, Value
Size (MMs):	$1,483.772
RRSP:	100%
Management Expense Ratio:	2.42% (Category Average: 2.08%)

COMMENTS

Gerry Coleman and Jerry Javasky have a long history of above-average performance in Canadian equity management. Their bottom up style is similar to Trimark's philosophy of buying into great businesses. The difference is Ivy's emphasis on value. Price criteria are much stricter, which can lead the managers to hold large positions in cash. Ivy was criticized for this during the market run up in '93, then praised for it as markets dropped in '94. Again in '96, a plus-20% cash and almost 5% gold bullion position has given Ivy Canadian unit holders a smoother ride, despite choppy markets. At the same time, Ivy has maintained above average performance. It has emerged as another safe haven fund along with several Trimark products.

RISK

The fund lost money in..............13 of 43 Months
The fund lost money in..............5 of 41 Quarters
Worst 3 Months ....-2.93% (1994)
Best 3 Months....................................8.65% (1996)

ASSET ALLOCATION

Canadian equities....................51.4%
Cash & equivalents.................24.8%
U.S. equities..............................13.2%
U.S. cash......................................4.9%
Other...5.7%

COMPARISON OF FUND TO INDEXES

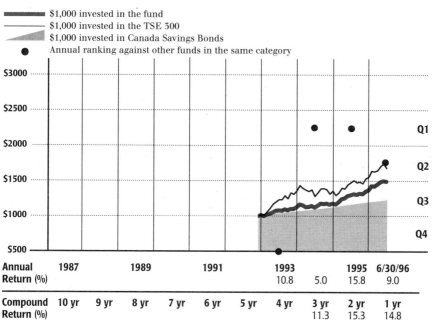

- ▬▬▬ $1,000 invested in the fund
- —— $1,000 invested in the TSE 300
- ◢ $1,000 invested in Canada Savings Bonds
- ● Annual ranking against other funds in the same category

	1987		1989		1991		1993		1995	6/30/96
Annual Return (%)							10.8	5.0	15.8	9.0

	10 yr	9 yr	8 yr	7 yr	6 yr	5 yr	4 yr	3 yr	2 yr	1 yr
Compound Return (%)								11.3	15.3	14.8

CANADIAN EQUITY

MAXXUM CANADIAN EQUITY GROWTH LOAD

Primary Objective:	Growth
Sponsor:	London Fund Management (formerly Prudential)
Fund Manager:	Jacqueline Pratt, Prudential
Style:	Bottom-up, Growth
Size (MMs):	$143.771
RRSP:	100%
Management Expense Ratio:	1.75% (Category Average: 2.08%)

COMMENTS

The departure of Veronika Hirsch in mid-'95 kept this fund from the Smart Funds list last year. However, Jacqueline Pratt, who took over from Hirsch, has proven worthy of the task. While the fund certainly benefited from some of the names Hirsch put into it, its make up is significantly different from a year ago. At the time of writing, it did not appear that the London Life buyout of Prudential would have any impact, other than in name, on the fund.

RISK

The fund lost money in..............45 of 114 Months
The fund lost money in ....36 of 112 Quarters
Worst 3 Months ....-29.56% (1987)
Best 3 Months....................................26.69% (1987)

ASSET ALLOCATION

Industrial products..................21.1%
Gold & silver............................14.8%
Metals & minerals..................13.1%
Oil & gas 12.2%
Other..38.8%

COMPARISON OF FUND TO INDEXES

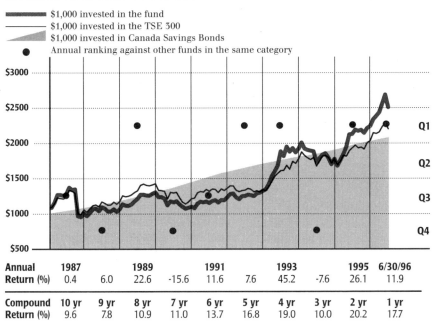

- $1,000 invested in the fund
- $1,000 invested in the TSE 300
- $1,000 invested in Canada Savings Bonds
- Annual ranking against other funds in the same category

Annual	1987		1989		1991		1993		1995	6/30/96
Return (%)	0.4	6.0	22.6	-15.6	11.6	7.6	45.2	-7.6	26.1	11.9

Compound	10 yr	9 yr	8 yr	7 yr	6 yr	5 yr	4 yr	3 yr	2 yr	1 yr
Return (%)	9.6	7.8	10.9	11.0	13.7	16.8	19.0	10.0	20.2	17.7

PH&N CANADIAN EQUITY

NO-LOAD

Primary Objective:	Growth
Sponsor:	Phillips, Hager & North
Fund Manager:	Team
Style:	Bottom-up Growth
Size (MMs):	$365.704
RRSP:	100%
Management Expense Ratio:	1.13% (Category Average: 2.08%)

COMMENTS

PH&N is one of Canada's pre-eminent money management firms, although the Vancouver location and lack of advertising makes it less familiar to many Canadian investors. Funds are managed by teams. The Canadian equity team is made up of five managers. This fund focuses on growing mid- to large-cap companies, although it will go into small-caps in certain sectors (e.g. oil and gas). It has achieved above-average return with below average risk. It also boasts one of the lowest MERs in the category at 1.13%. This compares with the TD Green Line Canadian Index Fund at 1.11%, a fund that has no active management.

RISK

The fund lost money in..............44 of 114 Months
The fund lost money in ....34 of 112 Quarters
Worst 3 Months ....-24.38% (1987)
Best 3 Months....................................19.20% (1987)

ASSET ALLOCATION

Financial services...................17.9%
Industrial products................17.4%
Oil & gas 13.3%
Merchandising 11.0%
Other...40.4%

COMPARISON OF FUND TO INDEXES

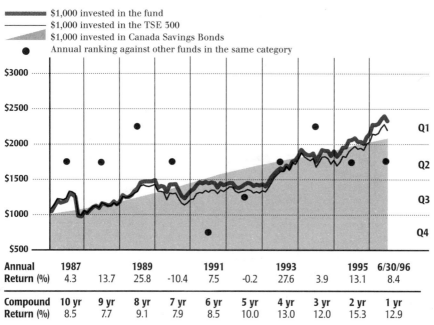

- $1,000 invested in the fund
- $1,000 invested in the TSE 300
- $1,000 invested in Canada Savings Bonds
- Annual ranking against other funds in the same category

Annual Return (%)	1987		1989		1991		1993		1995	6/30/96
	4.3	13.7	25.8	-10.4	7.5	-0.2	27.6	3.9	13.1	8.4

Compound Return (%)	10 yr	9 yr	8 yr	7 yr	6 yr	5 yr	4 yr	3 yr	2 yr	1 yr
	8.5	7.7	9.1	7.9	8.5	10.0	13.0	12.0	15.3	12.9

SCOTIA EXCELSIOR CANADIAN GROWTH NO-LOAD

Primary Objective:	Growth
Sponsor:	Scotia Mutual Funds
Fund Manager:	Denis Ouellet
Style:	Bottom-up Growth
Size (MMs):	$268.699
RRSP:	100%
Management Expense Ratio:	2.11% (Category Average: 2.08%)

COMMENTS

This fund may well have made the Smart Funds pages last year were it not for the fact that Scotia Securities was absorbing Montreal Trust, the former manager of this fund. One of the jewels in the Montreal Trust fund family, this fund is the exception to the vanilla large-cap bank-run funds. Credit manager Ouellet, whose bottom-up value-based style has made this fund a consistent top-quartile performer since its inception.

RISK

The fund lost money in..............42 of 114 Months
The fund lost money in ....35 of 112 Quarters
Worst 3 Months ....-20.62% (1987)
Best 3 Months....................................24.29% (1987)

ASSET ALLOCATION

Canadian equities....................96.2%
Cash & equivalents...................3.0%
Bonds...0.8%

COMPARISON OF FUND TO INDEXES

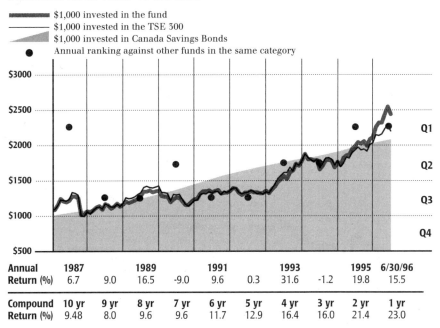

- $1,000 invested in the fund
- $1,000 invested in the TSE 300
- $1,000 invested in Canada Savings Bonds
- Annual ranking against other funds in the same category

Annual	1987		1989		1991		1993		1995	6/30/96
Return (%)	6.7	9.0	16.5	-9.0	9.6	0.3	31.6	-1.2	19.8	15.5

Compound	10 yr	9 yr	8 yr	7 yr	6 yr	5 yr	4 yr	3 yr	2 yr	1 yr
Return (%)	9.48	8.0	9.6	9.6	11.7	12.9	16.4	16.0	21.4	23.0

CANADIAN EQUITY

SPECTRUM UNITED CANADIAN EQUITY   LOAD

Primary Objective:	Growth
Sponsor:	Spectrum United Mutual Funds
Fund Manager:	Catherine (Kiki) Delaney, Delaney Capital Management
Style:	Bottom-up Growth
Size (MMs):	$551.942
RRSP:	100%
Management Expense Ratio:	2.30% (Category Average: 2.08%)

COMMENTS

This fund has a long history of high performance, resulting from two stewardships. Until 1992, it was managed by Gerry Coleman and Jerry Javasky, who moved to Mackenzie to run the Ivy funds (see Ivy Canadian entry). The Spectrum United fund is now run by Catherine (Kiki) Delaney with a growth at a reasonable price (GARP) style. Delaney first looks for companies that are growing at an above-average rate. Then she assesses their value. She will not buy if she feels a company is overvalued, regardless of how good it looks.

RISK

The fund lost money in..............41 of 114 Months
The fund lost money in ....31 of 112 Quarters
Worst 3 Months................................-17.81% (1987)
Best 3 Months.....................................17.32% (1993)

ASSET ALLOCATION

Oil & gas 21.20%
Industrial products.................16.30%
Financial services...................14.40%
Cash & equivalents...................7.60%
Other...40.50%

COMPARISON OF FUND TO INDEXES

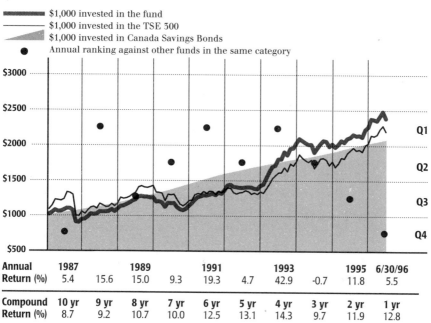

■■■■■ $1,000 invested in the fund
——— $1,000 invested in the TSE 300
▨▨▨ $1,000 invested in Canada Savings Bonds
● Annual ranking against other funds in the same category

Annual Return (%)	1987		1989		1991		1993		1995	6/30/96
	5.4	15.6	15.0	9.3	19.3	4.7	42.9	-0.7	11.8	5.5

Compound Return (%)	10 yr	9 yr	8 yr	7 yr	6 yr	5 yr	4 yr	3 yr	2 yr	1 yr
	8.7	9.2	10.7	10.0	12.5	13.1	14.3	9.7	11.9	12.8

TRIMARK CANADIAN

LOAD

Primary Objective:	Growth
Sponsor:	Trimark Investment Management
Fund Manager:	Vito Maida, Trimark
Style:	Bottom-up Growth
Size (MMs):	$1,485.346
RRSP:	100%
Management Expense Ratio:	1.54% (Category Average: 2.08%)

COMMENTS

The Trimark philosophy is to invest in businesses the managers know extremely well, and then stick with them. The primary focus is on growth companies that dominate their market. Given the screening that is required with this style, they have very concentrated portfolios. Maida, who took over as manager in the fall of '95 after an extensive search, has proven up to the task. Recent under performance is more style related than anything else. We recommend the Canadian fund, available only on a front-end basis, with an MER of 1.54%. Almost identical funds are available on a deferred sales charge basis. RSP Equity has an MER of 2.00% with a 9-year redemption schedule, and Select Canadian has an MER of 2.28% with a 6-year redemption schedule.

RISK

The fund lost money in	42 of 114 Months
The fund lost money in	28 of 112 Quarters
Worst 3 Months	-22.27% (1987)
Best 3 Months	17.94% (1987)

ASSET ALLOCATION

Canadian equities	65.00%
Foreign equities	21.80%
Cash & equivalents	12.90%
Convertible debentures	0.30%

COMPARISON OF FUND TO INDEXES

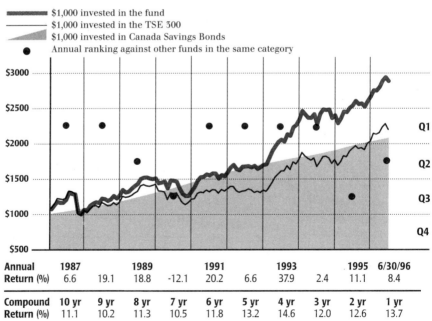

- $1,000 invested in the fund
- $1,000 invested in the TSE 300
- $1,000 invested in Canada Savings Bonds
- Annual ranking against other funds in the same category

Annual Return (%)	1987		1989		1991		1993		1995	6/30/96
	6.6	19.1	18.8	-12.1	20.2	6.6	37.9	2.4	11.1	8.4

Compound Return (%)	10 yr	9 yr	8 yr	7 yr	6 yr	5 yr	4 yr	3 yr	2 yr	1 yr
	11.1	10.2	11.3	10.5	11.8	13.2	14.6	12.0	12.6	13.7

ALTAMIRA U.S. LARGER COMPANIES NO-LOAD

Primary Objective:	Growth
Sponsor:	Altamira Investment Management
Fund Manager:	Ian Ainsworth, Altamira
Style:	Bottom-up, Growth
Size (MMs):	$94.343
RRSP:	20%
Management Expense Ratio:	2.36% (Category Average: 2.30%)

COMMENTS

Using a portfolio strategy that emphasizes growth, Ainsworth focuses on the big-cap companies in the U.S. The mandate of the fund is to give unit holders exposure to the U.S. in a relatively conservative manner. The fund is well diversified among industry sectors. While this fund is not insulated from broad-based market declines, its sector diversification and cap-size focus should allow it to meet its mandate. Investors who like high-tech and Ainsworth's style can access both through the Altamira Science & Technology Fund.

RISK

The fund lost money in ....11 of 34 Months
The fund lost money in ....6 of 32 Quarters
Worst 3 Months ....-5.20% (1994)
Best 3 Months 17.78% (1995)

ASSET ALLOCATION

Capital goods & technology...19.6%
Financial services....................16.4%
Consumer services..................15.8%
Basic industries.........................9.3%
Other..38.9%

COMPARISON OF FUND TO INDEXES

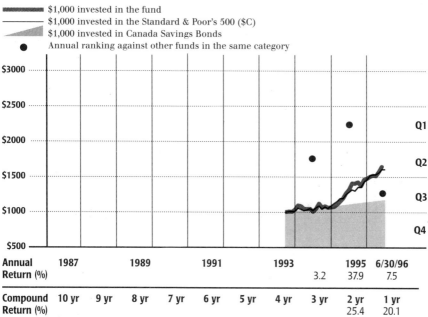

- $1,000 invested in the fund
- $1,000 invested in the Standard & Poor's 500 ($C)
- $1,000 invested in Canada Savings Bonds
- ● Annual ranking against other funds in the same category

Annual Return (%)	1987		1989		1991		1993		1995	6/30/96
								3.2	37.9	7.5

Compound Return (%)	10 yr	9 yr	8 yr	7 yr	6 yr	5 yr	4 yr	3 yr	2 yr	1 yr
									25.4	20.1

BPI AMERICAN SMALL COMPANIES LOAD

Primary Objective:	Aggressive Growth
Sponsor:	BPI
Fund Manager:	Michael Rome, Lazard Freres
Style:	Bottom-up, Value
Size (MMs):	$82.200
RRSP:	20%
Management Expense Ratio:	2.95% (Category Average: 2.30%)

COMMENTS

Using a bottom-up, value discipline, Michael Rome concentrates on about 60 stocks that appear to offer superior capital gains potential. BPI should be complimented since, in the year since we included it as a Smart Fund, the MER has been reduced from 3.49% to 2.95%. Given its focus on small caps, this fund will be relatively volatile within the U.S. equity category.

RISK

The fund lost money in ....47 of 114 Months
The fund lost money in ....39 of 112 Quarters
Worst 3 Months ....-33.48% (1987)
Best 3 Months 23.97% (1987)

ASSET ALLOCATION

Technology 18.4%
Consumer discretion 17.2%
Financial services....................16.1%
Producer manufacture...........13.7%
Other..34.6%

COMPARISON OF FUND TO INDEXES

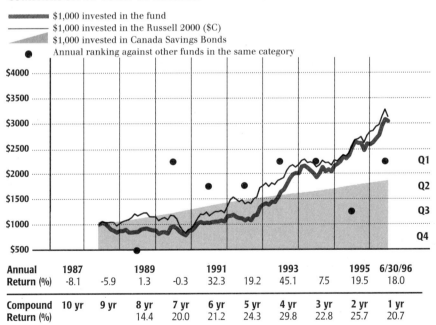

- $1,000 invested in the fund
- $1,000 invested in the Russell 2000 ($C)
- $1,000 invested in Canada Savings Bonds
- Annual ranking against other funds in the same category

Annual Return (%)	1987		1989		1991		1993		1995	6/30/96
	-8.1	-5.9	1.3	-0.3	32.3	19.2	45.1	7.5	19.5	18.0

Compound Return (%)	10 yr	9 yr	8 yr	7 yr	6 yr	5 yr	4 yr	3 yr	2 yr	1 yr
			14.4	20.0	21.2	24.3	29.8	22.8	25.7	20.7

U.S. EQUITY

C.I. AMERICAN

Primary Objective:	Growth
Sponsor:	C.I. Mutual Funds
Fund Manager:	Bill Priest, BEA Associates
Style:	Bottom-up, Growth
Size (MMs):	$161.542
RRSP:	20%
Management Expense Ratio:	2.48% (Category Average: 2.30%)

COMMENTS

Priest has a mid- to large-cap focus. Emphasis is on finding companies with above average growth characteristics. This is done on a company-by-company basis. Much time is spent getting to know the companies being considered and carefully analyzing their financial statements. In particular, price to cash flow is a key criterion. This fund rarely plays the technology sector due to Priest's admitted lack of understanding of the factors that make companies in the sector tick. Note too that C.I. now has a 100% RRSP-eligible version of the fund.

RISK

The fund lost money in ....12 of 45 Months
The fund lost money in ....4 of 43 Quarters
Worst 3 Months ....-4.07% (1994)
Best 3 Months 14.96% (1992)

ASSET ALLOCATION

Industrial products 26.0%
Consumer goods & services..25.9%
Communications & media.....10.6%
Financial services...................11.1%
Other...26.4%

COMPARISON OF FUND TO INDEXES

■■■■■ $1,000 invested in the fund
——— $1,000 invested in the Standard & Poor's 500 ($C)
░░░░ $1,000 invested in Canada Savings Bonds
● Annual ranking against other funds in the same category

Annual Return (%)	1987		1989		1991		1993		1995	6/30/96
							33.1	8.1	27.4	8.0

Compound Return (%)	10 yr	9 yr	8 yr	7 yr	6 yr	5 yr	4 yr	3 yr	2 yr	1 yr
								19.7	21.4	21.2

U.S. EQUITY

FIDELITY GROWTH AMERICA LOAD

Primary Objective:	Growth
Sponsor:	Fidelity Investments Canada
Fund Manager:	Brad Lewis, Fidelity Management Research
Style:	Top-Down, Growth
Size (MMs):	$887.486
RRSP:	20%
Management Expense Ratio:	2.36% (Category Average: 2.30%)

COMMENTS

Lewis is well known for his ability to construct and use sophisticated computer models. The models use the huge amount of statistical data Fidelity generates and, at speeds humans could never match, analyze it. The result is information Lewis uses to pick stocks. A key part of this work is focused on avoiding stocks that will underperform.

RISK

The fund lost money in...............23 of 69 Months
The fund lost money in.............14 of 67 Quarters
Worst 3 Months...................................-5.89% (1987)
Best 3 Months....................................24.18% (1987)

ASSET ALLOCATION

Financial services...................20.0%
Technology 14.1%
Utilities.....................................10.8%
Retail & wholesale....................9.0%
Other...46.1%

COMPARISON OF FUND TO INDEXES

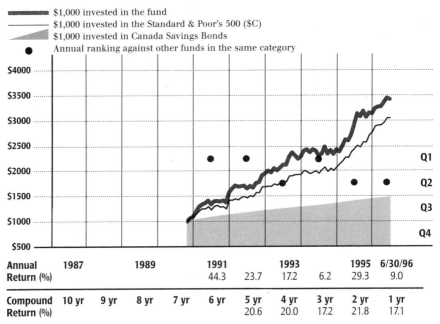

$1,000 invested in the fund
$1,000 invested in the Standard & Poor's 500 ($C)
$1,000 invested in Canada Savings Bonds
● Annual ranking against other funds in the same category

Annual Return (%)	1987		1989		1991		1993		1995	6/30/96
					44.3	23.7	17.2	6.2	29.3	9.0

Compound Return (%)	10 yr	9 yr	8 yr	7 yr	6 yr	5 yr	4 yr	3 yr	2 yr	1 yr
						20.6	20.0	17.2	21.8	17.1

U.S. EQUITY

GREEN LINE N. AMERICAN GROWTH   NO-LOAD

Primary Objective:	Aggressive Growth
Sponsor:	TD Bank
Fund Manager:	Brian Berghuis, T. Rowe Price
Style:	Bottom-up, Growth
Size (MMs):	$83.597
RRSP:	20%
Management Expense Ratio:	2.37% (Category Average: 2.30%)

COMMENTS

T. Rowe Price is a U.S. firm world renowned for its growth investing. The late Mr. Rowe Price is considered by many as the pioneer of growth stock investing. The fund, which is a clone of the Morningstar five-star-rated (3-year) fund run by Berghuis in the U.S., invests in mid-cap ($500 million to $1.5 billion) companies expected to increase earnings at high rates of growth. While the fund's focus will be the U.S., it can also invest in Canada and Mexico.

RISK

The fund lost money in ....10 of 30 Months
The fund lost money in ....5 of 28 Quarters
Worst 3 Months ....-4.12% (1994)
Best 3 Months 13.88% (1995)

ASSET ALLOCATION

U.S. equities 89.5%
Canadian equities 5.2%
Cash & equivalents...................3.3%
Global equities..........................2.0%

COMPARISON OF FUND TO INDEXES

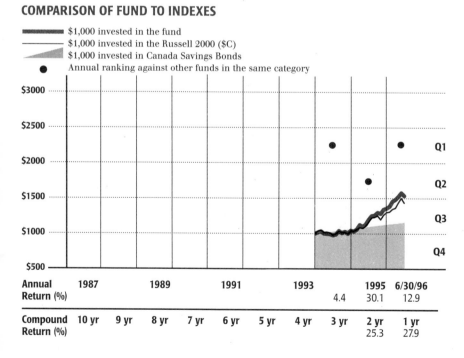

━━━ $1,000 invested in the fund
──── $1,000 invested in the Russell 2000 ($C)
▨ $1,000 invested in Canada Savings Bonds
● Annual ranking against other funds in the same category

	1987	1989	1991	1993	1995	6/30/96
Annual Return (%)				4.4	30.1	12.9

	10 yr	9 yr	8 yr	7 yr	6 yr	5 yr	4 yr	3 yr	2 yr	1 yr
Compound Return (%)									25.3	27.9

U.S. EQUITY

PH&N U.S. EQUITY

Primary Objective:	Growth
Sponsor:	Phillips, Hager & North
Fund Manager:	Team
Style:	Bottom-up Growth
Size (MMs):	$329.518
RRSP:	20%
Management Expense Ratio:	1.12%(Category Average: 2.30%)

COMMENTS

Launched in 1964, this fund has one of the lowest MERs in the category. PH&N uses a team approach to management. The U.S. equity team consists of five individuals who focus exclusively on the U.S. market. The team looks for mid-to larger-cap companies with high expected growth rates and low debt.

RISK

The fund lost money in..............41 of 114 Months
The fund lost money in ....29 of 112 Quarters
Worst 3 Months ....-32.34% (1987)
Best 3 Months 25.19% (1991)

ASSET ALLOCATION

Financial services....................14.3%
Consumer non-durables........11.5%
Healthcare 11.4%
Technology 8.9%
Other..53.9%

COMPARISON OF FUND TO INDEXES

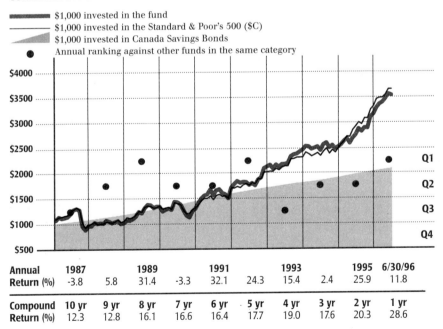

- $1,000 invested in the fund
- $1,000 invested in the Standard & Poor's 500 ($C)
- $1,000 invested in Canada Savings Bonds
- Annual ranking against other funds in the same category

Annual Return (%)	1987		1989		1991		1993		1995	6/30/96
	-3.8	5.8	31.4	-3.3	32.1	24.3	15.4	2.4	25.9	11.8

Compound Return (%)	10 yr	9 yr	8 yr	7 yr	6 yr	5 yr	4 yr	3 yr	2 yr	1 yr
	12.3	12.8	16.1	16.6	16.4	17.7	19.0	17.6	20.3	28.6

SPECTRUM UNITED AMERICAN EQUITY   LOAD

Primary Objective: Growth
Sponsor: Spectrum United Mutual Funds
Fund Manager: Kevin Parke, Massachusetts Financial
Style: Bottom-up, Growth
Size (MMs): $264.140
RRSP: 20%
Management Expense Ratio: 2.30% (Category Average: 2.30%)

COMMENTS

This fund has a best ideas portfolio, cloned from the top-quartile fund Massachusetts Financial Services has been running in the U.S. for years. Parke heads up the research group at MFS. All the analysts bring their best stock ideas to a monthly meeting and sell the others in the group on why their idea(s) should get a place in the portfolio. In order for an idea to get in, it has to beat out other new ideas and a holding already in the portfolio. While all individuals are recognized for their efforts, the performance of the team is also highly valued.

RISK

The fund lost money in..............39 of 114 Months
The fund lost money in ....26 of 112 Quarters
Worst 3 Months ....-27.72% (1987)
Best 3 Months 16.61% (1991)

ASSET ALLOCATION

Industrial products.................16.2%
Technology 12.5%
Consumer products...............11.4%
Financial services..................10.1%
Other...49.8%

COMPARISON OF FUND TO INDEXES

▬▬▬ $1,000 invested in the fund
──── $1,000 invested in the Standard & Poor's 500 ($C)
░░░░ $1,000 invested in Canada Savings Bonds
● Annual ranking against other funds in the same category

	1987		1989		1991		1993		1995	6/30/96
Annual Return (%)	-5.2	9.4	26.6	-6.6	23.2	16.1	4.0	-2.8	33.1	12.8

	10 yr	9 yr	8 yr	7 yr	6 yr	5 yr	4 yr	3 yr	2 yr	1 yr
Compound Return (%)	10.0	9.8	13.4	11.7	13.2	14.2	14.3	16.8	25.1	29.9

U.S. EQUITY

UNIVERSAL U.S. EMERGING GROWTH   LOAD

Primary Objective:	Aggressive Growth
Sponsor:	Mackenzie Financial
Fund Manager:	Jim Broadfoot, Mackenzie Investment Management
Style:	Bottom-up, Growth
Size (MMs):	$322.705
RRSP:	20%
Management Expense Ratio:	2.46% (Category Average: 2.30%)

COMMENTS

Broadfoot is the author of a respected book entitled *Investing in Emerging Growth Stocks*. He learned his growth style of management at T. Rowe Price, where he worked on the bellwether small-cap fund, New Horizons, prior to joining Mackenzie's U.S. operation. He uses a well-diversified approach (150+ names) as a risk management tool, but knows every one of the stocks in the portfolio.

RISK

The fund lost money in ....16 of 53 Months
The fund lost money in ....12 of 51 Quarters
Worst 3 Months ....-11.39% (1992)
Best 3 Months 30.17% (1992)

ASSET ALLOCATION

Technology 20.4%
Healthcare 13.8%
Software 11.9%
Business services......................9.9%
Other..44.0%

COMPARISON OF FUND TO INDEXES

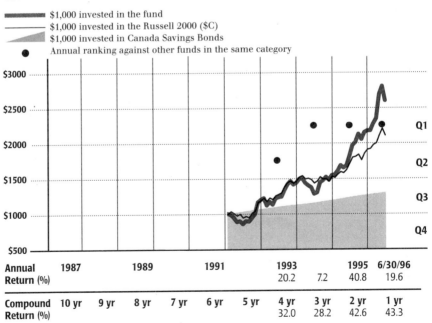

- $1,000 invested in the fund
- $1,000 invested in the Russell 2000 ($C)
- $1,000 invested in Canada Savings Bonds
- ● Annual ranking against other funds in the same category

Annual Return (%)	1987		1989		1991		1993		1995	6/30/96
							20.2	7.2	40.8	19.6

Compound Return (%)	10 yr	9 yr	8 yr	7 yr	6 yr	5 yr	4 yr	3 yr	2 yr	1 yr
							32.0	28.2	42.6	43.3

20/20 INTERNATIONAL VALUE LOAD

Primary Objective:	Growth
Sponsor:	AGF
Fund Manager:	Charles Brandes & Jeff Busby, Brandes Investment Partners
Style:	Bottom-up, Value
Size (MMs):	$341.723
RRSP:	20%
Management Expense Ratio:	2.89% (Category Average: 2.25%)

COMMENTS

While this fund has an MER 65 basis points higher than the category average, Charles Brandes is a proven performer. His value-based investment philosophy is heavily research based. Brandes has taken the work of the father of value investing, Benjamin Graham, and updated it in his own book, *Value Investing Today*. He pays little attention to market conditions or countries, focusing instead on the fundamentals of each business he invests in.

RISK

The fund lost money in................32 of 84 Months
The fund lost money in ....19 of 82 Quarters
Worst 3 Months ....-8.44% (1994)
Best 3 Months 16.62% (1991)

ASSET ALLOCATION

Europe.......................................55.0%
U.S. 26.0%
Pacific Rim 11.0%
Latin America & Africa 8.0%

COMPARISON OF FUND TO INDEXES

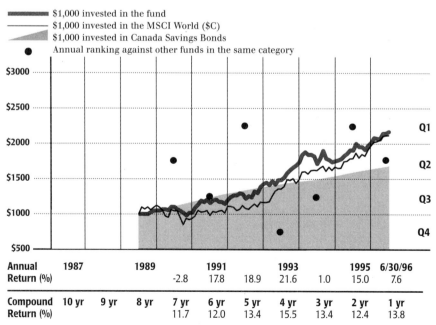

$1,000 invested in the fund
$1,000 invested in the MSCI World ($C)
$1,000 invested in Canada Savings Bonds
● Annual ranking against other funds in the same category

Annual Return (%)	1987		1989	1991		1993		1995	6/30/96
			-2.8	17.8	18.9	21.6	1.0	15.0	7.6

Compound Return (%)	10 yr	9 yr	8 yr	7 yr	6 yr	5 yr	4 yr	3 yr	2 yr	1 yr
				11.7	12.0	13.4	15.5	13.4	12.4	13.8

GLOBAL EQUITY

BPI GLOBAL SMALL COMPANIES   LOAD

Primary Objective:	Aggressive Growth
Sponsor:	BPI
Fund Manager:	John Reinsburg, Lazard Freres
Style:	Bottom-up, Value
Size (MMs):	$82.200
RRSP:	20%
Management Expense Ratio:	2.55% (Category Average: 2.25%)

COMMENTS

This fund is managed with a bottom-up value approach, focusing on companies around the world with a market cap of less than U.S. $750 million. Lazard has been in the wealth-management business for 140 years and uses the resources of offices and affiliates in 13 major centres around the world. Its research emphasizes corporate performance assessed through in-depth fundamental research.

RISK

The fund lost money in ....14 of 38 Months
The fund lost money in ....11 of 36 Quarters
Worst 3 Months ....-7.21% (1995)
Best 3 Months 21.75% (1994)

ASSET ALLOCATION

Europe 46.0%
North America 28.7%
Far East & Australia 18.7%
Japan 6.6%

COMPARISON OF FUND TO INDEXES

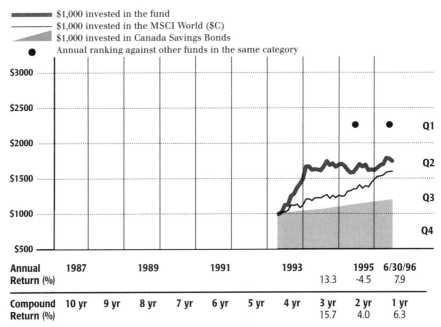

▬▬▬▬ $1,000 invested in the fund
────── $1,000 invested in the MSCI World ($C)
▨▨▨ $1,000 invested in Canada Savings Bonds
● Annual ranking against other funds in the same category

	1987	1989	1991	1993	1995	6/30/96
Annual Return (%)					13.3 -4.5	7.9

	10 yr	9 yr	8 yr	7 yr	6 yr	5 yr	4 yr	3 yr	2 yr	1 yr
Compound Return (%)								15.7	4.0	6.3

GLOBAL EQUITY

CUNDILL VALUE

Primary Objective:	Growth
Sponsor:	Peter Cundill & Associates
Fund Manager:	Peter Cundill
Style:	Bottom-up, Value
Size (MMs):	$402.258
RRSP:	20%
Management Expense Ratio:	2.06% (Category Average: 2.25%)

COMMENTS

While the Cundill name may not be as well recognized as Trimark or Templeton, this fund has been around for more than 20 years. Cundill is the most ardent value investor in Canada. He follows the investment disciplines of Benjamin Graham, which focus solely on a company's financial data. This fund may lag when markets are moving up quickly, but will cushion investors when markets are moving the other way. The fund has only lost money in one year (-9.4% in 1990). Cundill passes along his value approach in the form of an MER well below the category average.

RISK

The fund lost money in..............33 of 114 Months
The fund lost money in ....26 of 112 Quarters
Worst 3 Months ....-14.44% (1987)
Best 3 Months 16.63% (1993)

ASSET ALLOCATION

France..14.7%
Japan..11.1%
Canada..9.3%
U.S. 8.5%
Other...56.4%

COMPARISON OF FUND TO INDEXES

$1,000 invested in the fund
$1,000 invested in the MSCI World ($C)
$1,000 invested in Canada Savings Bonds
● Annual ranking against other funds in the same category

Annual Return (%)	1987 12.9	19.1	1989 10.0	-9.4	1991 5.5	7.1	1993 43.1	15.4	1995 8.2	6/30/96 7.8

Compound Return (%)	10 yr 11.2	9 yr 10.6	8 yr 10.7	7 yr 10.7	6 yr 12.3	5 yr 16.3	4 yr 18.0	3 yr 15.7	2 yr 12.0	1 yr 12.8

GLOBAL EQUITY

FIDELITY INTERNATIONAL PORTFOLIO LOAD

Primary Objective:	Growth
Sponsor:	Fidelity Investments Canada
Fund Manager:	Richard Habermann, Fidelity Management Research
Style:	Top-Down, Growth
Size (MMs):	$950.003
RRSP:	20%
Management Expense Ratio:	2.75% (Category Average: 2.25%)

COMMENTS

A team of Fidelity's best regional specialists meet regularly to manage the fund. Team leader Haberman uses Fidelity's in-house research to allocate portions of the fund to each specialist. Using Fidelity's fundamental, bottom-up stock-selection approach, these managers look for the most promising investments in their regions. If the company's financial statements prove attractive, company visits are next. Finally, a macro-economic analysis is applied in an effort to determine how economic trends might affect each investment.

RISK

The fund lost money in ....35 of 102 Months
The fund lost money in ....28 of 100 Quarters
Worst 3 Months................................-17.86% (1990)
Best 3 Months.....................................17.51% (1989)

ASSET ALLOCATION

U.S..42.9%
Japan..17.8%
U.K..7.2%
France..3.1%
Other...29.0%

COMPARISON OF FUND TO INDEXES

━━━━━ $1,000 invested in the fund
──────── $1,000 invested in the MSCI World ($C)
▨ $1,000 invested in Canada Savings Bonds
● Annual ranking against other funds in the same category

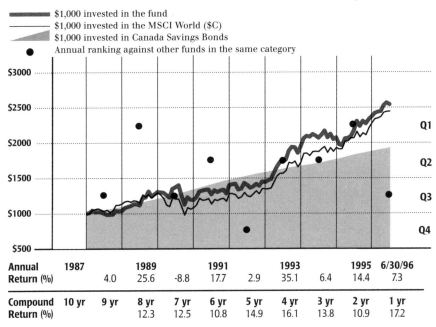

Annual Return (%)	1987		1989		1991		1993		1995	6/30/96
		4.0	25.6	-8.8	17.7	2.9	35.1	6.4	14.4	7.3

Compound Return (%)	10 yr	9 yr	8 yr	7 yr	6 yr	5 yr	4 yr	3 yr	2 yr	1 yr
			12.3	12.5	10.8	14.9	16.1	13.8	10.9	17.2

GLOBAL EQUITY

GLOBAL STRATEGY WORLD EMERGING CO. LOAD

Primary Objective:	Aggressive Growth
Sponsor:	Global Strategy
Fund Manager:	Perpetual, Rothschild, & Montgomery
Style:	Blend
Size (MMs):	$80.739
RRSP:	20%
Management Expense Ratio:	2.95% (Category Average: 2.25%)

COMMENTS

Global Strategy is one of the few fund companies to offer a multi-manager strategy within one fund. The three managers on this fund are well respected global equity managers. Montgomery, applying a bottom-up stock-selection strategy, has particular strength in Asia and Latin America. Perpetual applies a top-down approach to country allocation, complemented by five regional teams that blend value and growth styles in their security selection. Rothschild also uses a top-down approach, focusing on the larger cap stocks in emerging markets.

RISK

The fund lost money in ....2 of 18 Months
The fund lost money in ....0 of 16 Quarters
Worst 3 Months 1995
Best 3 Months 1995

ASSET ALLOCATION

European equities....................22.2%
U.S. equities..............................17.5%
Asia Pacific (ex. Japan) 17.0%
Japanese equities.....................10.2%
Other..33.1%

COMPARISON OF FUND TO INDEXES

$1,000 invested in the fund
$1,000 invested in the MSCI World ($C)
$1,000 invested in Canada Savings Bonds
● Annual ranking against other funds in the same category

Annual Return (%)	1987	1989	1991	1993	1995	6/30/96
					52.8	17.6

Compound Return (%)	10 yr	9 yr	8 yr	7 yr	6 yr	5 yr	4 yr	3 yr	2 yr	1 yr
										40.0

GLOBAL EQUITY

GLOBAL STRATEGY WORLD EQUITY LOAD

Primary Objective:	Growth
Sponsor:	Global Strategy
Fund Manager:	Rothschild, Schroders, Capital Int'l.
Style:	Blend
Size (MMs):	$104.782
RRSP:	20%
Management Expense Ratio:	2.95% (Category Average: 2.25%)

COMMENTS

Another multi-manager fund. Capital International, the second-largest mutual fund company in the U.S. and the CI in the MSCI indices, applies a stock-driven value philosophy based on fundamental research. Schroders Capital Management Ltd. is also stock driven, but favours growth stocks with small- to mid-cap sizes. Rothschild utilizes detailed economic analysis to support a top-down investment approach focusing on the larger caps in both developed and developing markets.

RISK

The fund lost money in ....6 of 18 Months
The fund lost money in ....2 of 16 Quarters
Worst 3 Months ....-3.04% (1995)
Best 3 Months...................................8.52% (1996)

ASSET ALLOCATION

U.S. equities 33.0%
Europe.......................................31.9%
Japan 21.6%
Asia-Pacific (ex. Japan) 8.3%
Other..5.2%

COMPARISON OF FUND TO INDEXES

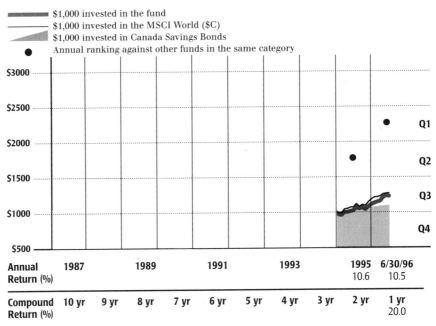

- $1,000 invested in the fund
- $1,000 invested in the MSCI World ($C)
- $1,000 invested in Canada Savings Bonds
- Annual ranking against other funds in the same category

Annual Return (%)	1987	1989	1991	1993	1995	6/30/96
					10.6	10.5

Compound Return (%)	10 yr	9 yr	8 yr	7 yr	6 yr	5 yr	4 yr	3 yr	2 yr	1 yr
										20.0

GLOBAL EQUITY

GREEN LINE GLOBAL SELECT NO-LOAD

Primary Objective:	Growth
Sponsor:	TD Bank
Fund Manager:	Kathryn Langridge, Perpetual
Style:	Top-Down, Growth
Size (MMs):	$65.739
RRSP:	20%
Management Expense Ratio:	2.47% (Category Average: 2.25%)

COMMENTS

Perpetual Portfolio Management has more than 20 years of investment management experience and has more than $7.5 billion under management. It applies a top-down approach to country allocation, complemented by five regional teams that blend value and growth styles in their security selection. Perpetual is also one of three managers on the Global Strategy World Emerging Companies Fund.

RISK

The fund lost money in ....10 of 30 Months
The fund lost money in ....4 of 28 Quarters
Worst 3 Months ....-4.89% (1995)
Best 3 Months 11.32% (1996)

ASSET ALLOCATION

U.S. 36.0%
Japan...17.7%
U.K...10.8%
Hong Kong...................................5.9%
Other..29.6%

COMPARISON OF FUND TO INDEXES

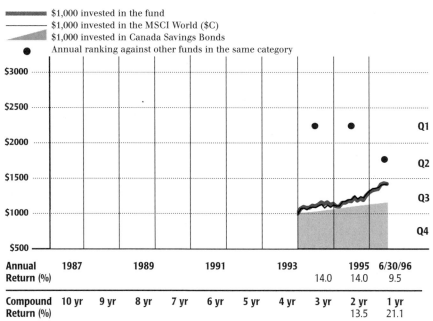

- $1,000 invested in the fund
- $1,000 invested in the MSCI World ($C)
- $1,000 invested in Canada Savings Bonds
- Annual ranking against other funds in the same category

Annual Return (%)	1987		1989		1991		1993		1995	6/30/96
								14.0	14.0	9.5

Compound Return (%)	10 yr	9 yr	8 yr	7 yr	6 yr	5 yr	4 yr	3 yr	2 yr	1 yr
									13.5	21.1

MD GROWTH

Primary Objective:	Growth
Sponsor:	MD Management
Fund Manager:	Templeton International & Marvin Palmer
Style:	Bottom-up, Value
Size (MMs):	$2,152.397
RRSP:	20%
Management Expense Ratio:	1.08% (Category Average: 2.25%)

COMMENTS

See Templeton Growth.

RISK

The fund lost money in..............40 of 114 Months
The fund lost money in ....28 of 112 Quarters
Worst 3 Months ....-27.89% (1987)
Best 3 Months 17.43% (1993)

ASSET ALLOCATION

U.S. 27.3%
Cash & equivalents...................8.8%
Switzerland...............................7.2%
France.......................................7.0%
Other...49.7%

COMPARISON OF FUND TO INDEXES

$1,000 invested in the fund
$1,000 invested in the MSCI World ($C)
$1,000 invested in Canada Savings Bonds
● Annual ranking against other funds in the same category

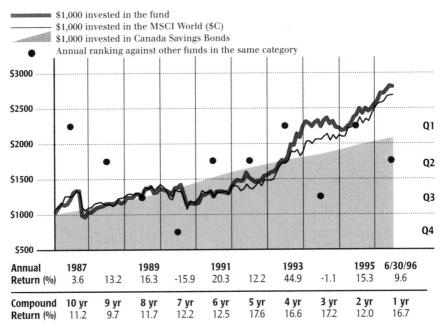

Annual Return (%)	1987 3.6	13.2	1989 16.3	-15.9	1991 20.3	12.2	1993 44.9	-1.1	1995 15.3	6/30/96 9.6

Compound Return (%)	10 yr 11.2	9 yr 9.7	8 yr 11.7	7 yr 12.2	6 yr 12.5	5 yr 17.6	4 yr 16.6	3 yr 17.2	2 yr 12.0	1 yr 16.7

GLOBAL EQUITY

SAXON WORLD GROWTH

NO-LOAD

Primary Objective:	Growth
Sponsor:	Saxon Group of Funds
Fund Manager:	Bob Tattersall, Howson Tattersall
Style:	Bottom-up, Growth
Size (MMs):	$32.833
RRSP:	20%
Management Expense Ratio:	1.87% (Category Average: 2.25%)

COMMENTS

Tattersall runs this fund with a strict fundamental, value-based discipline. Since the portfolio is so numbers-based, it favours the U.S. and other major markets where accounting standards are meaningful. Given the fund's small size, it should be viewed as more aggressive than some of the larger, more diversified funds in the category.

RISK

The fund lost money in	37 of 114 Months
The fund lost money in	29 of 112 Quarters
Worst 3 Months	-28.61% (1987)
Best 3 Months	23.22% (1989)

ASSET ALLOCATION

U.S.	60.8%
U.K.	10.9%
Czech Republic	4.1%
Korea	2.6%
Other	21.6%

COMPARISON OF FUND TO INDEXES

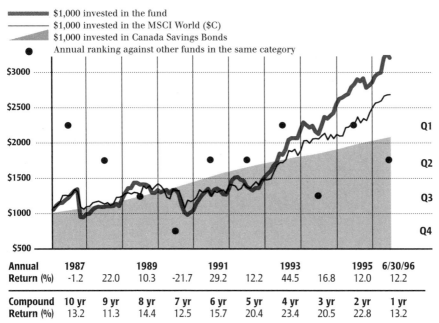

- ▬ $1,000 invested in the fund
- ─ $1,000 invested in the MSCI World ($C)
- ◣ $1,000 invested in Canada Savings Bonds
- ● Annual ranking against other funds in the same category

Annual	1987		1989		1991		1993		1995	6/30/96
Return (%)	-1.2	22.0	10.3	-21.7	29.2	12.2	44.5	16.8	12.0	12.2

Compound	10 yr	9 yr	8 yr	7 yr	6 yr	5 yr	4 yr	3 yr	2 yr	1 yr
Return (%)	13.2	11.3	14.4	12.5	15.7	20.4	23.4	20.5	22.8	13.2

GLOBAL EQUITY

SCEPTRE INTERNATIONAL EQUITY NO-LOAD

Primary Objective:	Growth
Sponsor:	Sceptre Mutual Funds
Fund Manager:	Lennox McNeely, Sceptre Investment Counsel
Style:	Top-Down, Growth
Size (MMs):	$143.470
RRSP:	20%
Management Expense Ratio:	2.10% (Category Average: 2.25%)

COMMENTS

McNeely is the asset allocator on the fund, supported by three regional specialists (Europe, the Far East and the U.S.). A unique feature of the fund is the number of stocks – averaging around 250. No single position exceeds 2% of the portfolio. With a focus on the mid- to large-cap market, McNeely employs a value-based discipline to country and security selection. Both developed and emerging markets are included.

RISK

The fund lost money in..............35 of 114 Months
The fund lost money in ....29 of 112 Quarters
Worst 3 Months ....-24.65% (1987)
Best 3 Months 26.18% (1993)

ASSET ALLOCATION

Japan	17.8%
U.S.	12.7%
Hong Kong	8.4%
Australia	5.0%
Other	56.1%

COMPARISON OF FUND TO INDEXES

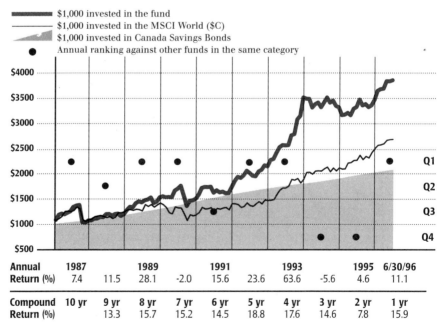

━━━━━ $1,000 invested in the fund
─────── $1,000 invested in the MSCI World ($C)
▨▨▨ $1,000 invested in Canada Savings Bonds
● Annual ranking against other funds in the same category

Annual Return (%)	1987		1989		1991		1993		1995	6/30/96
	7.4	11.5	28.1	-2.0	15.6	23.6	63.6	-5.6	4.6	11.1

Compound Return (%)	10 yr	9 yr	8 yr	7 yr	6 yr	5 yr	4 yr	3 yr	2 yr	1 yr
		13.3	15.7	15.2	14.5	18.8	17.6	14.6	7.8	15.9

GLOBAL EQUITY

SCUDDER GLOBAL

Primary Objective:	Growth
Sponsor:	Scudder Canada
Fund Manager:	William Holzer, Scudder, Stevens & Clark
Style:	Top-Down, Growth
Size (MMs):	$7.754
RRSP:	20%
Management Expense Ratio:	1.75%(Category Average: 2.25%)

COMMENTS

Holzer is the manager of the same fund in the U.S. This fund has a 10-year record of outperforming the MSCI World index by a considerable margin. While the U.S. fund is only three-star ranked by Morningstar, the ranking is against all equity funds, and hence has favoured the U.S. equity funds considerably over the last couple of years. In this fund, country and stock selection is value based and is theme driven. Holzer will move to bonds if he cannot find the value he is looking for.

RISK

The fund lost money in	0 of 8 Months
The fund lost money in	0 of 6 Quarters
Worst 3 Months	4.31% (1996)
Best 3 Months	6.71% (1996)

ASSET ALLOCATION

U.S.	22.0%
Germany	16.0%
Japan	13.0%
U.K.	10.0%
Other	39.0%

COMPARISON OF FUND TO INDEXES

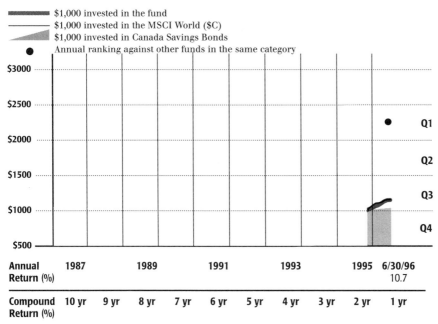

- ▬▬ $1,000 invested in the fund
- —— $1,000 invested in the MSCI World ($C)
- ◢ $1,000 invested in Canada Savings Bonds
- ● Annual ranking against other funds in the same category

	1987	1989	1991	1993	1995	6/30/96
Annual Return (%)						10.7

	10 yr	9 yr	8 yr	7 yr	6 yr	5 yr	4 yr	3 yr	2 yr	1 yr
Compound Return (%)										

GLOBAL EQUITY

TEMPLETON GLOBAL SMALL COMPANIES LOAD

Primary Objective:	Aggressive Growth
Sponsor:	Templeton Management Limited
Fund Manager:	Marc Joseph, Templeton
Style:	Bottom-up, Value
Size (MMs):	$221.145
RRSP:	20%
Management Expense Ratio:	2.62% (Category Average: 2.25%)

COMMENTS

Joseph is the head of Templeton's small-cap research group. Like all Templeton managers, he applies a bottom-up value style to portfolio management. The fund's broad country diversification (36 countries) is a result of the stock picking process supported by more than 20 Templeton offices worldwide.

RISK

The fund lost money in	29 of 89 Months
The fund lost money in	29 of 87 Quarters
Worst 3 Months	-19.42% (1990)
Best 3 Months	22.17% (1991)

ASSET ALLOCATION

Healthcare	6.0%
Merchandising	5.8%
Transportation	5.4%
Business & public service	4.5%
Other	78.3%

COMPARISON OF FUND TO INDEXES

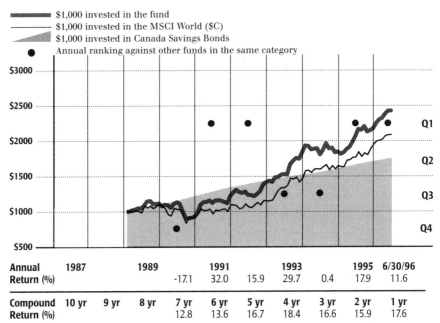

- $1,000 invested in the fund
- $1,000 invested in the MSCI World ($C)
- $1,000 invested in Canada Savings Bonds
- ● Annual ranking against other funds in the same category

Annual Return (%)	1987		1989		1991		1993		1995	6/30/96
				-17.1	32.0	15.9	29.7	0.4	17.9	11.6

Compound Return (%)	10 yr	9 yr	8 yr	7 yr	6 yr	5 yr	4 yr	3 yr	2 yr	1 yr
				12.8	13.6	16.7	18.4	16.6	15.9	17.6

GLOBAL EQUITY

TEMPLETON GROWTH

Primary Objective:	Growth
Sponsor:	Templeton Management Limited
Fund Manager:	Mark Holowesko, Templeton
Style:	Bottom-up, Value
Size (MMs):	$5,249.709
RRSP:	20%
Management Expense Ratio:	2.10% (Category Average: 2.25%)

COMMENTS

Formerly run by Sir John himself, the mountain chart on this fund is one of the best advertisements the mutual fund industry has. A person investing $10,000 in the fund in 1954 would have more than $3 million today. Holowesko continues in his mentor's footsteps, applying the stock-by-stock value-based approach that has made Templeton a household name. Templeton now has more than 20 offices around the world. Those in the medical community can get a similar fund run by Templeton in MD Growth, with an MER of only 1.08%. Under Don Reed, Templeton International Stock utilizes the same global resources but excludes the U.S. and Canada.

RISK

The fund lost money in..............35 of 114 Months
The fund lost money in ....22 of 112 Quarters
Worst 3 Months ....-27.17% (1987)
Best 3 Months....................................15.69% (1987)

ASSET ALLOCATION

Banking...8.9%
Telecommunications................6.5%
Automobiles 5.7%
Paper & forest products...........5.2%
Other..73.7%

COMPARISON OF FUND TO INDEXES

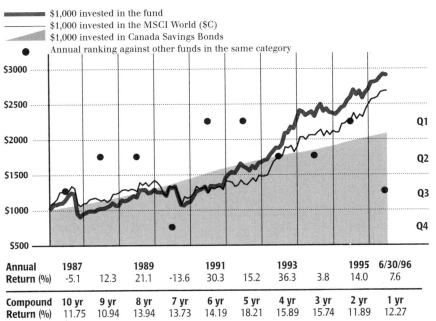

- $1,000 invested in the fund
- $1,000 invested in the MSCI World ($C)
- $1,000 invested in Canada Savings Bonds
- Annual ranking against other funds in the same category

Annual Return (%)	1987		1989		1991		1993		1995	6/30/96
	-5.1	12.3	21.1	-13.6	30.3	15.2	36.3	3.8	14.0	7.6

Compound Return (%)	10 yr	9 yr	8 yr	7 yr	6 yr	5 yr	4 yr	3 yr	2 yr	1 yr
	11.75	10.94	13.94	13.73	14.19	18.21	15.89	15.74	11.89	12.27

GLOBAL EQUITY

TEMPLETON INTERNATIONAL STOCK LOAD

Primary Objective:	Growth
Sponsor:	Templeton
Fund Manager:	Don Reed, Templeton
Style:	Bottom-up, Value
Size (MMs):	$1,591.401
RRSP:	20%
Management Expense Ratio:	2.55% (Category Average: 2.25%)

COMMENTS

See Templeton Growth.

RISK

The fund lost money in................31 of 89 Months
The fund lost money in..............23 of 87 Quarters
Worst 3 Months ....-15.34% (1990)
Best 3 Months 23.43% (1992)

ASSET ALLOCATION

Banking.......................................8.9%
Telecommunications................6.5%
Automobiles 5.7%
Paper & forest products............5.2%
Other..73.7%

COMPARISON OF FUND TO INDEXES

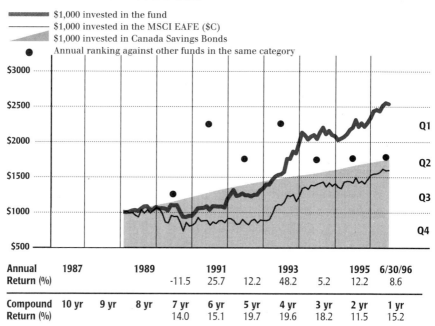

- $1,000 invested in the fund
- $1,000 invested in the MSCI EAFE ($C)
- $1,000 invested in Canada Savings Bonds
- Annual ranking against other funds in the same category

Annual Return (%)	1987		1989		1991		1993		1995	6/30/96
				-11.5	25.7	12.2	48.2	5.2	12.2	8.6

Compound Return (%)	10 yr	9 yr	8 yr	7 yr	6 yr	5 yr	4 yr	3 yr	2 yr	1 yr
				14.0	15.1	19.7	19.6	18.2	11.5	15.2

GLOBAL EQUITY

TRIMARK FUND

Primary Objective:	Growth
Sponsor:	Trimark
Fund Manager:	Bob Krembil, Trimark
Style:	Bottom-up, Growth
Size (MMs):	$2,155.256
RRSP:	20%
Management Expense Ratio:	1.52% (Category Average: 2.25%)

COMMENTS

This fund deserves the recognition it is given. Virtually everyone recommends it. Krembil's discipline of buying good growth companies he knows well, and sticking with them, has paid off. The fund invests globally but only in major markets and primarily in the U.S. The corporate financial data Krembil and his team emphasize is most reliable in major markets and most familiar in the U.S. While the fund is over weighted in the U.S., many of the U.S. stocks are themselves multinationals diversified globally, and derive a significant amount of their revenue from outside the U.S. This fund, only available on a front-end basis, has an MER of 1.52%. Its sister fund, Select Growth, is available on a DSC basis, but has an MER of 2.25%.

RISK

The fund lost money in ....37 of 114 Months
The fund lost money in ....23 of 112 Quarters
Worst 3 Months................................-29.97% (1987)
Best 3 Months 24.22% (1992)

ASSET ALLOCATION

U.S. 63.6%
Japan...7.6%
Germany 3.7%
Canada...3.1%
Other..22.0%

COMPARISON OF FUND TO INDEXES

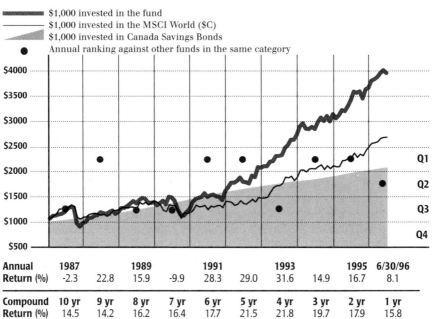

- $1,000 invested in the fund
- $1,000 invested in the MSCI World ($C)
- $1,000 invested in Canada Savings Bonds
- Annual ranking against other funds in the same category

Annual	1987		1989		1991		1993		1995	6/30/96
Return (%)	-2.3	22.8	15.9	-9.9	28.3	29.0	31.6	14.9	16.7	8.1

Compound	10 yr	9 yr	8 yr	7 yr	6 yr	5 yr	4 yr	3 yr	2 yr	1 yr
Return (%)	14.5	14.2	16.2	16.4	17.7	21.5	21.8	19.7	17.9	15.8

GLOBAL EQUITY

UNIVERSAL WORLD EQUITY

LOAD

Primary Objective:	Growth
Sponsor:	Mackenzie Financial
Fund Manager:	Iain Clark & Nitin Metha, Henderson Administration
Style:	Top-Down, Growth
Size (MMs):	$297.034
RRSP:	20%
Management Expense Ratio:	2.46% (Category Average: 2.25%)

COMMENTS

Henderson International has been directing global investment portfolios since 1932. It was one of the first to invest in emerging markets and global smaller companies. Clark and Mehta apply a top-down approach to country allocation, followed by a blend of growth and value styles in security selection. They are supported by more than 60 in-house specialists concentrating on various geographic regions and asset classes. The fund does not invest in Canada or the U.S.

RISK

The fund lost money in..............49 of 114 Months
The fund lost money in ....35 of 112 Quarters
Worst 3 Months ....-18.92% (1987)
Best 3 Months 17.40% (1993)

ASSET ALLOCATION

Europe & Scandinavia............34.0%
Asia & Australia (ex. Japan)..12.0%
Latin America............................1.0%
Other..53.0%

COMPARISON OF FUND TO INDEXES

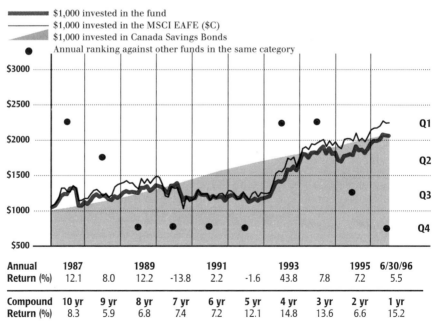

- $1,000 invested in the fund
- $1,000 invested in the MSCI EAFE ($C)
- $1,000 invested in Canada Savings Bonds
- Annual ranking against other funds in the same category

Annual	1987		1989		1991		1993		1995	6/30/96
Return (%)	12.1	8.0	12.2	-13.8	2.2	-1.6	43.8	7.8	7.2	5.5

Compound	10 yr	9 yr	8 yr	7 yr	6 yr	5 yr	4 yr	3 yr	2 yr	1 yr
Return (%)	8.3	5.9	6.8	7.4	7.2	12.1	14.8	13.6	6.6	15.2

GLOBAL EQUITY

UNIVERSAL WORLD GROWTH RRSP LOAD

Primary Objective:	Aggressive Growth
Sponsor:	Mackenzie Financial
Fund Manager:	Barbara Trebbi & Michael Landry
Style:	Top-Down, Growth
Size (MMs):	$157.817
RRSP:	100%
Management Expense Ratio:	2.46% (Category Average: 2.25%)

COMMENTS

This fund allows Canadians to invest globally within the Canadian content portion of
their RRSP. This is achieved by buying futures contracts on various market indices
around the world. These purchases are guaranteed using 80% of the fund, which is
kept in T-bills. The managers' value is in their world market allocation decisions.

RISK

The fund lost money in ....8 of 21 Months
The fund lost money in ....5 of 19 Quarters
Worst 3 Months ....-6.83% (1995)
Best 3 Months 10.09% (1996)

ASSET ALLOCATION

Continental Europe................31.0%
Emerging markets..................13.0%
Canada 12.0%
Asia (ex. Japan).......................11.0%
Other...33.0%

COMPARISON OF FUND TO INDEXES

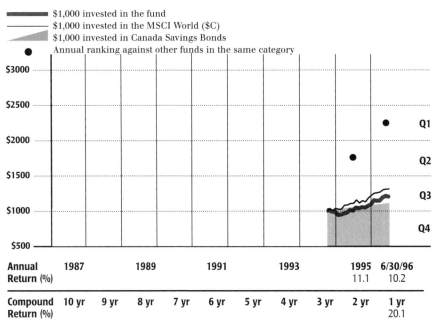

- $1,000 invested in the fund
- $1,000 invested in the MSCI World ($C)
- $1,000 invested in Canada Savings Bonds
- Annual ranking against other funds in the same category

Annual Return (%)	1987		1989		1991		1993		1995 11.1	6/30/96 10.2

Compound Return (%)	10 yr	9 yr	8 yr	7 yr	6 yr	5 yr	4 yr	3 yr	2 yr	1 yr 20.1

20/20 DIVIDEND

DIVIDEND

Primary Objective:	Growth
Sponsor:	AGF
Fund Manager:	Gordon MacDougall & Martin Gerber, Connor Clark & Lunn
Style:	Bottom-up, Value
Size (MMs):	$253.969
RRSP:	100%
Management Expense Ratio:	1.98% (Category Average: 1.84%)

COMMENTS

Fund focuses on conservative common equity. MER around category average. Variable monthly distributions.

RISK

The fund lost money in..............41 of 114 Months
The fund lost money in ....28 of 112 Quarters
Worst 3 Months ....-14.17% (1987)
Best 3 Months 11.08% (1993)

ASSET ALLOCATION

Financial services....................27.1%
Industrial products.................17.7%
Oil & gas 13.5%
Consumer products.................8.3%
Other..33.4%

COMPARISON OF FUND TO INDEXES

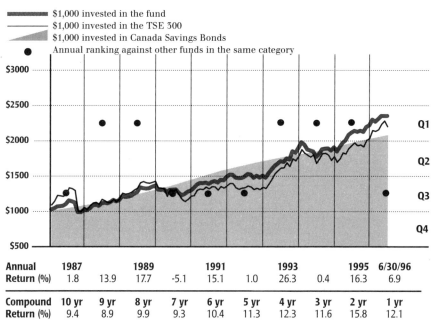

- $1,000 invested in the fund
- $1,000 invested in the TSE 300
- $1,000 invested in Canada Savings Bonds
- Annual ranking against other funds in the same category

Annual	1987		1989		1991		1993		1995	6/30/96
Return (%)	1.8	13.9	17.7	-5.1	15.1	1.0	26.3	0.4	16.3	6.9

Compound	10 yr	9 yr	8 yr	7 yr	6 yr	5 yr	4 yr	3 yr	2 yr	1 yr
Return (%)	9.4	8.9	9.9	9.3	10.4	11.3	12.3	11.6	15.8	12.1

BISSETT DIVIDEND INCOME   NO-LOAD

Primary Objective:	Growth & Income
Sponsor:	Bissett & Associates
Fund Manager:	Fred Pynn, Bissett & Associates
Style:	Bottom-up Growth
Size (MMs):	$9.319
RRSP:	100%
Management Expense Ratio:	1.50% (Category Average: 1.84%)

DIVIDEND

COMMENTS

Focus on common equities, both U.S. and Canadian. Below average MER. Variable
quarterly distributions.

RISK

The fund lost money in...............10 of 43 Months
The fund lost money in...............7 of 41 Quarters
Worst 3 Months..................................-3.89% (1994)
Best 3 Months.....................................9.81% (1996)

ASSET ALLOCATION

Canadian equities....................50.3%
U.S. equities 21.7%
Preferred equities....................17.3%
Corporate bonds.......................5.7%
Other...5.0%

COMPARISON OF FUND TO INDEXES

■■■■■■■ $1,000 invested in the fund
——— $1,000 invested in the TSE 300
▰▰▰ $1,000 invested in Canada Savings Bonds
● Annual ranking against other funds in the same category

Annual Return (%)	1987		1989		1991		1993		1995	6/30/96
			12.0	-7.2	15.1	1.8	18.7	0.7	22.9	7.3

Compound Return (%)	10 yr	9 yr	8 yr	7 yr	6 yr	5 yr	4 yr	3 yr	2 yr	1 yr
			8.3	8.3	9.9	11.3	12.8	12.8	17.8	18.8

BPI INCOME

LOAD

Primary Objective: Growth
Sponsor: BPI Capital
Fund Manager: Eric Bushell
Style: Bottom-up
Size (MMs): $34.800
RRSP: 100%
Management Expense Ratio: 1.20% (Category Average: 1.84%)

COMMENTS

Combination of high yield and preferred equity. MER well below average. Variable monthly distributions.

RISK

The fund lost money in..............35 of 114 Months
The fund lost money in ....24 of 112 Quarters
Worst 3 Months..................................-6.86% (1987)
Best 3 Months.....................................8.00% (1991)

ASSET ALLOCATION

High yield equities..................45.7%
Preferred equities....................34.2%
Cash & equivalents.................16.5%
Other...3.6%

COMPARISON OF FUND TO INDEXES

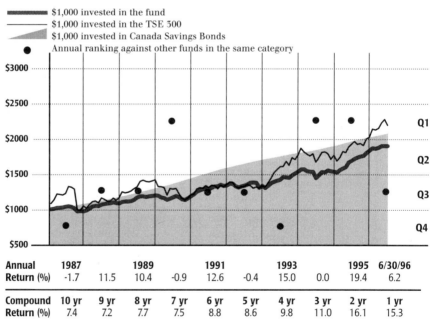

■■■■■ $1,000 invested in the fund
——— $1,000 invested in the TSE 300
▨ $1,000 invested in Canada Savings Bonds
● Annual ranking against other funds in the same category

Annual	1987		1989		1991		1993		1995	6/30/96
Return (%)	-1.7	11.5	10.4	-0.9	12.6	-0.4	15.0	0.0	19.4	6.2

Compound	10 yr	9 yr	8 yr	7 yr	6 yr	5 yr	4 yr	3 yr	2 yr	1 yr
Return (%)	7.4	7.2	7.7	7.5	8.8	8.6	9.8	11.0	16.1	15.3

GT GLOBAL CANADA INCOME CLASS LOAD

Primary Objective:	Growth & Income
Sponsor:	GT Global Canada
Fund Manager:	Derek Webb, LGT Management
Style:	Bottom-up, Growth
Size (MMs):	$18.106
RRSP:	100%
Management Expense Ratio:	2.45% (Category Average: 1.84%)

COMMENTS

Asset mix is that of a balanced fund. Above average MER. Fixed monthly distribution (totaling forty cents a year) of dividend income – including, when necessary, returned capital, and qualifies for the dividend tax credit. Will typically maximize foreign content.

RISK

The fund lost money in ....of Months
The fund lost money in ....N/A of N/A Quarters
Worst 3 Months ....N/A
Best 3 Months ....N/A

ASSET ALLOCATION

Canada...74.7%
U.S. 25.3%

COMPARISON OF FUND TO INDEXES

■■■■■ $1,000 invested in the fund
——— $1,000 invested in the TSE 300
▨ $1,000 invested in Canada Savings Bonds
● Annual ranking against other funds in the same category

Annual Return (%)	1987		1989		1991		1993		1995	6/30/96

Compound Return (%)	10 yr	9 yr	8 yr	7 yr	6 yr	5 yr	4 yr	3 yr	2 yr	1 yr

GUARDIAN MONTHLY DIVIDEND A LOAD

Primary Objective:	Income
Sponsor:	Guardian Group of Funds
Fund Manager:	John Priestman, Guardian
Style:	Bottom-up
Size (MMs):	$117.707
RRSP:	100%
Management Expense Ratio:	1.25% (Category Average: 1.84%)

COMMENTS

At least 80% of portfolio invested in Canadian preferred shares. This fund qualifies for trust investments. Low MER. Fixed monthly distributions of five cents, declining to 4 1/2 cents on October 31, 1996. All distributions qualify for the dividend tax credit.

RISK

The fund lost money in..............20 of 114 Months
The fund lost money in ....21 of 112 Quarters
Worst 3 Months ....-5.35% (1994)
Best 3 Months....................................6.48% (1988)

ASSET ALLOCATION

Preferreds-retractable and ex...40.4%
Preferreds-floating rate 23.7%
Bonds..16.4%
Commons, RTUs, REITS........14.2%
Other 5.3%

COMPARISON OF FUND TO INDEXES

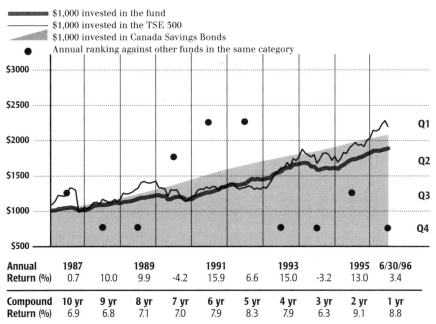

$1,000 invested in the fund
$1,000 invested in the TSE 300
$1,000 invested in Canada Savings Bonds
● Annual ranking against other funds in the same category

Annual Return (%)	1987		1989		1991		1993		1995	6/30/96
	0.7	10.0	9.9	-4.2	15.9	6.6	15.0	-3.2	13.0	3.4

Compound Return (%)	10 yr	9 yr	8 yr	7 yr	6 yr	5 yr	4 yr	3 yr	2 yr	1 yr
	6.9	6.8	7.1	7.0	7.9	8.3	7.9	6.3	9.1	8.8

MAXXUM DIVIDEND FUND OF CANADA   LOAD

Primary Objective:	Growth & Income
Sponsor:	London Fund Management (formerly Prudential)
Fund Manager:	Jacqueline Pratt, Prudential
Style:	Bottom-up, Growth
Size (MMs):	$74.865
RRSP:	100%
Management Expense Ratio:	1.51% (Category Average: 1.84%)

COMMENTS

Low MER. Combination of high-yield common and preferred shares. Variable quarterly distributions.

RISK

The fund lost money in..............39 of 114 Months
The fund lost money in ....30 of 112 Quarters
Worst 3 Months ....-9.88% (1990)
Best 3 Months....................................16.13% (1993)

ASSET ALLOCATION

Financial services....................17.9%
Utilities......................................12.8%
Consumer products..................9.0%
Merchandising..........................8.3%
Other..52.0%

COMPARISON OF FUND TO INDEXES

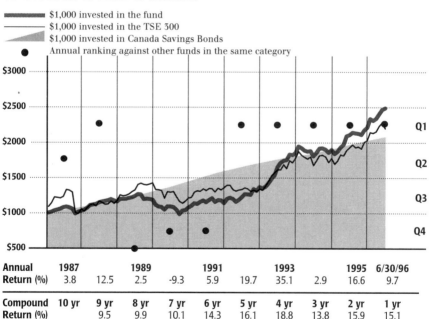

- $1,000 invested in the fund
- $1,000 invested in the TSE 300
- $1,000 invested in Canada Savings Bonds
- Annual ranking against other funds in the same category

Annual Return (%)	1987		1989		1991		1993		1995	6/30/96
	3.8	12.5	2.5	-9.3	5.9	19.7	35.1	2.9	16.6	9.7

Compound Return (%)	10 yr	9 yr	8 yr	7 yr	6 yr	5 yr	4 yr	3 yr	2 yr	1 yr
		9.5	9.9	10.1	14.3	16.1	18.8	13.8	15.9	15.1

PH&N DIVIDEND INCOME NO-LOAD

Primary Objective: Growth
Sponsor: Phillips, Hager & North
Fund Manager: Team
Style: Bottom-up Growth
Size (MMs): $71.650
RRSP: 100%
Management Expense Ratio: 1.19% (Category Average: 1.84%)

COMMENTS

Low MER. Focus favours common equity. Variable quarterly distributions.

RISK

The fund lost money in.............36 of 114 Months
The fund lost money in..........28 of 112 Quarters
Worst 3 Months ....-15.90% (1987)
Best 3 Months....................................12.60% (1987)

ASSET ALLOCATION

Common stocks.......................80.4%
Preferred stocks.......................10.9%
Cash 8.7%

COMPARISON OF FUND TO INDEXES

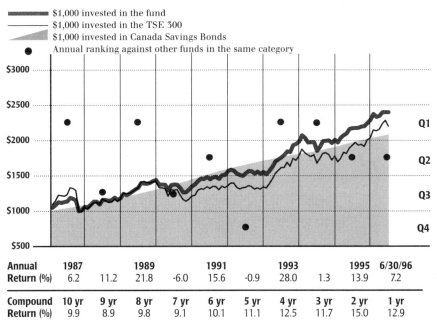

▬▬▬ $1,000 invested in the fund
——— $1,000 invested in the TSE 300
▨ $1,000 invested in Canada Savings Bonds
● Annual ranking against other funds in the same category

Annual	1987		1989		1991		1993		1995	6/30/96
Return (%)	6.2	11.2	21.8	-6.0	15.6	-0.9	28.0	1.3	13.9	7.2

Compound	10 yr	9 yr	8 yr	7 yr	6 yr	5 yr	4 yr	3 yr	2 yr	1 yr
Return (%)	9.9	8.9	9.8	9.1	10.1	11.1	12.5	11.7	15.0	12.9

SCOTIA EXCELSIOR DIVIDEND FUND NO-LOAD

Primary Objective:	Growth & Income
Sponsor:	Scotia Mutual Funds
Fund Manager:	Michael Evans
Style:	Bottom-up Growth
Size (MMs):	$41.951
RRSP:	100%
Management Expense Ratio:	1.07% (Category Average: 1.84%)

COMMENTS

Very low MER. Combination of high-yield common and preferred shares. Variable quarterly distributions.

RISK

The fund lost money in..............36 of 114 Months
The fund lost money in..........28 of 112 Quarters
Worst 3 Months ....-10.19% (1987)
Best 3 Months 7.78% (1992)

ASSET ALLOCATION

Financial services...................44.9%
Utilities.......................................35.1%
Communications & media.....12.4%
Pipelines......................................4.5%
Other..3.1%

COMPARISON OF FUND TO INDEXES

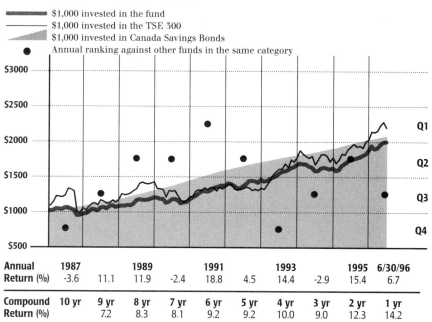

- $1,000 invested in the fund
- $1,000 invested in the TSE 300
- $1,000 invested in Canada Savings Bonds
- Annual ranking against other funds in the same category

Annual	1987		1989		1991		1993		1995	6/30/96
Return (%)	-3.6	11.1	11.9	-2.4	18.8	4.5	14.4	-2.9	15.4	6.7

Compound	10 yr	9 yr	8 yr	7 yr	6 yr	5 yr	4 yr	3 yr	2 yr	1 yr
Return (%)		7.2	8.3	8.1	9.2	9.2	10.0	9.0	12.3	14.2

FIDELITY EUROPEAN GROWTH   LOAD

Primary Objective: Growth
Sponsor: Fidelity Investments Canada
Fund Manager: Sally Walden
Style: Bottom-up, Value
Size (MMs): $795.549
RRSP: 20%
Management Expense Ratio: 2.81% (Category Average: 2.51%)

COMMENTS

By effectively utilizing Fidelity's huge research capabilities (she has more than 40 analysts supporting her), Walden has been able to flush out the growth stories in Europe and stay ahead of most of the competition. Walden manages the fund from Fidelity's London office, using a bottom-up style that emphasizes growth. The fund has no exposure to Eastern Europe. Instead, growth opportunities are sought in the mid-and small-cap sectors of developed nations.

RISK

The fund lost money in ....15 of 48 Months
The fund lost money in ....11 of 46 Quarters
Worst 3 Months ....-5.00% (1992)
Best 3 Months 14.63% (1993)

ASSET ALLOCATION

U.K. 31.6%
France...12.1%
Sweden 9.4%
Switzerland..................................8.0%
Other...38.9%

COMPARISON OF FUND TO INDEXES

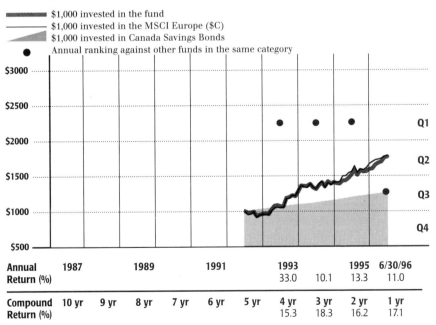

$1,000 invested in the fund
$1,000 invested in the MSCI Europe ($C)
$1,000 invested in Canada Savings Bonds
● Annual ranking against other funds in the same category

Annual Return (%)	1987	1989	1991	1993		1995	6/30/96
				33.0	10.1	13.3	11.0

Compound Return (%)	10 yr	9 yr	8 yr	7 yr	6 yr	5 yr	4 yr	3 yr	2 yr	1 yr
							15.3	18.3	16.2	17.1

GLOBAL STRATEGY EUROPE PLUS   LOAD

Primary Objective:	Growth
Sponsor:	Global Strategy
Fund Manager:	UBS, Rothschild, Gartmore
Style:	Blend
Size (MMs):	$75.624
RRSP:	20%
Management Expense Ratio:	2.95%(Category Average: 2.51%)

COMMENTS

One of the unique multi-manager funds offered by Global Strategy, this fund brings together the bottom-up, value discipline of UBS with the bottom-up growth expertise of Gartmore and combines that with the top-down approach of Rothschild. Each manager invests a third of the portfolio money independently. Given the differences in management style, the fund should display good performance with reduced volatility.

RISK

The fund lost money in	3 of 18 Months
The fund lost money in	2 of 16 Quarters
Worst 3 Months	-3.48% (1995)
Best 3 Months	8.04% (1995)

ASSET ALLOCATION

U.K.	28.7%
France	17.1%
Germany	11.5%
Eastern Europe	7.3%
Other	35.4%

COMPARISON OF FUND TO INDEXES

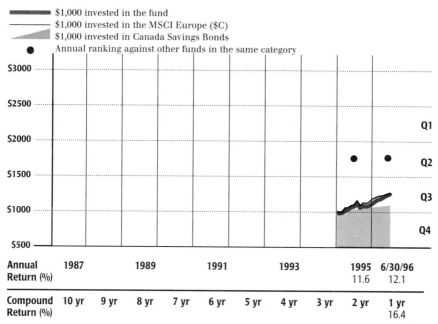

- $1,000 invested in the fund
- $1,000 invested in the MSCI Europe ($C)
- $1,000 invested in Canada Savings Bonds
- ● Annual ranking against other funds in the same category

Annual Return (%)	1987	1989	1991	1993	1995	6/30/96
					11.6	12.1

Compound Return (%)	10 yr	9 yr	8 yr	7 yr	6 yr	5 yr	4 yr	3 yr	2 yr	1 yr
										16.4

SPECTRUM UNITED EUROPEAN ENTERPRISE LOAD

Primary Objective:	Aggressive Growth
Sponsor:	Spectrum United Mutual Funds
Fund Manager:	James Hordern Mercury Asset Management
Style:	Bottom-up, Growth
Size (MMs):	$30.1
RRSP:	20%
Management Expense Ratio:	2.30% (Category Average: 2.51%)

COMMENTS

Formerly the Bullock European Enterprise Fund, this small-cap fund benefits from the resources of Mercury's 80-person European equity team. This coverage allows for an intensive bottom-up stock selection process. The team meets, on average, with two companies a day. Eastern Europe represents less than 5% of the portfolio at present.

RISK

The fund lost money in ....3 of 16 Months
The fund lost money in ....1 of 14 Quarters
Worst 3 Months ....-1.90% (1995)
Best 3 Months 14.44% (1995)

ASSET ALLOCATION

U.K. 28.1%
France...10.7%
Germany 9.4%
Sweden 8.8%
Other...43.0%

COMPARISON OF FUND TO INDEXES

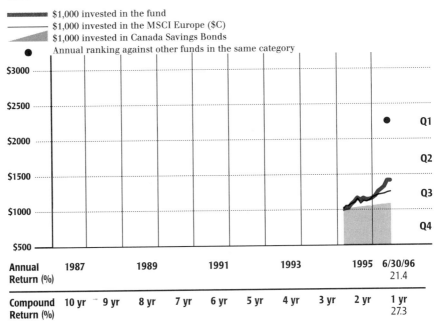

- $1,000 invested in the fund
- $1,000 invested in the MSCI Europe ($C)
- $1,000 invested in Canada Savings Bonds
- Annual ranking against other funds in the same category

Annual Return (%)	1987	1989	1991	1993	1995	6/30/96
						21.4

Compound Return (%)	10 yr	9 yr	8 yr	7 yr	6 yr	5 yr	4 yr	3 yr	2 yr	1 yr
										27.3

UNIVERSAL EUROPEAN OPPORTUNITIES LOAD

Primary Objective:	Aggressive Growth
Sponsor:	Mackenzie Financial
Fund Manager:	Stephen Peak, Henderson Administration
Style:	Bottom-up, Growth
Size (MMs):	$119.270
RRSP:	20%
Management Expense Ratio:	2.58% (Category Average: 2.51%)

COMMENTS

This fund has a smaller-company bias within the developed markets and also invests
in some of the emerging Eastern European markets. Henderson, based in London, is
a fundamental, research-driven organization that has been in business since 1934.
The fund is not restricted to any minimum or maximum country or sector weighting.
Peak is a recognized authority in European small cap investing and has more than 19
years of research and portfolio management experience.

RISK

The fund lost money in ....2 of 21 Months
The fund lost money in ....0 of 19 Quarters
Worst 3 Months...
Best 3 Months 1987

ASSET ALLOCATION

France..12.0%
Finland 10.0%
Germany 9.0%
Denmark 6.0%
Other..63.0%

COMPARISON OF FUND TO INDEXES

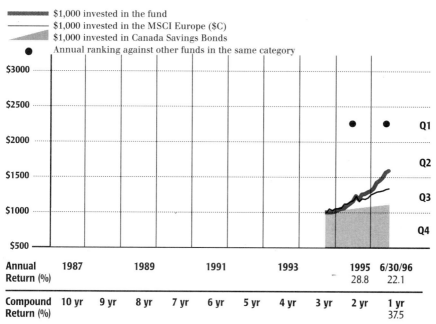

- $1,000 invested in the fund
- $1,000 invested in the MSCI Europe ($C)
- $1,000 invested in Canada Savings Bonds
- ● Annual ranking against other funds in the same category

Annual Return (%)	1987	1989	1991	1993	1995	6/30/96
					28.8	22.1

Compound Return (%)	10 yr	9 yr	8 yr	7 yr	6 yr	5 yr	4 yr	3 yr	2 yr	1 yr
										37.5

European Equity

AGF ASIAN GROWTH A LOAD

Primary Objective:	Aggressive Growth
Sponsor:	AGF Management
Fund Manager:	David Chan, AGF Singapore
Style:	Bottom-up, Growth
Size (MMs):	$113.233
RRSP:	20%
Management Expense Ratio:	2.41% (Category Average: 2.67%)

COMMENTS

This fund does not invest in Japan. (AGF has a separate fund with Japan as its sole focus). The fund is still run by David Chan. However, in the spring of 1996, Chan left Nomura, where he had been a director to establish AGF Asset Management Asia Ltd. (Singapore). Chan, who has run Asian equities for more than ten years, will still focus his energies on picking companies using a wide range of institutional research. As such, he may well end up with over and under weightings of countries, as these weightings reflect the result of, not the beginning of the process.

RISK

The fund lost money in	21 of 56 Months
The fund lost money in	16 of 54 Quarters
Worst 3 Months	-17.64% (1995)
Best 3 Months	39.55% (1993)

ASSET ALLOCATION

Hong Kong	27.0%
Malaysia	26.0%
Singapore	15.0%
Thailand	9.0%
Other	23.0%

COMPARISON OF FUND TO INDEXES

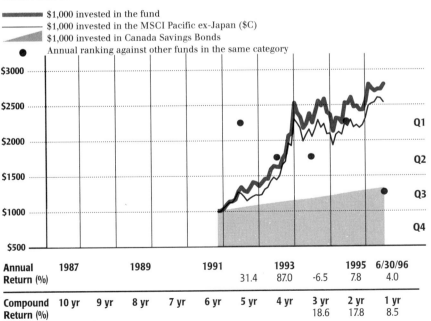

- $1,000 invested in the fund
- $1,000 invested in the MSCI Pacific ex-Japan ($C)
- $1,000 invested in Canada Savings Bonds
- Annual ranking against other funds in the same category

Annual Return (%)	1987	1989	1991		1993			1995	6/30/96
				31.4	87.0	-6.5		7.8	4.0

Compound Return (%)	10 yr	9 yr	8 yr	7 yr	6 yr	5 yr	4 yr	3 yr	2 yr	1 yr
								18.6	17.8	8.5

FAR EAST EQUITY

CIBC FAR EAST PROSPERITY

NO-LOAD

Primary Objective:	Aggressive Growth
Sponsor:	CIBC Securities
Fund Manager:	Duncan Mount, CEF Investment Management
Style:	Bottom-up, Growth
Size (MMs):	$278.443
RRSP:	20%
Management Expense Ratio:	2.85% (Category Average: 2.67%)

COMMENTS

See Hyperion Asian

RISK

The fund lost money in	18 of 33 Months
The fund lost money in	13 of 31 Quarters
Worst 3 Months	-21.78% (1993)
Best 3 Months	36.00% (1994)

ASSET ALLOCATION

Hong Kong	24.3%
Japan	15.5%
Thailand	15.3%
Malaysia	15.1%
Other	29.8%

COMPARISON OF FUND TO INDEXES

- $1,000 invested in the fund
- $1,000 invested in the MSCI Pacific ex-Japan ($C)
- $1,000 invested in Canada Savings Bonds
- Annual ranking against other funds in the same category

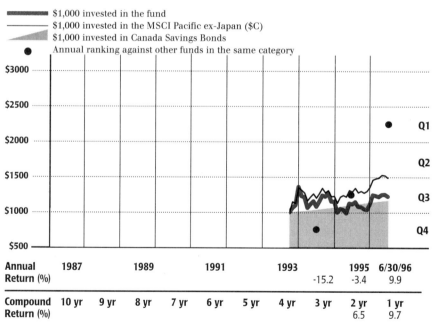

Annual Return (%)	1987		1989		1991		1993		1995	6/30/96
								-15.2	-3.4	9.9

Compound Return (%)	10 yr	9 yr	8 yr	7 yr	6 yr	5 yr	4 yr	3 yr	2 yr	1 yr
									6.5	9.7

EVEREST ASIAGROWTH

Primary Objective:	Aggressive Growth
Sponsor:	Canada Trust
Fund Manager:	David Patterson, Newcastle Capital Management
Style:	Index Matching
Size (MMs):	$208.397
RRSP:	100%
Management Expense Ratio:	2.44% (Category Average: 2.67%)

COMMENTS

This is the way to play the Asian markets within the Canadian content portion of your RRSP. Patterson and his team at Newcastle, using a non-leveraged derivatives strategy, use a top down approach on the region, determining which of the Asian or Australian markets they want to be in. Once this decision is made, they use futures contracts, backed by Canadian T-Bills, to buy these markets.

RISK

The fund lost money in................13 of 29 Months	
The fund lost money in................8 of 27 Quarters	
Worst 3 Months ....-15.70% (1995)	
Best 3 Months 13.81% (1996)	

ASSET ALLOCATION

Canadian T-Bills 100%

COMPARISON OF FUND TO INDEXES

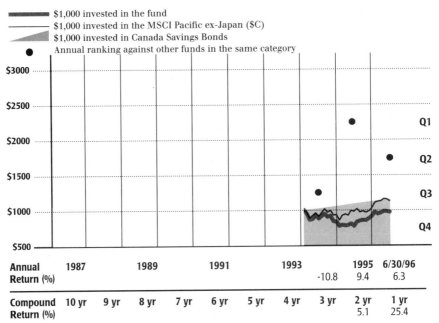

FAR EAST EQUITY

- $1,000 invested in the fund
- $1,000 invested in the MSCI Pacific ex-Japan ($C)
- $1,000 invested in Canada Savings Bonds
- Annual ranking against other funds in the same category

	1987		1989		1991		1993		1995	6/30/96
Annual Return (%)								-10.8	9.4	6.3

	10 yr	9 yr	8 yr	7 yr	6 yr	5 yr	4 yr	3 yr	2 yr	1 yr
Compound Return (%)									5.1	25.4

FIDELITY FAR EAST

Primary Objective:	Aggressive Growth
Sponsor:	Fidelity Investments Canada
Fund Manager:	K.C. Lee, Fidelity
Style:	Bottom-up, Growth
Size (MMs):	$1,629.531
RRSP:	20%
Management Expense Ratio:	2.82% (Category Average: 2.67%)

COMMENTS

This fund was not a Smart Fund last year because the authors felt a regional fund that was so overweight in one market (Hong Kong) did not conform to our view of a Smart Fund. (We applied the same view to the then Regent Tiger Fund, which was at the time completely out of Hong Kong). However, Lee has proven that, although it may take its hits, Hong Kong is the premier market in the Far East. At June 30, he was still almost 60% in Hong Kong. While there is no denying this fund deserves Smart Fund status, we remind investors that the magnitude of the overweighting makes this fund very sensitive to shocks to Hong Kong. The fund will never include Japan.

RISK

The fund lost money in ....21 of 57 Months
The fund lost money in ....11 of 55 Quarters
Worst 3 Months ....-16.25% (1994)
Best 3 Months 33.99% (1993)

ASSET ALLOCATION

Hong Kong................................56.6%
Korea..9.6%
Malaysia 5.1%
Singapore....................................4.2%
Other..24.5%

COMPARISON OF FUND TO INDEXES

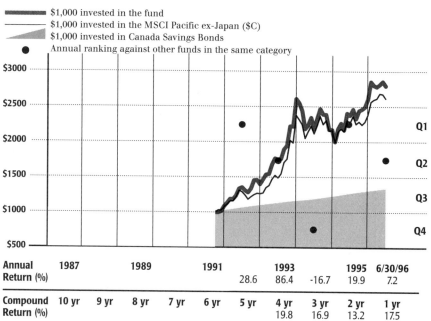

FAR EAST EQUITY

- $1,000 invested in the fund
- $1,000 invested in the MSCI Pacific ex-Japan ($C)
- $1,000 invested in Canada Savings Bonds
- Annual ranking against other funds in the same category

Q1
Q2
Q3
Q4

Annual Return (%)	1987		1989		1991		1993		1995	6/30/96
						28.6	86.4	-16.7	19.9	7.2

Compound Return (%)	10 yr	9 yr	8 yr	7 yr	6 yr	5 yr	4 yr	3 yr	2 yr	1 yr
							19.8	16.9	13.2	17.5

HONGKONG BANK ASIAN GROWTH   NO-LOAD

Primary Objective:	Aggressive Growth
Sponsor:	Stella Yiu, HSBC Asset Management
Fund Manager:	HSBC
Style:	Bottom-up, Growth
Size (MMs):	$46.471
RRSP:	20%
Management Expense Ratio:	2.46% (Category Average: 2.67%)

COMMENTS

Managers at Hongkong Shanghai Bank Asset Management manage money world-wide, based on a global economic view reviewed quarterly by the entire group. Using a top down view, they endeavour to determine which assets will outperform, and when applied to a regionally focused fund like this, which country will outperform. This fund's benchmark is the MSCI Pacific (ex-Japan). The portfolio will, therefore, resemble the index weightings. Actual stock picking employs a growth style applied to the mid- to large-cap stocks, most of which would be represented in the Asian indexes. Manager Stella Yiu is another alumna of G.T. Management.

RISK

The fund lost money in ....15 of 31 Months
The fund lost money in ....13 of 29 Quarters
Worst 3 Months................................-17.08% (1995)
Best 3 Months 15.49% (1996)

ASSET ALLOCATION

Hong Kong................................22.8%
Australia....................................21.4%
Malaysia 13.4%
Thailand...................................10.5%
Other...31.9%

COMPARISON OF FUND TO INDEXES

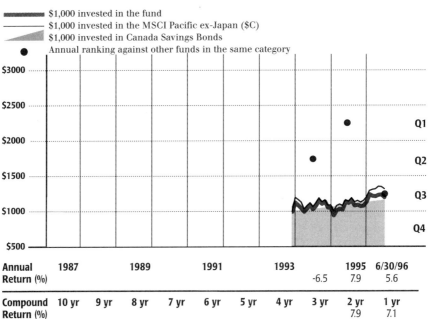

- $1,000 invested in the fund
- $1,000 invested in the MSCI Pacific ex-Japan ($C)
- $1,000 invested in Canada Savings Bonds
- ● Annual ranking against other funds in the same category

Annual Return (%)	1987		1989		1991		1993		1995	6/30/96
								-6.5	7.9	5.6

Compound Return (%)	10 yr	9 yr	8 yr	7 yr	6 yr	5 yr	4 yr	3 yr	2 yr	1 yr
									7.9	7.1

FAR EAST EQUITY

HYPERION ASIAN

Primary Objective:	Aggressive Growth
Sponsor:	Talvest
Fund Manager:	Duncan Mount, CEF Investment Management
Style:	Bottom-up Growth
Size (MMs):	$200.377
RRSP:	20%
Management Expense Ratio:	3.25% (Category Average: 2.67%)

COMMENTS

This fund uses a bottom up growth style to choose companies from the entire Asian marketplace including Japan. Because the manager is more interested in the companies than the countries he invests in, the fund will rarely track any regional index. Mount has been running Asian equities since 1974 and specifically for CEF since 1988. CEF was sold by the CIBC to Talvest, its money management arm in the early summer of 1996. For those that want the manager on a no load basis, he also manages the CIBC Far East Prosperity Fund.

RISK

The fund lost money in ....36 of 78 Months
The fund lost money in ....26 of 76 Quarters
Worst 3 Months ....-24.00% (1990)
Best 3 Months 49.19% (1993)

ASSET ALLOCATION

Hong Kong...............................25.2%
Malaysia 16.3%
Japan...15.8%
Thailand....................................13.5%
Other..29.2%

COMPARISON OF FUND TO INDEXES

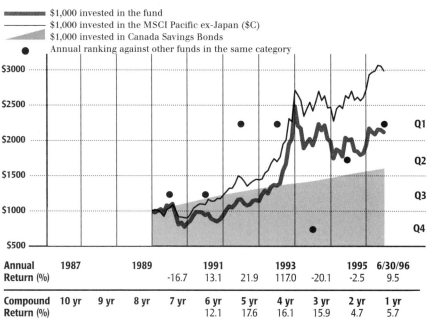

- $1,000 invested in the fund
- $1,000 invested in the MSCI Pacific ex-Japan ($C)
- $1,000 invested in Canada Savings Bonds
- Annual ranking against other funds in the same category

Annual Return (%)	1987		1989		1991		1993		1995	6/30/96
				-16.7	13.1	21.9	117.0	-20.1	-2.5	9.5

Compound Return (%)	10 yr	9 yr	8 yr	7 yr	6 yr	5 yr	4 yr	3 yr	2 yr	1 yr
					12.1	17.6	16.1	15.9	4.7	5.7

FAR EAST EQUITY

INVESTORS JAPANESE GROWTH LOAD

Primary Objective: Aggressive Growth
Sponsor: Investors Group
Fund Manager: Colin Abraham, Carlson Investment Management
Style: Bottom-up Growth
Size (MMs): $707.200
RRSP: 20%
Management Expense Ratio: 2.42% (Category Average: 2.67%)

COMMENTS

Investors uses Carlson Asset Management to advise them on this fund as well
Investors Pacific International; see that fund's entry for Carlson's philosophy and
style. This was one of the first Japan funds in Canada and has maintained a
competitive positioning despite more recent challengers. This fund seems to have
come through some very difficult years and may well be ready to surprise on the
upside.

RISK

The fund lost money in.............53 of 114 Months
The fund lost money in ....48 of 112 Quarters
Worst 3 Months 1990
Best 3 Months 1993

ASSET ALLOCATION

Industrial products.................32.3%
Consumer products................17.9%
Real estate & construction.....13.6%
Financial services...................12.6%
Other...23.6%

COMPARISON OF FUND TO INDEXES

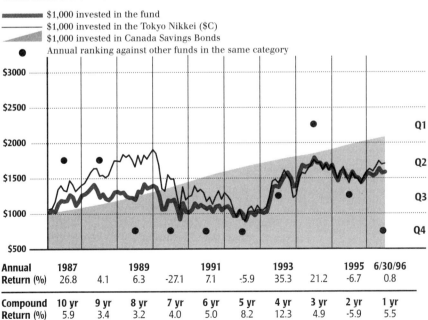

$1,000 invested in the fund
$1,000 invested in the Tokyo Nikkei ($C)
$1,000 invested in Canada Savings Bonds
● Annual ranking against other funds in the same category

Annual Return (%)	1987		1989		1991		1993		1995	6/30/96
	26.8	4.1	6.3	-27.1	7.1	-5.9	35.3	21.2	-6.7	0.8

Compound Return (%)	10 yr	9 yr	8 yr	7 yr	6 yr	5 yr	4 yr	3 yr	2 yr	1 yr
	5.9	3.4	3.2	4.0	5.0	8.2	12.3	4.9	-5.9	5.5

INVESTORS PACIFIC INTERNATIONAL LOAD

Primary Objective:	Aggressive Growth
Sponsor:	Investors Group
Fund Manager:	Jeremy Higgs, Carlson Investment Management
Style:	Bottom-up, Growth
Size (MMs):	$1,280.000
RRSP:	20%
Management Expense Ratio:	2.53% (Category Average: 2.67%)

COMMENTS

Investors' sub-adviser on this fund is Carlson Investment Management, a Swedish firm established in 1990. Its investment philosophy is to balance risk in a disciplined way. They focus more on the risk/return balance as it pertains to their clients than trying to compete with an index. Emphasis is on long-term structural changes, such as political flux, new growth areas, and long investment cycles. Portfolios are concentrated. Companies are chosen as a result of a complete understanding of both a company and its industry. This fund excludes Japan and invests broadly throughout the rest of the region. While it primarily focuses on common shares, it can also utilize bonds and other investment products.

RISK

The fund lost money in .... 30 of 69 Months
The fund lost money in .... 19 of 67 Quarters
Worst 3 Months .... -13.83% (1995)
Best 3 Months 34.96% (1993)

ASSET ALLOCATION

Hong Kong 21.8%
Malaysia 12.8%
Singapore 12.7%
Thailand 9.1%
Other 43.6%

COMPARISON OF FUND TO INDEXES

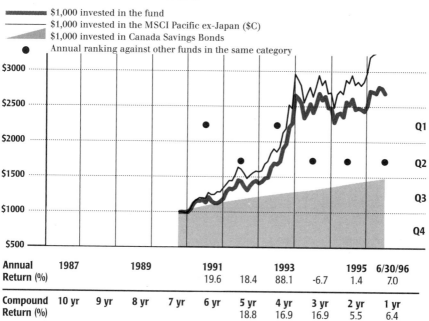

- $1,000 invested in the fund
- $1,000 invested in the MSCI Pacific ex-Japan ($C)
- $1,000 invested in Canada Savings Bonds
- Annual ranking against other funds in the same category

Annual Return (%)	1987		1989		1991		1993		1995	6/30/96
					19.6	18.4	88.1	-6.7	1.4	7.0

Compound Return (%)	10 yr	9 yr	8 yr	7 yr	6 yr	5 yr	4 yr	3 yr	2 yr	1 yr
						18.8	16.9	16.9	5.5	6.4

FAR EAST EQUITY

TRIMARK INDO-PACIFIC

LOAD

Primary Objective:	Growth
Sponsor:	Trimark Financial
Fund Manager:	Robert Lloyd George & Pamela Chan, Lloyd George Management
Style:	Bottom-up, Value
Size (MMs):	$210.470
RRSP:	20%
Management Expense Ratio:	2.74% (Category Average: 2.67%)

COMMENTS

This fund represents the only foray into external money management by Trimark. Lloyd George's management philosophy is very much like Trimark's, so much so that Trimark took an equity position in the company. Using a bottom up growth style, Pamela Chan will be investing in the traditional Far East markets as well as those of India and Pakistan.

RISK

The fund lost money in ....10 of 21 Months
The fund lost money in ....6 of 19 Quarters
Worst 3 Months ....-7.00% (1995)
Best 3 Months 13.92% (1996)

ASSET ALLOCATION

Hong Kong................................23.3%
Malaysia....................................13.0%
Thailand......................................9.1%
Singapore....................................7.4%
Other 47.2%

COMPARISON OF FUND TO INDEXES

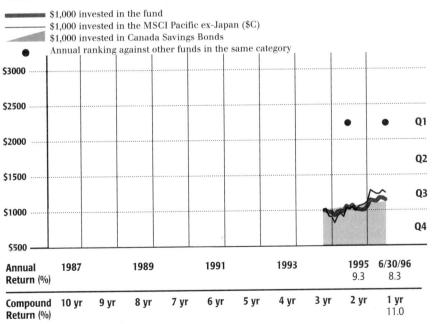

■■■■■ $1,000 invested in the fund
──── $1,000 invested in the MSCI Pacific ex-Japan ($C)
◤ $1,000 invested in Canada Savings Bonds
● Annual ranking against other funds in the same category

Annual Return (%)	1987	1989	1991	1993	1995	6/30/96
					9.3	8.3

Compound Return (%)	10 yr	9 yr	8 yr	7 yr	6 yr	5 yr	4 yr	3 yr	2 yr	1 yr
										11.0

20/20 LATIN AMERICA LOAD

Primary Objective:	Aggressive Growth
Sponsor:	AGF
Fund Manager:	Peter Gruber, GlobeInvest, Globalvest
Style:	Top-Down
Size (MMs):	$193.407
RRSP:	20%
Management Expense Ratio:	3.22% (Category Average: 2.81%)

COMMENTS

This is the Latin American equivalent to the Fidelity Far East fund in that Gruber tends to overweight a single country – in this case Brazil. Like many managers in the region, Gruber first applies a top-down analysis to determine which country he should be in. He then uses a value-based stock selection process to determine which companies to buy.

RISK

The fund lost money in ....15 of 28 Months
The fund lost money in ....11 of 26 Quarters
Worst 3 Months ....-28.04% (1995)
Best 3 Months 38.52% (1994)

ASSET ALLOCATION

Brazil...73.0%
Venezuela...................................11.0%
Mexico 8.0%
Ecuador.......................................3.0%
Other...5.0%

COMPARISON OF FUND TO INDEXES

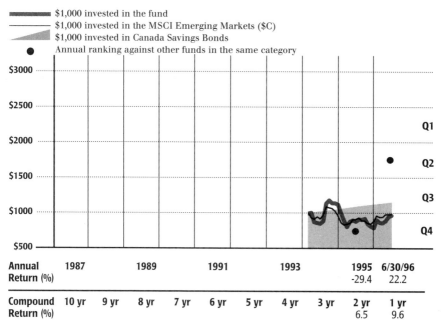

- $1,000 invested in the fund
- $1,000 invested in the MSCI Emerging Markets ($C)
- $1,000 invested in Canada Savings Bonds
- ● Annual ranking against other funds in the same category

Annual Return (%)	1987		1989		1991		1993		1995	6/30/96
									-29.4	22.2

Compound Return (%)	10 yr	9 yr	8 yr	7 yr	6 yr	5 yr	4 yr	3 yr	2 yr	1 yr
									6.5	9.6

EMERGING MARKETS EQUITY

GREEN LINE EMERGING MARKETS NO-LOAD

Primary Objective:	Aggressive Growth
Sponsor:	TD Asset Management
Fund Manager:	Madhav Dhar, Morgan Stanley Asset Management
Style:	Top-down
Size (MMs):	$168.728
RRSP:	20%
Management Expense Ratio:	2.68% (Category Average: 2.81%)

COMMENTS

Morgan Stanley Asset Management is generally recognized as a pioneer in emerging market asset management. It is the MS in the MSCI indices, which are commonly used benchmarks for global asset management. The company's success has been in identifying undervalued markets that are set for rapid growth. The fund does invest in India.

RISK

The fund lost money in ....18 of 42 Months
The fund lost money in ....13 of 40 Quarters
Worst 3 Months ....-23.06% (1995)
Best 3 Months 29.91% (1994)

ASSET ALLOCATION

Brazil 15.6%
Mexico 10.8%
India..10.3%
Indonesia 8.4%
Other...54.9%

COMPARISON OF FUND TO INDEXES

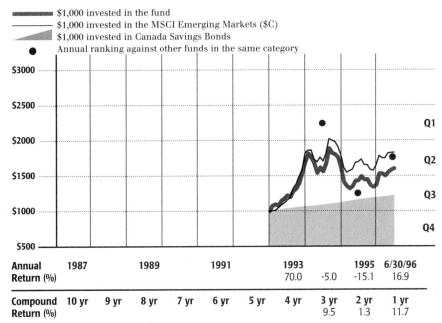

- $1,000 invested in the fund
- $1,000 invested in the MSCI Emerging Markets ($C)
- $1,000 invested in Canada Savings Bonds
- Annual ranking against other funds in the same category

Annual Return (%)	1987	1989	1991	1993		1995	6/30/96
				70.0	-5.0	-15.1	16.9

Compound Return (%)	10 yr	9 yr	8 yr	7 yr	6 yr	5 yr	4 yr	3 yr	2 yr	1 yr
								9.5	1.3	11.7

GT GLOBAL LATIN AMERICA CLASS LOAD

Primary Objective:	Aggressive Growth
Sponsor:	GT Global Canada
Fund Manager:	Soraya Betterton, LGT
Style:	Bottom-up, Value
Size (MMs):	$9.509
RRSP:	20%
Management Expense Ratio:	2.95% (Category Average: 2.81%)

COMMENTS

Timing is everything. This is the only Latin American fund that has made money for unit holders who have owned it since inception. This is because it was launched at the time of the Mexican peso crisis and was largely in cash. However, Betterton has capitalized on the advantage and remained top quartile. GT's approach, like many in the region, is a top-down country allocation, followed by a bottom-up stock selection process.

RISK

The fund lost money in	8 of 20 Months
The fund lost money in	6 of 18 Quarters
Worst 3 Months	-26.30% (1995)
Best 3 Months	23.71% (1995)

ASSET ALLOCATION

Mexico	29.2%
Brazil	28.5%
U.S.	10.7%
Chile	9.8%
Other	21.8%

COMPARISON OF FUND TO INDEXES

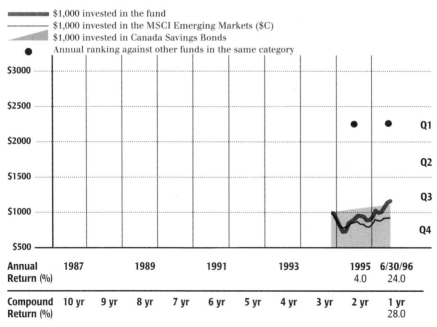

- $1,000 invested in the fund
- $1,000 invested in the MSCI Emerging Markets ($C)
- $1,000 invested in Canada Savings Bonds
- Annual ranking against other funds in the same category

Annual Return (%)	1987	1989	1991	1993	1995	6/30/96
					4.0	24.0

Compound Return (%)	10 yr	9 yr	8 yr	7 yr	6 yr	5 yr	4 yr	3 yr	2 yr	1 yr
										28.0

EMERGING MARKETS EQUITY

GUARDIAN EMERGING MARKETS A LOAD

Primary Objective:	Aggressive Growth
Sponsor:	Guardian Group of Funds
Fund Manager:	Kenneth King, Kleinwort Benson
Style:	Top-Down
Size (MMs):	$1.360
RRSP:	20%
Management Expense Ratio:	2.02% (Category Average: 2.81%)

COMMENTS

This fund minimizes the volatility of emerging markets by limiting exposure to any one country to 10%. Countries are ranked by their capitalization. The top 50% are given twice the portfolio weighting as the bottom 50%. The manager takes profits in the markets that have risen over a 12-month period and redeploys the capital into markets that have under performed. Kleinwort has back-tested this methodology and shown it to be an effective way to reduce volatility while maintaining performance.

RISK

The fund lost money in ....9 of 22 Months
The fund lost money in ....5 of 20 Quarters
Worst 3 Months ....-9.56% (1995)
Best 3 Months 14.47% (1996)

ASSET ALLOCATION

Far East 45.0%
Latin America 35.0%
Europe & Africa 16.0%
Cash & equivalents..................4.0%

COMPARISON OF FUND TO INDEXES

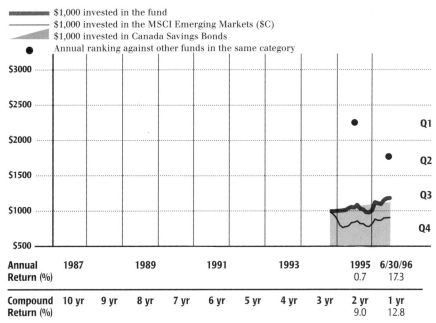

- $1,000 invested in the fund
- $1,000 invested in the MSCI Emerging Markets ($C)
- $1,000 invested in Canada Savings Bonds
- ● Annual ranking against other funds in the same category

Annual Return (%)	1987	1989	1991	1993	1995	6/30/96
					0.7	17.3

Compound Return (%)	10 yr	9 yr	8 yr	7 yr	6 yr	5 yr	4 yr	3 yr	2 yr	1 yr
									9.0	12.8

EMERGING MARKETS EQUITY

MD EMERGING MARKETS

NO-LOAD

Primary Objective:	Aggressive Growth
Sponsor:	MD Management
Fund Manager:	Mark Mobius, Templeton
Style:	Bottom-up, Value
Size (MMs):	$45.121
RRSP:	20%
Management Expense Ratio:	2.49% (Category Average: 2.81%)

COMMENTS

See Templeton Emerging Markets Fund.

RISK

The fund lost money in	11 of 19 Months
The fund lost money in	5 of 17 Quarters
Worst 3 Months	-7.91% (1995)
Best 3 Months	13.30% (1996)

ASSET ALLOCATION

Brazil	14.1%
Mexico	13.6%
Argentina	11.4%
Indonesia	9.9%
Other	51.0%

COMPARISON OF FUND TO INDEXES

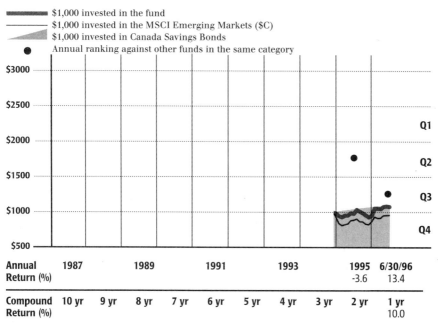

- ▬▬▬ $1,000 invested in the fund
- ———— $1,000 invested in the MSCI Emerging Markets ($C)
- ◢ $1,000 invested in Canada Savings Bonds
- ● Annual ranking against other funds in the same category

Annual Return (%)	1987		1989		1991		1993		1995	6/30/96
									-3.6	13.4

Compound Return (%)	10 yr	9 yr	8 yr	7 yr	6 yr	5 yr	4 yr	3 yr	2 yr	1 yr
										10.0

EMERGING MARKETS EQUITY

SPECTRUM UNITED EMERGING MARKETS LOAD

Primary Objective:	Aggressive Growth
Sponsor:	Spectrum United Mutual Funds
Fund Manager:	Ewen Cameron-Watt, Mercury Asset Management
Style:	Top-Down, Blend
Size (MMs):	$8.647
RRSP:	20%
Management Expense Ratio:	2.33% (Category Average: 2.81%)

COMMENTS

Formerly the Bullock Emerging Markets Fund. Cameron Watt, head of the emerging markets team at Mercury Asset Management, applies a bottom-up, stock-selection style to markets in a similar manner to that of Templeton. Similarities end there. Unlike Templeton, which averages a five-year hold, Mercury's style incorporates more turnover (approximately 90% per year). It is not interested in buying value stories that will some day pay off. It screens on value and then tries to determine the economic risks of buying a stock.

RISK

The fund lost money in ....13 of 30 Months
The fund lost money in ....12 of 28 Quarters
Worst 3 Months ....-20.87% (1995)
Best 3 Months 15.55% (1996)

ASSET ALLOCATION

Far East, ex. Japan 35.4%
Latin America..........................29.4%
Europe.......................................21.5%
Mid East & Africa....................6.2%
Other...7.5%

COMPARISON OF FUND TO INDEXES

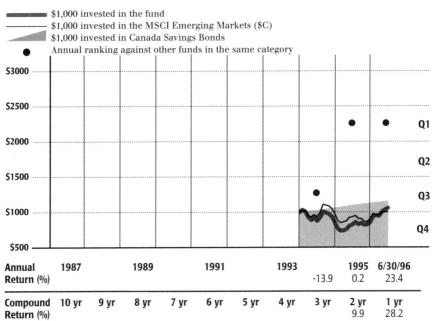

■■■■ $1,000 invested in the fund
——— $1,000 invested in the MSCI Emerging Markets ($C)
▨ $1,000 invested in Canada Savings Bonds
● Annual ranking against other funds in the same category

Annual Return (%)	1987	1989	1991	1993	1995	6/30/96
					-13.9	0.2 23.4

Compound Return (%)	10 yr	9 yr	8 yr	7 yr	6 yr	5 yr	4 yr	3 yr	2 yr	1 yr
									9.9	28.2

EMERGING MARKETS EQUITY

TEMPLETON EMERGING MARKETS LOAD

Primary Objective:	Aggressive Growth
Sponsor:	Templeton Investment Management
Fund Manager:	Mark Mobius, Templeton
Style:	Bottom-up, Value
Size (MMs):	$950.061
RRSP:	20%
Management Expense Ratio:	3.28% (Category Average: 2.81%)

COMMENTS

Mobius is regarded as the dean of emerging-markets investing (see profile in 1996 edition). He heads a 40-person emerging markets team that draws on Templeton's on-the-ground research in more than 20 countries. The Templeton style of buying value (at the point of maximum pessimism) is well known. Mobius travels ten months of the year visiting companies they hold or are interested in. Country allocation is a by-product of the stock selection process. Those in the medical community can buy the same management expertise no-load, and at a reduced MER, through Templeton's MD Emerging Markets.

RISK

The fund lost money in	22 of 56 Months
The fund lost money in	19 of 54 Quarters
Worst 3 Months	-12.66% (1995)
Best 3 Months	21.37% (1993)

ASSET ALLOCATION

Banking	24.5%
Multi-industry	11.0%
Telecommunications	8.4%
Real estate	7.2%
Other	48.9%

COMPARISON OF FUND TO INDEXES

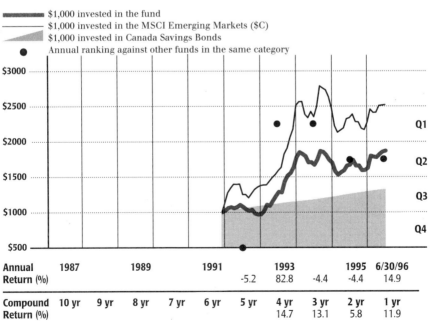

- $1,000 invested in the fund
- $1,000 invested in the MSCI Emerging Markets ($C)
- $1,000 invested in Canada Savings Bonds
- Annual ranking against other funds in the same category

Annual Return (%)	1987	1989	1991	1993	1995	6/30/96
				-5.2 82.8 -4.4	-4.4	14.9

Compound Return (%)	10 yr	9 yr	8 yr	7 yr	6 yr	5 yr	4 yr	3 yr	2 yr	1 yr
							14.7	13.1	5.8	11.9

EMERGING MARKETS EQUITY

20/20 MANAGED FUTURES VALUE LOAD

Primary Objective:	Growth
Sponsor:	AGF
Fund Manager:	John Di Thomasso
Style:	Bottom-up, Value
Size (MMs):	$49.890
RRSP:	100%
Management Expense Ratio:	3%+ (Category Average: 3.24%)

COMMENTS

This fund is not for everyone. It has recently done well because of its focus on hard commodities and the fact that they have been, as is typical in the latter stages of the economic cycle, experiencing upward price pressure. Managed futures can be an attractive asset class because historically they have been non correlated to equities and bonds. In portfolios of adequate size, this additional asset class may help smooth out portfolio returns. Fewer will be attracted to this fund as a pure play on hard commodities, although Di Tomasso's methodology is extremely sound in this area.

RISK

The fund lost money in	4 of 13 Months
The fund lost money in	1 of 11 Quarters
Worst 3 Months	-2.41% (1995)
Best 3 Months	8.46% (1996)

ASSET ALLOCATION

Livestock	17.0%
Metals	26.0%
Grains & oilseeds	17.0%
Softs	20.0%
Miscellaneous	20.0%

COMPARISON OF FUND TO INDEXES

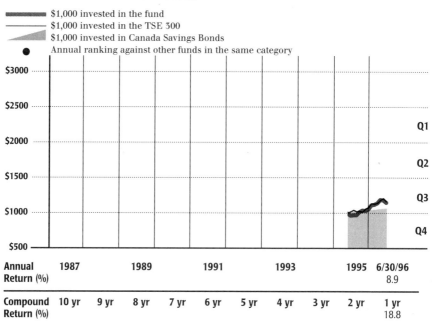

$1,000 invested in the fund
$1,000 invested in the TSE 300
$1,000 invested in Canada Savings Bonds
● Annual ranking against other funds in the same category

Annual Return (%)	1987	1989	1991	1993	1995	6/30/96
						8.9

Compound Return (%)	10 yr	9 yr	8 yr	7 yr	6 yr	5 yr	4 yr	3 yr	2 yr	1 yr
										18.8

ADMAX GLOBAL HEALTH SCIENCES LOAD

Primary Objective:	Aggressive Growth
Sponsor:	Admax Group of Funds
Fund Manager:	John Schroer, Invesco
Style:	Bottom-up, Growth
Size (MMs):	$111.210
RRSP:	20%
Management Expense Ratio:	2.58% (Category Average: 3.24%)

COMMENTS

This formerly unique fund now has competition from GT Global and C.I. Mutual Funds. It uses a bottom-up growth style of management to pick companies around the world and across industry segments that will benefit from the increased demographic demand for health care. The intuitive appeal of the sector has been proven out in the performance of the fund. The on-going success of the fund, despite two manager changes, is a testament to the depth and expertise of Invesco in this area.

RISK

The fund lost money in..............15 of 44 Months
The fund lost money in..............8 of 42 Quarters
Worst 3 Months.............................-12.68% (1993)
Best 3 Months.................................29.77% (1993)

ASSET ALLOCATION

Pharmaceuticals......................27.3%
Healthcare...............................23.7%
Healthcare delivery................22.8%
Cash & equivalents.................19.5%
Biotechnology...........................6.7%

COMPARISON OF FUND TO INDEXES

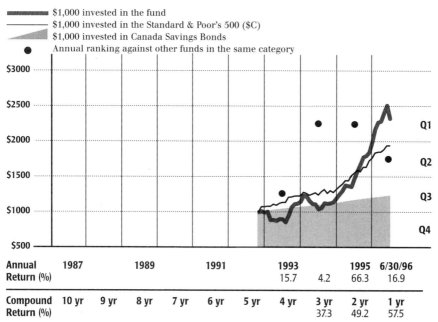

- $1,000 invested in the fund
- $1,000 invested in the Standard & Poor's 500 ($C)
- $1,000 invested in Canada Savings Bonds
- Annual ranking against other funds in the same category

Q1									
Q2									
Q3									
Q4									

Annual Return (%)	1987		1989		1991		1993		1995	6/30/96
							15.7	4.2	66.3	16.9

Compound Return (%)	10 yr	9 yr	8 yr	7 yr	6 yr	5 yr	4 yr	3 yr	2 yr	1 yr
								37.3	49.2	57.5

AGF CANADIAN RESOURCES A LOAD

Primary Objective:	Aggressive Growth
Sponsor:	AGF Management
Fund Manager:	Bob Farquharson
Style:	Bottom-up, Growth
Size (MMs):	$67.825
RRSP:	100%
Management Expense Ratio:	2.56% (Category Average: 3.24%)

COMMENTS

This fund is now in its 37th year. Farquharson has managed it since 1975 using a bottom-up growth style. This type of fund is a cyclical play. Its volatility has been close to twice that of the Canadian mid- to large-cap category.

RISK

The fund lost money in..............45 of 114 Months
The fund lost money in ....50 of 112 Quarters
Worst 3 Months ....-27.59% (1987)
Best 3 Months 37.86% (1993)

ASSET ALLOCATION

Oil & gas 39.0%
Gold & silver.............................24.0%
Metals & minerals 15.0%
Resource services....................12.0%
Other..10.0%

COMPARISON OF FUND TO INDEXES

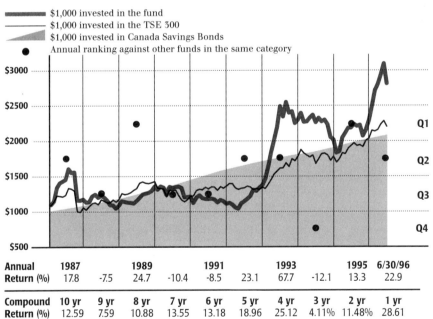

$1,000 invested in the fund
$1,000 invested in the TSE 300
$1,000 invested in Canada Savings Bonds
● Annual ranking against other funds in the same category

Annual Return (%)	1987		1989		1991		1993		1995	6/30/96
	17.8	-7.5	24.7	-10.4	-8.5	23.1	67.7	-12.1	13.3	22.9

Compound Return (%)	10 yr	9 yr	8 yr	7 yr	6 yr	5 yr	4 yr	3 yr	2 yr	1 yr
	12.59	7.59	10.88	13.55	13.18	18.96	25.12	4.11%	11.48%	28.61

AIC ADVANTAGE

Primary Objective:	Growth
Sponsor:	AIC
Fund Manager:	Jonathan Wellum, AIC
Style:	Bottom-up, Growth
Size (MMs):	$667.408
RRSP:	100%
Management Expense Ratio:	2.55% (Category Average: 3.24%)

COMMENTS

This fund is a play on the Canadian financial services industry, and particularly the mutual fund industry. AIC literature points out that the stock of a publicly-traded mutual fund company has a history of outperforming its best funds. But it is also Wellum's discipline that makes this fund stand out. Emulating the bottom-up buy-and-hold strategies of Warren Buffett's Berkshire Hathaway and Trimark, both of which Wellum holds, he buys companies and will hold them for long periods of time. Turnover is low as are distributions, which makes this fund particularly attractive for non-RRSP accounts.

RISK

The fund lost money in..............38 of 114 Months
The fund lost money in ....38 of 112 Quarters
Worst 3 Months ....-30.46% (1987)
Best 3 Months 25.02% (1992)

ASSET ALLOCATION

Financial services...................65.4%
Communications & media.....13.2%
Gold & precious metals...........7.5%
Other.......................................13.9%

COMPARISON OF FUND TO INDEXES

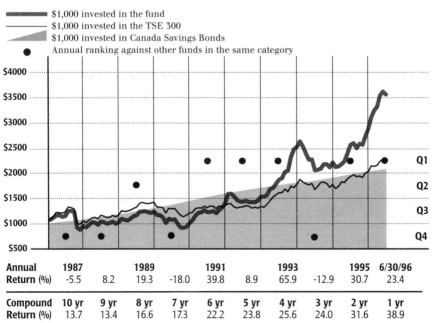

- $1,000 invested in the fund
- $1,000 invested in the TSE 300
- $1,000 invested in Canada Savings Bonds
- Annual ranking against other funds in the same category

Annual	1987		1989		1991		1993		1995	6/30/96
Return (%)	-5.5	8.2	19.3	-18.0	39.8	8.9	65.9	-12.9	30.7	23.4

Compound	10 yr	9 yr	8 yr	7 yr	6 yr	5 yr	4 yr	3 yr	2 yr	1 yr
Return (%)	13.7	13.4	16.6	17.3	22.2	23.8	25.6	24.0	31.6	38.9

THE 125 SMART FUNDS   231

DYNAMIC PRECIOUS METALS   LOAD

Primary Objective:	Aggressive Growth
Sponsor:	Dynamic Mutual Funds
Fund Manager:	Jonathan Goodman, Goodman & Co.
Style:	Bottom-up, Value
Size (MMs):	$327.625
RRSP:	100%
Management Expense Ratio:	2.57% (Category Average: 3.24%)

COMMENTS

This fund did not participate in some of the hot exploration stocks of 1995. As a result, it finished the year with a 0% return, compared to the 20% of its competitors: Prudential and Royal, also mentioned in this section. Exploration is a tough category for Goodman to manage because of his value discipline. These companies, with no earnings, are hard to value. Goodman et al did not miss some of the stocks that did well; they were aware of them but passed them over. Despite the impact on performance, we respect Dynamic's ability to avoid the temptation to stray from a management style that has made them successful.

RISK

The fund lost money in.............46 of 114 Months
The fund lost money in ....49 of 112 Quarters
Worst 3 Months ....-17.79% (1987)
Best 3 Months 50.41% (1993)

ASSET ALLOCATION

Gold & silver.............................54.5%
Metals & minerals 16.9%
Cash 17.2%
Other..11.4%

COMPARISON OF FUND TO INDEXES

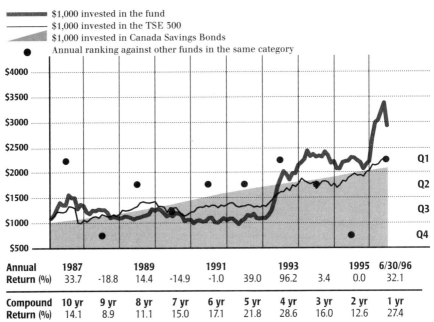

▬▬▬▬ $1,000 invested in the fund
——— $1,000 invested in the TSE 300
▨▨▨ $1,000 invested in Canada Savings Bonds
● Annual ranking against other funds in the same category

Annual Return (%)	1987		1989		1991		1993		1995	6/30/96
	33.7	-18.8	14.4	-14.9	-1.0	39.0	96.2	3.4	0.0	32.1

Compound Return (%)	10 yr	9 yr	8 yr	7 yr	6 yr	5 yr	4 yr	3 yr	2 yr	1 yr
	14.1	8.9	11.1	15.0	17.1	21.8	28.6	16.0	12.6	27.4

DYNAMIC REAL ESTATE

Primary Objective:	Growth
Sponsor:	Dynamic Mutual Funds
Fund Manager:	Anne McLean & Michael Cooper
Style:	Bottom-up, Value
Size (MMs):	$13.602
RRSP:	20%
Management Expense Ratio:	3.70% (Category Average: 3.24%)

COMMENTS

Like 20/20 Managed Futures, this should be purchased by investors looking for an asset class that is not correlated to equities and bonds. Unlike some real estate investments, this fund is fully liquid and may be redeemed at any time. Cooper and McLean focus on asset quality, growth prospects, conservative leverage ratios and management's ability to add value when making their security selection. All the securities are publicly listed.

RISK

The fund lost money in .... 1 of 13 Months
The fund lost money in .... 0 of 11 Quarters
Worst 3 Months 2.46% (1995)
Best 3 Months 16.90% (1996)

ASSET ALLOCATION

Real estate & construction 58.5%
Cash & equivalents 41.5%

COMPARISON OF FUND TO INDEXES

- $1,000 invested in the fund
- $1,000 invested in the TSE 300
- $1,000 invested in Canada Savings Bonds
- Annual ranking against other funds in the same category

Annual Return (%)	1987	1989	1991	1993	1995	6/30/96
						23.0

Compound Return (%)	10 yr	9 yr	8 yr	7 yr	6 yr	5 yr	4 yr	3 yr	2 yr	1 yr
										42.8

GLOBAL STRATEGY GOLD PLUS   LOAD

Primary Objective:	Growth
Sponsor:	Global Strategy
Fund Manager:	Tony Massie
Style:	Bottom-up, Growth
Size (MMs):	$121.243
RRSP:	100%
Management Expense Ratio:	2.95% (Category Average: 3.24%)

COMMENTS

While a relative newcomer to picking gold stocks, Massie has quickly proven he can excel at it. The fund uses a bottom-up style that blends value and growth criteria into the security selection process. Massie will buy senior and junior producers. His Vancouver location keeps him close to early stage developments in the exploration sector. This fund is one of the purest gold plays in the industry.

RISK

The fund lost money in ....10 of 33 Months
The fund lost money in ....13 of 31 Quarters
Worst 3 Months ....-10.35% (1995)
Best 3 Months 54.20% (1996)

ASSET ALLOCATION

Common equities....................99.3%
Cash & equivalents..................0.7%

COMPARISON OF FUND TO INDEXES

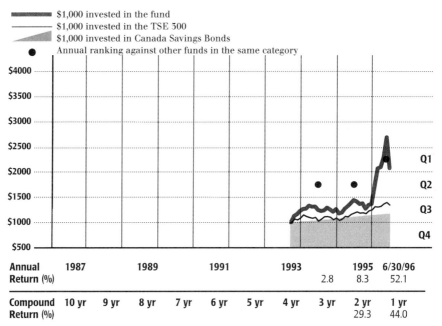

- $1,000 invested in the fund
- $1,000 invested in the TSE 300
- $1,000 invested in Canada Savings Bonds
- Annual ranking against other funds in the same category

Annual Return (%)	1987		1989		1991		1993			1995	6/30/96
									2.8	8.3	52.1

Compound Return (%)	10 yr	9 yr	8 yr	7 yr	6 yr	5 yr	4 yr	3 yr	2 yr	1 yr
									29.3	44.0

GREEN LINE SCIENCE & TECHNOLOGY　NO-LOAD

Primary Objective:	Aggressive Growth
Sponsor:	TD Bank
Fund Manager:	Charles Morris, T. Rowe Price
Style:	Bottom-up, Growth
Size (MMs):	$144.257
RRSP:	20%
Management Expense Ratio:	2.64% (Category Average: 3.24%)

COMMENTS

There are other funds with similar names (CIBC, Royal and Altamira) but if you want sci-tech, this one has the edge, as well as the longest track record. T. Rowe Price is one of the most respected money management firms in the U.S. The late Mr. Rowe Price is considered the pioneer of growth-stock investing. This is a clone of the top-ranked, $2-billion fund that Morris runs in the U.S. The fund's focus is NASDAQ-listed companies positioned to gain from scientific and technological advance. NASDAQ stocks are, of course, volatile.

RISK

The fund lost money in ....12 of 30 Months
The fund lost money in ....4 of 28 Quarters
Worst 3 Months ....-5.99% (1994)
Best 3 Months................................29.78% (1995)

ASSET ALLOCATION

Computer software.................26.3%
Semiconductor 16.1%
Networking..............................14.8%
Media & telecommunication 10.6%
Other......................................32.2%

COMPARISON OF FUND TO INDEXES

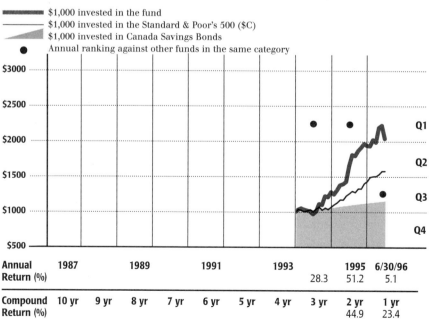

- $1,000 invested in the fund
- $1,000 invested in the Standard & Poor's 500 ($C)
- $1,000 invested in Canada Savings Bonds
- ● Annual ranking against other funds in the same category

Annual Return (%)	1987	1989	1991	1993	1995	6/30/96
					28.3	51.2	5.1

Compound Return (%)	10 yr	9 yr	8 yr	7 yr	6 yr	5 yr	4 yr	3 yr	2 yr	1 yr
									44.9	23.4

GT GLOBAL INFRASTRUCTURE CLASS LOAD

Primary Objective:	Aggressive Growth
Sponsor:	GT Global Canada
Fund Manager:	LGT
Style:	Bottom-up, Growth
Size (MMs):	$45.961
RRSP:	20%
Management Expense Ratio:	2.95% (Category Average: 3.24%)

COMMENTS

This is a theme fund with appeal similar to GT sector funds such as telecommunications and health care. Both developing and developed countries will have to build or rebuild their roads, power plants airports, etc. David Sherry and Michael Mahoney apply top-down macro-economic research to determine country allocation and then a bottom-up growth style when picking individual securities.

RISK

The fund lost money in ....8 of 20 Months
The fund lost money in ....5 of 18 Quarters
Worst 3 Months ....-7.12% (1995)
Best 3 Months 14.03% (1995)

ASSET ALLOCATION

U.S. 27.3%
Canada 23.3%
Spain 4.9%
Sweden 4.5%
Other..40.0%

COMPARISON OF FUND TO INDEXES

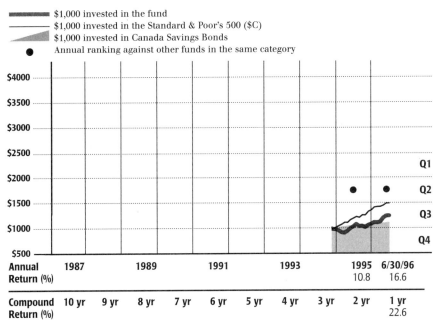

▬▬▬▬▬ $1,000 invested in the fund
———— $1,000 invested in the Standard & Poor's 500 ($C)
◢ $1,000 invested in Canada Savings Bonds
● Annual ranking against other funds in the same category

	1987	1989	1991	1993	1995	6/30/96
Annual Return (%)					10.8	16.6

	10 yr	9 yr	8 yr	7 yr	6 yr	5 yr	4 yr	3 yr	2 yr	1 yr
Compound Return (%)										22.6

GT GLOBAL TELECOMMUNICATIONS CLASS LOAD

Primary Objective:	Aggressive Growth
Sponsor:	GT Global Canada
Fund Manager:	Michael Mahoney, LGT
Style:	Bottom-up Growth
Size (MMs):	$362.900
RRSP:	20%
Management Expense Ratio:	2.95% (Category Average: 3.24%)

COMMENTS

This is another GT theme fund with appeal similar to infrastructure and health care. While global in approach, telecommunications is much narrower in scope than the several rival Science and & Technology funds. So far, the emphasis on such high-growth areas as networking and the Internet has resulted in superior performance that has justified its narrow focus.

RISK

The fund lost money in .... 4 of 20 Months
The fund lost money in .... 2 of 18 Quarters
Worst 3 Months .... -4.40% (1995)
Best 3 Months 19.52% (1995)

ASSET ALLOCATION

U.S. 58.1%
Canada 11.4%
Sweden 4.2%
Japan 3.4%
Other 22.9%

COMPARISON OF FUND TO INDEXES

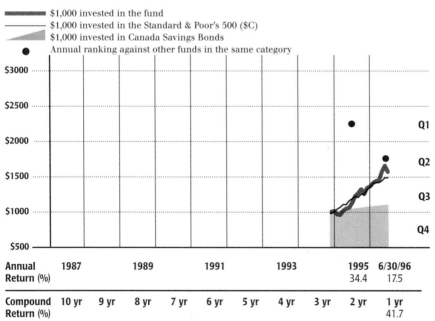

- $1,000 invested in the fund
- $1,000 invested in the Standard & Poor's 500 ($C)
- $1,000 invested in Canada Savings Bonds
- Annual ranking against other funds in the same category

Annual Return (%)	1987		1989		1991		1993		1995	6/30/96
									34.4	17.5

Compound Return (%)	10 yr	9 yr	8 yr	7 yr	6 yr	5 yr	4 yr	3 yr	2 yr	1 yr
										41.7

INDUSTRIAL FUTURE

LOAD

Primary Objective:	Aggressive Growth
Sponsor:	Mackenzie Financial
Fund Manager:	John Rohr, Mackenzie
Style:	Bottom-up, Growth
Size (MMs):	$490.057
RRSP:	100%
Management Expense Ratio:	2.41% (Category Average: 3.24%)

COMMENTS

If you want consistent exposure to science and technology stocks, but need 100%
RRSP eligibility, this may be the fund to do it. Using the Industrial team's top-down
growth criteria, Rohr maintains approximately 50% (30% Canadian and 20% U.S.) of
this fund in technology stocks. The balance of the fund is invested using the top-
down, sector-allocation models that drive the other Industrial funds. The remaining
50% of the fund is invested chiefly in Canadian natural resource stocks, buffering the
volatility that a pure technology portfolio would entail.

RISK

The fund lost money in	41 of 102 Months
The fund lost money in	37 of 100 Quarters
Worst 3 Months	-12.88% (1990)
Best 3 Months	25.54% (1993)

ASSET ALLOCATION

Canadian equities	60.3%
Cash & equivalents	22.9%
Foreign equities	16.8%

COMPARISON OF FUND TO INDEXES

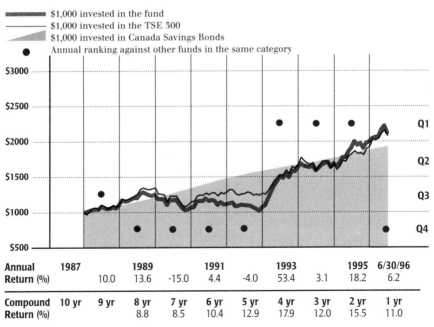

- $1,000 invested in the fund
- $1,000 invested in the TSE 300
- $1,000 invested in Canada Savings Bonds
- Annual ranking against other funds in the same category

Annual Return (%)	1987		1989		1991		1993		1995	6/30/96
		10.0	13.6	-15.0	4.4	-4.0	53.4	3.1	18.2	6.2

Compound Return (%)	10 yr	9 yr	8 yr	7 yr	6 yr	5 yr	4 yr	3 yr	2 yr	1 yr
			8.8	8.5	10.4	12.9	17.9	12.0	15.5	11.0

MAXXUM NATURAL RESOURCE LOAD

Primary Objective:	Aggressive Growth
Sponsor:	London Life Insurance
Fund Manager:	Jacqueline Pratt, Prudential
Style:	Bottom-up, Growth
Size (MMs):	$88.536
RRSP:	100%
Management Expense Ratio:	1.76% (Category Average: 3.24%)

COMMENTS

Although this fund has had consistent top-quartile performance, it was not a Smart Fund last year due to the then-recent departure of its former manager, Veronika Hirsch. Pratt, and her boss Martin Anstee, have maintained the bottom-up, sector-rotator style used by Hirsch, and proved they are worthy of the task. The fund continues to benefit from some of the investments for which Hirsch was responsible, but Anstee and Pratt have been actively adding new companies since her departure.

RISK

The fund lost money in ....38 of 101 Months
The fund lost money in ....26 of 99 Quarters
Worst 3 Months ....-11.02% (1993)
Best 3 Months 45.35% (1993)

ASSET ALLOCATION

Gold & silver............................36.7%
Metals & minerals.................25.3%
Oil & gas 22.3%
Paper & forest products..........4.6%
Other..11.1%

COMPARISON OF FUND TO INDEXES

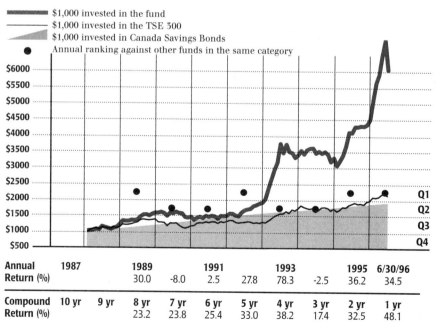

- ▬▬▬ $1,000 invested in the fund
- ──── $1,000 invested in the TSE 300
- ▨▨▨ $1,000 invested in Canada Savings Bonds
- ● Annual ranking against other funds in the same category

Annual Return (%)	1987		1989		1991		1993		1995	6/30/96
			30.0	-8.0	2.5	27.8	78.3	-2.5	36.2	34.5

Compound Return (%)	10 yr	9 yr	8 yr	7 yr	6 yr	5 yr	4 yr	3 yr	2 yr	1 yr
			23.2	23.8	25.4	33.0	38.2	17.4	32.5	48.1

MAXXUM PRECIOUS METALS LOAD

Primary Objective: Aggressive Growth
Sponsor: London Life
Fund Manager: Martin Anstee
Style: Bottom-up, Growth
Size (MMs): $17.520
RRSP: 100%
Management Expense Ratio: 1.79% (Category Average: 3.24%)

COMMENTS

The situation here is similar to that of Prudential Natural Resources: both funds were excluded from the Smart Funds list last year, based on the fact that its former manager had just left. However, it has consistently been and remains a top-quartile fund. Anstee has added value. While having maintained some of the stocks he inherited, others are new. He employs a bottom-up, sector-rotation style within this sub-sector grouping.

RISK

The fund lost money in ....45 of 101 Months
The fund lost money in ....43 of 99 Quarters
Worst 3 Months ....-20.68% (1990)
Best 3 Months 49.83% (1996)

ASSET ALLOCATION

Gold & silver 67.2%
Metals & minerals 16.7%
Cash & equivalents.................16.1%

COMPARISON OF FUND TO INDEXES

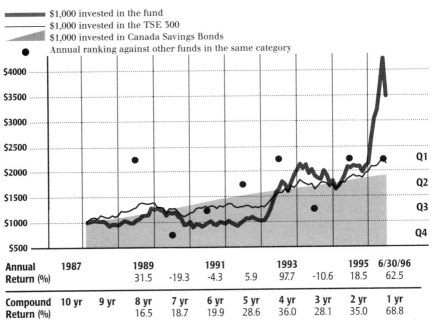

- $1,000 invested in the fund
- $1,000 invested in the TSE 300
- $1,000 invested in Canada Savings Bonds
- Annual ranking against other funds in the same category

Annual Return (%)	1987		1989		1991		1993		1995	6/30/96
			31.5	-19.3	-4.3	5.9	97.7	-10.6	18.5	62.5

Compound Return (%)	10 yr	9 yr	8 yr	7 yr	6 yr	5 yr	4 yr	3 yr	2 yr	1 yr
			16.5	18.7	19.9	28.6	36.0	28.1	35.0	68.8

ROYAL PRECIOUS METALS

NO-LOAD

Primary Objective:	Progressive Growth
Sponsor:	Royal Mutual Funds
Fund Manager:	John Embry, RBIM
Style:	Bottom-up Growth
Size (MMs):	$293.236
RRSP:	100%
Management Expense Ratio:	2.21% (Category Average: 3.24%)

COMMENTS

Having been a money manager for years (seven at Royal), John Embry, who uses a bottom-up, sector-rotation approach, stepped into the spotlight in '95 with the hottest metals fund in the country. A conservative investor by nature, Embry also took pains to tell potential investors of the volatile nature of such a focused fund. Embry's success came from committing early to high-performing stocks in the sector. He was the first to point out that such success stories are few and far between.

RISK

The fund lost money in ....35 of 91 Months
The fund lost money in ....35 of 89 Quarters
Worst 3 Months ....-15.77% (1995)
Best 3 Months 55.56% (1996)

ASSET ALLOCATION

Canadian equities...................59.0%
Silver.......................................11.8%
U.S. equities.............................11.5%
Gold...9.5%
Cash & equivalents..................8.2%

COMPARISON OF FUND TO INDEXES

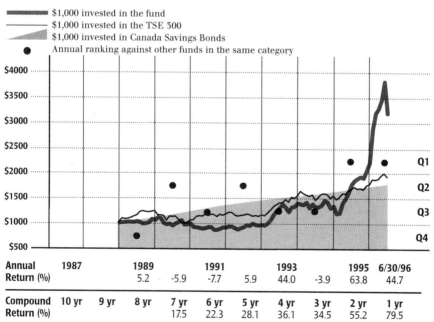

- $1,000 invested in the fund
- $1,000 invested in the TSE 300
- $1,000 invested in Canada Savings Bonds
- Annual ranking against other funds in the same category

Annual Return (%)	1987		1989		1991		1993		1995	6/30/96
			5.2	-5.9	-7.7	5.9	44.0	-3.9	63.8	44.7

Compound Return (%)	10 yr	9 yr	8 yr	7 yr	6 yr	5 yr	4 yr	3 yr	2 yr	1 yr
				17.5	22.3	28.1	36.1	34.5	55.2	79.5

UNIVERSAL CANADIAN RESOURCE LOAD

Primary Objective:	Aggressive Growth
Sponsor:	Mackenzie Financial
Fund Manager:	Fred Sturm
Style:	Bottom-up, Growth
Size (MMs):	$209.691
RRSP:	100%
Management Expense Ratio:	243.00% (Category Average: 3.24%)

COMMENTS

Sturm utilizes the top-down, sector-allocation models that drive the other Industrial funds, but focuses them specifically on the resource sector. Like its competitors, this fund has benefited from commodity price increases. The fund will err on the conservative side as shown by its withdrawal from the gold and silver sector in early '96 as a speculative tone appeared to be taking hold. At the same time, Sturm was taking a somewhat contrarian view, buying into paper and forest products at a time when prices were depressed due to high inventory levels.

RISK

The fund lost money in..............51 of 114 Months
The fund lost money in ....50 of 112 Quarters
Worst 3 Months ....-22.18% (1987)
Best 3 Months 51.60% (1993)

ASSET ALLOCATION

Metals & minerals....................35.0%
Oil & gas 34.0%
Paper & forest products.........23.0%
Cash & equivalents....................6.0%
Other 2.0%

COMPARISON OF FUND TO INDEXES

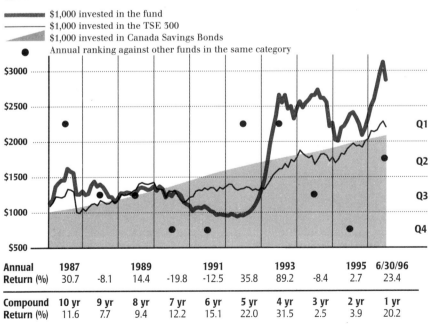

— $1,000 invested in the fund
— $1,000 invested in the TSE 300
— $1,000 invested in Canada Savings Bonds
● Annual ranking against other funds in the same category

Annual	1987		1989		1991		1993		1995	6/30/96
Return (%)	30.7	-8.1	14.4	-19.8	-12.5	35.8	89.2	-8.4	2.7	23.4

Compound	10 yr	9 yr	8 yr	7 yr	6 yr	5 yr	4 yr	3 yr	2 yr	1 yr
Return (%)	11.6	7.7	9.4	12.2	15.1	22.0	31.5	2.5	3.9	20.2

AGF CANADIAN BOND A
LOAD

Primary Objective:	Income
Sponsor:	AGF Management
Fund Manager:	Clive Coombs & Warren Goldring
Style:	Interest Rate Anticipator
Size (MMs):	$167.705
RRSP:	100%
Management Expense Ratio:	1.40% (Category Average: 1.64%)

RISK

The fund lost money in..............41 of 114 Months
The fund lost money in ....28 of 112 Quarters
Worst 3 Months ....-10.41% (1994)
Best 3 Months 12.55% (1992)

ASSET ALLOCATION

Gov't. of Canada bonds 78.0%
Provincial Bonds......................16.0%
Cash & Equivalents 6.0%

Annual	1987		1989		1991		1993		1995	6/30/96
Return (%)	0.9	9.9	12.1	5.5	20.6	10.0	19.6	-8.5	20.6	0.4

Compound	10 yr	9 yr	8 yr	7 yr	6 yr	5 yr	4 yr	3 yr	2 yr	1 yr
Return (%)	9.3	9.7	10.0	9.6	11.1	11.3	8.8	7.0%	12.9%	9.0

CANADIAN BOND

ALTAMIRA INCOME
NO-LOAD

Primary Objective:	Income
Sponsor:	Altamira Investment Management
Fund Manager:	Will Sutherland
Style:	Interest Rate Anticipator
Size (MMs):	$594.474
RRSP:	100%
Management Expense Ratio:	1.00% (Category Average: 1.64%)

RISK

The fund lost money in..............34 of 114 Months
The fund lost money in ....22 of 112 Quarters
Worst 3 Months ....-9.19% (1994)
Best 3 Months 13.56% (1992)

ASSET ALLOCATION

Bonds-long term 74.2%
Bonds-mid term........................12.3%
Bonds-short term....................11.9%
Cash & Equivalents 1.6%

Annual	1987		1989		1991		1993		1995	6/30/96
Return (%)	6.4	12.4	11.5	10.7	22.8	12.7	20.1	-6.6	22.8	-0.8

Compound	10 yr	9 yr	8 yr	7 yr	6 yr	5 yr	4 yr	3 yr	2 yr	1 yr
Return (%)	11.3	11.8	11.9	11.7	12.7	12.3	10.1	8.0	14.0	6.5

ATLAS CANADIAN HIGH YIELD   NO-LOAD

Primary Objective:	Income
Sponsor:	Atlas Asset Management
Fund Manager:	Doug Knight, Deans Knight
Style:	Corporate Bonds
Size (MMs):	$45.220
RRSP:	100%
Management Expense Ratio:	1.91% (Category Average: 1.64%)

RISK

The fund lost money in.................4 of 20 Months
The fund lost money in.............2 of 18 Quarters
Worst 3 Months ....-0.76% (1995)
Best 3 Months...................................5.36% (1996)

ASSET ALLOCATION

Corporate bonds 82.1%
Foreign bonds...........................9.1%
Equities....................................0.1%
Other 8.7%

Annual Return (%)	1987		1989		1991		1993		1995	6/30/96
									15.1	3.5

Compound Return (%)	10 yr	9 yr	8 yr	7 yr	6 yr	5 yr	4 yr	3 yr	2 yr	1 yr
										10.3

DYNAMIC INCOME   LOAD

Primary Objective:	Income
Sponsor:	Dynamic Mutual Funds
Fund Manager:	Norm Bengough
Style:	Interest Rate Anticipator
Size (MMs):	$334.909
RRSP:	100%
Management Expense Ratio:	1.68% (Category Average: 1.64%)

RISK

The fund lost money in..............30 of 114 Months
The fund lost money in ....15 of 112 Quarters
Worst 3 Months ....-5.12% (1990)
Best 3 Months 10.32% (1992)

ASSET ALLOCATION

Cdn.-foreign pay bonds..........30.3%
Gov't. of Canada bonds...........25.5%
Cash & equivalents..................20.8%
Foreign bonds..........................19.6%
Other 3.8%

Annual Return (%)	1987		1989		1991		1993		1995	6/30/96
	5.5	6.7	16.2	6.8	16.9	14.5	8.2	6.6	14.5	-0.3

Compound Return (%)	10 yr	9 yr	8 yr	7 yr	6 yr	5 yr	4 yr	3 yr	2 yr	1 yr
	10.0	10.28	10.6	10.2	11.1	11.0	9.7	8.7	8.8	9.1

GBC CANADIAN BOND

Primary Objective:	Income
Sponsor:	GBC Asset Management
Fund Manager:	Jake Greydanus, Greydanus Boeckh
Style:	Interest Rate Anticipator
Size (MMs):	$32.891
RRSP:	100%
Management Expense Ratio:	1.18% (Category Average: 1.64%)

RISK

The fund lost money in..............36 of 114 Months
The fund lost money in ....29 of 112 Quarters
Worst 3 Months ....-8.77% (1994)
Best 3 Months....................................11.07% (1992)

ASSET ALLOCATION

Government of Canada bonds76.0%
Ontario bonds...........................14.0%
British Columbia bonds...........8.0%
Cash & equivalents...................2.0%

Annual Return (%)	1987		1989		1991		1993		1995	6/30/96
	3.5	9.7	13.1	7.6	19.5	9.4	17.3	-5.6	20.2	0.7

Compound Return (%)	10 yr	9 yr	8 yr	7 yr	6 yr	5 yr	4 yr	3 yr	2 yr	1 yr
	9.9	10.2	10.3	10.0	11.4	10.9	8.9	7.6	12.7	8.7

GREEN LINE CDN GOVERNMENT BOND

Primary Objective:	Income
Sponsor:	TD Asset Management
Fund Manager:	Team
Style:	Index Matching
Size (MMs):	$120.347
RRSP:	100%
Management Expense Ratio:	0.97% (Category Average: 1.64%)

RISK

The fund lost money in ....36 of 105 Months
The fund lost money in ....25 of 103 Quarters
Worst 3 Months ....-8.50% (1990)
Best 3 Months 11.49% (1992)

ASSET ALLOCATION

Corporate bonds 82.1%
Foreign bonds...........................9.1%
Equities..0.1%
Other 8.7%

Annual Return (%)	1987		1989		1991		1993		1995	6/30/96
		9.3	12.8	2.0	16.4	7.8	14.9	-5.2	19.7	1.0

Compound Return (%)	10 yr	9 yr	8 yr	7 yr	6 yr	5 yr	4 yr	3 yr	2 yr	1 yr
			8.8	8.2	9.8	9.5	8.3	7.4	12.6	9.5

CANADIAN BOND

O'DONNELL HIGH INCOME

Primary Objective:	Income
Sponsor:	O'Donnell
Fund Manager:	Doug Knight, Deans Knight
Style:	Corporate Bonds
Size (MMs):	$28.322
RRSP:	100%
Management Expense Ratio:	2.00% (Category Average: 1.64%)

RISK

The fund lost money in ....2 of 6 Months
The fund lost money in ....2 of 4 Quarters
Worst 3 Months ....-0.53% (1996)
Best 3 Months....................................2.02% (1996)

ASSET ALLOCATION

Canadian bonds.......................85.0%
Cash & equivalents.................14.0%
Other..1.0%

Annual Return (%)	1987	1989	1991	1993	1995	6/30/96
						1.5

Compound Return (%)	10 yr	9 yr	8 yr	7 yr	6 yr	5 yr	4 yr	3 yr	2 yr	1 yr

PH&N BOND

Primary Objective:	Income
Sponsor:	Phillips, Hager & North
Fund Manager:	Team
Style:	Interest Rate Anticipator
Size (MMs):	$876.368
RRSP:	100%
Management Expense Ratio:	0.60% (Category Average: 1.64%)

RISK

The fund lost money in ....34 of 114 Months
The fund lost money in ....21 of 112 Quarters
Worst 3 Months...............................-7.70% (1994)
Best 3 Months 10.50% (1992)

ASSET ALLOCATION

Government of Canada 61.6%
Corporate bonds.......................17.0%
Provincial bonds 14.1%
Cash 3.6%
Other..3.7%

Annual Return (%)	1987		1989		1991		1993		1995	6/30/96
	5.8	10.5	13.4	8.1	21.7	9.9	17.8	-4.1	20.4	1.2

Compound Return (%)	10 yr	9 yr	8 yr	7 yr	6 yr	5 yr	4 yr	3 yr	2 yr	1 yr
	10.8	11.0	11.2	10.9	12.2	11.6	9.6	8.5	13.1	10.1

CANADIAN BOND

TRIMARK CANADIAN BOND

LOAD

Primary Objective:	Income
Sponsor:	Trimark
Fund Manager:	Patrick Farmer
Style:	Interest Rate Anticipator
Size (MMs):	$38.464
RRSP:	100%
Management Expense Ratio:	1.25% (Category Average: 1.64%)

RISK

The fund lost money in ....3 of 19 Months
The fund lost money in ....2 of 17 Quarters
Worst 3 Months ....-1.60% (1996)
Best 3 Months 7.20% (1995)

ASSET ALLOCATION

Long-term bonds 74.2%
Mid-term bonds 12.3%
Short-term bonds....................11.9%
Cash & equivalents...................1.6%

Annual Return (%)	1987		1989		1991		1993		1995	6/30/96
									21.6	1.5

Compound Return (%)	10 yr	9 yr	8 yr	7 yr	6 yr	5 yr	4 yr	3 yr	2 yr	1 yr
										10.4

CANADIAN BOND

DYNAMIC GLOBAL BOND

LOAD

Primary Objective:	Income
Sponsor:	Dynamic Mutual Funds
Fund Manager:	Norm Bengough, Goodman & Company
Style:	Interest Rate Anticipator
Size (MMs):	$462.290
RRSP:	100%
Management Expense Ratio:	1.94% (Category Average: 2.06%)

RISK

The fund lost money in...............37 of 96 Months
The fund lost money in.............27 of 94 Quarters
Worst 3 Months ....-8.92% (1991)
Best 3 Months 11.01% (1991)

ASSET ALLOCATION

U.S. 22.8%
Germany 22.0%
U.K. 14.7%
Denmark 11.2%
Other 29.3%

Annual Return (%)	1987		1989		1991		1993		1995	6/30/96
			5.1	11.3	7.5	9.1	14.8	4.9	19.8	-2.4

Compound Return (%)	10 yr	9 yr	8 yr	7 yr	6 yr	5 yr	4 yr	3 yr	2 yr	1 yr
			9.0	9.9	10.7	13.1	10.3	9.9	9.2	6.7

ELLIOTT & PAGE GLOBAL BOND

LOAD

Primary Objective:	Income
Sponsor:	Elliott & Page Mutual Funds
Fund Manager:	David Boardman, Flemings
Style:	Interest Rate Anticipator
Size (MMs):	$15.331
RRSP:	20%
Management Expense Ratio:	1.70% (Category Average: 2.06%)

RISK

The fund lost money in.................9 of 23 Months
The fund lost money in...............7 of 21 Quarters
Worst 3 Months ....-5.81% (1995)
Best 3 Months...................................9.72% (1995)

ASSET ALLOCATION

U.S. 17.3%
Japan..13.4%
Italy 12.0%
Germany 10.7%
Other 46.6%

Annual Return (%)	1987	1989	1991	1993	1995	6/30/96
					12.0	-1.0

Compound Return (%)	10 yr	9 yr	8 yr	7 yr	6 yr	5 yr	4 yr	3 yr	2 yr	1 yr
									6.7	-0.5

GLOBAL BOND

FIRST CANADIAN INTERNATIONAL BOND   NO-LOAD

Primary Objective:	Income
Sponsor:	Bank of Montreal
Fund Manager:	Brian Luck, Edinburgh Fund Managers
Style:	Interest Rate Anticipator
Size (MMs):	$86.620
RRSP:	20%
Management Expense Ratio:	2.01% (Category Average: 2.06%)

RISK

The fund lost money in ....16 of 34 Months
The fund lost money in ....10 of 32 Quarters
Worst 3 Months ....-3.03% (1995)
Best 3 Months 12.32% (1995)

ASSET ALLOCATION

Germany 18.7%
Japan..17.5%
France...10.6%
U.K..9.7%
Other..43.5%

Annual Return (%)	1987	1989	1991	1993		1995	6/30/96
					5.7	17.6	-0.7

Compound Return (%)	10 yr	9 yr	8 yr	7 yr	6 yr	5 yr	4 yr	3 yr	2 yr	1 yr
									9.0	1.9

GUARDIAN INTERNATIONAL INCOME A   LOAD

Primary Objective:	Income
Sponsor:	Guardian Group of Funds
Fund Manager:	Kenneth King, Kleinwort Benson
Style:	Interest Rate Anticipator
Size (MMs):	$63.545
RRSP:	100%
Management Expense Ratio:	2.09% (Category Average: 2.06%)

RISK

The fund lost money in ....40 of 114 Months
The fund lost money in ....38 of 112 Quarters
Worst 3 Months ....-5.95% (1988)
Best 3 Months 9.71% (1987)

ASSET ALLOCATION

Europe.......................................55.0%
U.S..40.0%
Pacific...5.0%

Annual Return (%)	1987		1989		1991		1993		1995	6/30/96
	4.9	-6.2	2.7	7.3	7.9	16.9	16.7	-6.3	17.8	0.9

Compound Return (%)	10 yr	9 yr	8 yr	7 yr	6 yr	5 yr	4 yr	3 yr	2 yr	1 yr
		6.7	7.8	8.6	9.5	10.7	9.1	6.9	8.8	9.9

GLOBAL BOND

HERCULES WORLD BOND NO-LOAD

Primary Objective: Income
Sponsor: Atlas Asset Management
Fund Manager: David Scott, Salomon Brothers
Asset Management
Style: Interest Rate Anticipator
Size (MMs): $51.328
RRSP: 100%
Management Expense Ratio: 2.06% (Category Average: 2.06%)

RISK

The fund lost money in .... 10 of 30 Months
The fund lost money in .... 9 of 28 Quarters
Worst 3 Months .... -4.43% (1994)
Best 3 Months .... -6.23% (1995)

ASSET ALLOCATION

Canada 83.3%
Italy 6.3%
U.K. 5.7%
Spain 2.6%
Other 2.1%

Annual Return (%)	1987	1989	1991	1993		1995	6/30/96
					-4.4	18.1	1.4

Compound Return (%)	10 yr	9 yr	8 yr	7 yr	6 yr	5 yr	4 yr	3 yr	2 yr	1 yr
									10.5	10.3

TALVEST FOREIGN PAY CANADIAN BOND LOAD

Primary Objective: Income
Sponsor: Talvest Funds
Fund Manager: Gordon Fife, TAL Investment
Style: Interest Rate Anticipator
Size (MMs): $145.648
RRSP: 100%
Management Expense Ratio: 2.15% (Category Average: 2.06%)

RISK

The fund lost money in .... 14 of 44 Months
The fund lost money in .... 14 of 42 Quarters
Worst 3 Months .... -4.82% (1994)
Best 3 Months 8.06% (1995)

ASSET ALLOCATION

Supranational bonds 47.0%
Cdn. foreign-pay bonds 26.5%
Denmark 9.6%
Gov't. of Canada bonds 6.4%
Other 10.5%

Annual Return (%)	1987	1989	1991	1993		1995	6/30/96
				15.1	-0.1	13.6	-1.1

Compound Return (%)	10 yr	9 yr	8 yr	7 yr	6 yr	5 yr	4 yr	3 yr	2 yr	1 yr
								6.0	5.8	1.2

CIBC MORTGAGE INVESTMENT   NO-LOAD

Primary Objective:	Income
Sponsor:	CIBC Securities
Fund Manager:	Bert Pearsoll, TAL Investment Counsel
Style:	N/A
Size (MMs):	$1,323.359
RRSP:	100%
Management Expense Ratio:	1.60% (Category Average: 1.57%)

RISK

The fund lost money in..............18 of 114 Months
The fund lost money in ....14 of 112 Quarters
Worst 3 Months ....-3.48% (1994)
Best 3 Months.................................6.80% (1992)

ASSET ALLOCATION

Mortgages...................................92.8%
Short term notes.........................5.4%
Cash & equivalents...................1.7%
Other 0.1%

Annual	1987		1989		1991		1993		1995	6/30/96
Return (%)	8.3	6.0	12.9	10.6	17.4	9.2	10.7	0.0	12.0	3.5

Compound	10 yr	9 yr	8 yr	7 yr	6 yr	5 yr	4 yr	3 yr	2 yr	1 yr
Return (%)	9.4	9.5	9.7	9.8	10.2	8.9	7.5	7.0	10.0	7.3

FIRST CANADIAN MORTGAGE   NO-LOAD

Primary Objective:	Income
Sponsor:	Bank of Montreal
Fund Manager:	Mary Jane Yule
Style:	N/A
Size (MMs):	$1,956.915
RRSP:	100%
Management Expense Ratio:	1.19% (Category Average: 1.57%)

RISK

The fund lost money in..............28 of 114 Months
The fund lost money in ....11 of 112 Quarters
Worst 3 Months ....-4.27% (1994)
Best 3 Months.................................5.93% (1991)

ASSET ALLOCATION

Mortgages...................................95.0%
Canada T-bills............................4.9%
Other 0.1%

Annual	1987		1989		1991		1993		1995	6/30/96
Return (%)	8.5	8.3	11.5	12.4	16.9	8.7	11.6	-0.5	12.9	3.3

Compound	10 yr	9 yr	8 yr	7 yr	6 yr	5 yr	4 yr	3 yr	2 yr	1 yr
Return (%)	9.9	9.8	9.9	10.0	10.4	8.8	7.6	7.2	10.5	7.3

MORTGAGE

HONGKONG BANK MORTGAGE NO-LOAD

Primary Objective:	Income
Sponsor:	Hongkong Bank of Canada
Fund Manager:	N/A
Style:	N/A
Size (MMs):	$128.702
RRSP:	100%
Management Expense Ratio:	1.76% (Category Average: 1.57%)

RISK

The fund lost money in.................7 of 42 Months
The fund lost money in...............6 of 40 Quarters
Worst 3 Months ....-1.61% (1994)
Best 3 Months...................................6.33% (1994)

ASSET ALLOCATION

Mortgages-residential.............91.0%
Cash & equivalents...................5.9%
Bonds...3.1%

Annual Return (%)	1987	1989	1991	1993		1995	6/30/96
				12.4	3.6	13.1	2.7

Compound Return (%)	10 yr	9 yr	8 yr	7 yr	6 yr	5 yr	4 yr	3 yr	2 yr	1 yr
								8.7	9.4	6.5

TALVEST INCOME LOAD

Primary Objective:	Income
Sponsor:	Talvest
Fund Manager:	John Braive, T.A.L. Investment Counsel
Style:	Spread Trader
Size (MMs):	$99.504
RRSP:	100%
Management Expense Ratio:	1.50% (Category Average: 1.57%)

RISK

The fund lost money in...............24 of 114 Months
The fund lost money in ....18 of 112 Quarters
Worst 3 Months ....-5.62% (1994)
Best 3 Months 7.16% (1992)

ASSET ALLOCATION

Corporate bonds 43.5%
Government of Canada bonds27.9%
Provincial bonds 16.7%
Municipal bonds 9.7%
Other..2.2%

Annual Return (%)	1987		1989		1991		1993		1995	6/30/96
	4.6	9.4	10.8	8.5	15.6	7.4	13.8	-2.9	14.5	2.1

Compound Return (%)	10 yr	9 yr	8 yr	7 yr	6 yr	5 yr	4 yr	3 yr	2 yr	1 yr
	8.8	8.8	8.9	8.9	9.4	8.7	7.4	6.6	10.1	8.5

MORTGAGE

ALTAMIRA GROWTH & INCOME   NO-LOAD

Primary Objective:	Growth & Income
Sponsor:	Altamira
Fund Manager:	Cedric Rabin
Style:	Top-Down, Growth
Size (MMs):	$297.171
RRSP:	100%
Management Expense Ratio:	1.41% (Category Average: 2.54%)

COMMENTS

Rabin has more than 30 years experience as a portfolio manager and analyst. This fund is unique to the category in that Rabin uses equity for income more than bonds (i.e. convertible bonds and preferreds). His style is top-down growth in equities and interest-rate anticipation in bonds.

RISK

The fund lost money in..............35 of 114 Months
The fund lost money in ....25 of 112 Quarters
Worst 3 Months ....-10.89% (1995)
Best 3 Months 19.83% (1996)

ASSET ALLOCATION

Industrial products.................16.6%
Gold & silver............................15.4%
Oil & gas 14.5%
Conglomerates 13.1%
Other..40.4%

COMPARISON OF FUND TO INDEXES

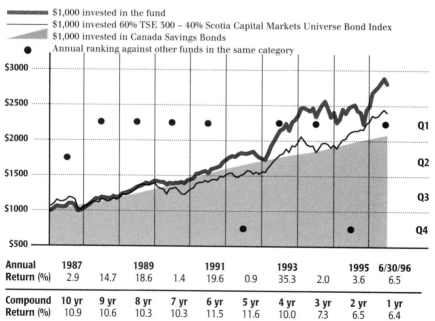

- ▬▬▬ $1,000 invested in the fund
- ——— $1,000 invested 60% TSE 300 – 40% Scotia Capital Markets Universe Bond Index
- $1,000 invested in Canada Savings Bonds
- ● Annual ranking against other funds in the same category

Annual Return (%)	1987		1989		1991		1993		1995	6/30/96
	2.9	14.7	18.6	1.4	19.6	0.9	35.3	2.0	3.6	6.5

Compound Return (%)	10 yr	9 yr	8 yr	7 yr	6 yr	5 yr	4 yr	3 yr	2 yr	1 yr
	10.9	10.6	10.3	10.3	11.5	11.6	10.0	7.3	6.5	6.4

ELLIOTT & PAGE BALANCED

LOAD

Primary Objective:	Growth & Income
Sponsor:	Elliott & Page Mutual Funds
Fund Manager:	Nereo Piticco, PCJ Investment Counsel & Jim Crysdale, E&P
Style:	Sector Rotation
Size (MMs):	$166.804
RRSP:	100%
Management Expense Ratio:	1.97% (Category Average: 2.54%)

COMMENTS

This is another fund not constrained to upper and lower limits of any one asset class, although big bets should not be expected. The equities are managed using a sector-rotator style, while fixed income is managed using a combination of interest-rate anticipation and spread trading. Foreign components of the fund are managed by E&P's international advisers, Goldman Sachs, Flemings and Jardine Fleming.

RISK

The fund lost money in ....33 of 97 Months
The fund lost money in ....26 of 95 Quarters
Worst 3 Months ....-6.18% (1994)
Best 3 Months 13.05% (1993)

ASSET ALLOCATION

Canadian equities 47.9%
Gov't. of Canada Bonds..........34.5%
Foreign equities.......................5.0%
Provincial bonds 4.9%
Other...7.7%

COMPARISON OF FUND TO INDEXES

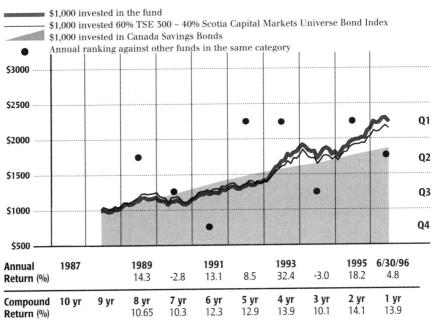

- $1,000 invested in the fund
- $1,000 invested 60% TSE 300 – 40% Scotia Capital Markets Universe Bond Index
- $1,000 invested in Canada Savings Bonds
- ● Annual ranking against other funds in the same category

Annual Return (%)	1987		1989		1991		1993		1995	6/30/96
			14.3	-2.8	13.1	8.5	32.4	-3.0	18.2	4.8

Compound Return (%)	10 yr	9 yr	8 yr	7 yr	6 yr	5 yr	4 yr	3 yr	2 yr	1 yr
			10.65	10.3	12.3	12.9	13.9	10.1	14.1	13.9

GLOBAL STRATEGY INCOME PLUS   LOAD

Primary Objective:	Growth & Income
Sponsor:	Global Strategy
Fund Manager:	Tony Massie
Style:	Bottom-up Growth
Size (MMs):	$345.373
RRSP:	100%
Management Expense Ratio:	2.64% (Category Average: 2.54%)

COMMENTS

This fund has been able to deliver above-average performance with below-average volatility. Massie's investment style was promoted by Global as "win by not losing" and that philosophy has been applied successfully here. Equity and fixed income investments are made with an emphasis on capital preservation. The fund pays a regular quarterly distribution of 30 cents. A clone of this fund is available to Investors Group clients through the Rothschild Select Canadian Balanced fund.

RISK

The fund lost money in ....14 of 50 Months
The fund lost money in ....9 of 48 Quarters
Worst 3 Months ....-5.56% (1994)
Best 3 Months 8.37% (1996)

ASSET ALLOCATION

Common equities....................58.7%
Bonds.......................................23.8%
Preferred equities....................9.3%
Cash & equivalents..................8.2%

COMPARISON OF FUND TO INDEXES

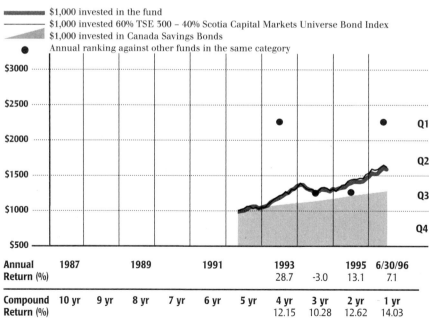

- $1,000 invested in the fund
- $1,000 invested 60% TSE 300 – 40% Scotia Capital Markets Universe Bond Index
- $1,000 invested in Canada Savings Bonds
- Annual ranking against other funds in the same category

Annual Return (%)	1987		1989		1991		1993		1995	6/30/96
							28.7	-3.0	13.1	7.1

Compound Return (%)	10 yr	9 yr	8 yr	7 yr	6 yr	5 yr	4 yr	3 yr	2 yr	1 yr
							12.15	10.28	12.62	14.03

GUARDIAN CANADIAN BALANCED A LOAD

Primary Objective:	Growth & Income
Sponsor:	Guardian Group of Funds
Fund Manager:	Larry Kennedy, Guardian
Style:	Bottom-up, Growth
Size (MMs):	$52.397
RRSP:	100%
Management Expense Ratio:	1.92% (Category Average: 2.54%)

COMMENTS

The long-term asset mix policy of this fund is 55% equity, 45% bonds. These targets are never exceeded by more than 5%. Kennedy uses a fundamental-based, bottom-up approach to equity selection and an interest-rate-anticipation style for fixed income management. While this fund's pure performance numbers may not be immediately impressive, this fund is the runaway winner on a risk versus return basis. This is the fund for the conservative investor who wants one fund to cover the entire equity and bond market.

RISK

The fund lost money in..............32 of 114 Months
The fund lost money in ....16 of 112 Quarters
Worst 3 Months..................................-8.15% (1987)
Best 3 Months 7.69% (1987)

ASSET ALLOCATION

Bonds...34.0%
Canadian equities..................31.0%
Cash & equivalents................28.0%
Foreign equities.........................7.0%

COMPARISON OF FUND TO INDEXES

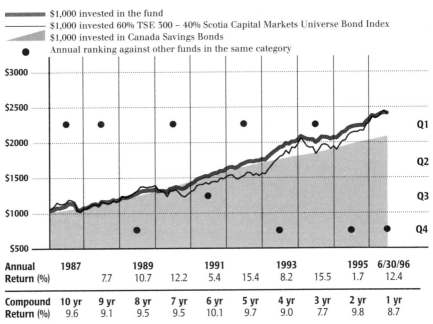

▬▬▬ $1,000 invested in the fund
——— $1,000 invested 60% TSE 300 – 40% Scotia Capital Markets Universe Bond Index
░░░ $1,000 invested in Canada Savings Bonds
● Annual ranking against other funds in the same category

Annual Return (%)	1987		1989		1991		1993		1995	6/30/96
	7.7	10.7	12.2	5.4	15.4	8.2	15.5	1.7	12.4	

Compound Return (%)	10 yr	9 yr	8 yr	7 yr	6 yr	5 yr	4 yr	3 yr	2 yr	1 yr
	9.6	9.1	9.5	9.5	10.1	9.7	9.0	7.7	9.8	8.7

INDUSTRIAL MORTGAGE SECURITIES LOAD

Primary Objective:	Growth & Income
Sponsor:	Mackenzie Financial
Fund Manager:	Fred Sturm, Mackenzie
Style:	Top-Down
Size (MMs):	$749.825
RRSP:	100%
Management Expense Ratio:	1.88% (Category Average: 2.02%)

COMMENTS

This fund invests in a balanced combination of mortgage-backed securities (MBSs), corporate and government bonds and equities of Canadian companies – with the equity portion not expected to exceed 30%. The fund emphasizes MBSs and will keep a 50% weighting in these. MBSs represent pools of residential first mortgages, secured by the underlying real estate and by mortgage insurance. Investors are guaranteed timely repayment of principle and interest by the Canadian Mortgage and Housing Corporation (CMHC), a government agency.

RISK

The fund lost money in.............34 of 114 Months
The fund lost money in ....23 of 112 Quarters
Worst 3 Months ....-9.03% (1990)
Best 3 Months....................................9.30% (1992)

ASSET ALLOCATION

Mortgage-backed securities ..50.3%
Fixed income 25.0%
Canadian equities 19.6%
Foreign equities.........................4.5%
Cash & equivalents..................0.6%

COMPARISON OF FUND TO INDEXES

▬▬▬ $1,000 invested in the fund
──── $1,000 invested 60% TSE 300 – 40% Scotia Capital Markets Universe Bond Index
░░░░ $1,000 invested in Canada Savings Bonds
● Annual ranking against other funds in the same category

Annual Return (%)	1987		1989		1991		1993		1995	6/30/96
	13.5	12.2	14.3	-2.0	16.7	7.5	20.4	-6.2	15.7	1.7

Compound Return (%)	10 yr	9 yr	8 yr	7 yr	6 yr	5 yr	4 yr	3 yr	2 yr	1 yr
	9.4	9.1	8.6	7.9	9.5	9.5	8.4	5.5	9.5	8.6

PH&N BALANCED

Primary Objective:	Growth & Income
Sponsor:	Phillips, Hager & North
Fund Manager:	Team, Phillips, Hager & North
Style:	Bottom-up, Growth
Size (MMs):	$187.069
RRSP:	100%
Management Expense Ratio:	0.92% (Category Average: 2.54%)

COMMENTS

This is perhaps the premier fund in the category. It is a model balanced fund with consistent good performance, an extremely low MER and one of the lowest standard deviations in the category. The PH&N team uses a bottom-up, growth style in equities and an interest-rate-anticipation style in bonds.

RISK

The fund lost money in ....16 of 57 Months
The fund lost money in ....11 of 55 Quarters
Worst 3 Months ....-4.77% (1994)
Best 3 Months...............................8.89% (1996)

ASSET ALLOCATION

Common stocks........................52.4%
Government bonds.................34.7%
Cash 7.2%
Corporate bonds......................5.7%

COMPARISON OF FUND TO INDEXES

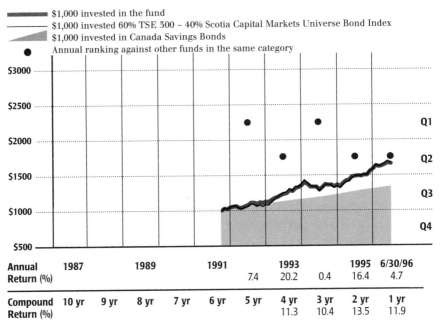

■■■■■ $1,000 invested in the fund
――――― $1,000 invested 60% TSE 300 – 40% Scotia Capital Markets Universe Bond Index
◢ $1,000 invested in Canada Savings Bonds
● Annual ranking against other funds in the same category

Annual Return (%)	1987		1989		1991		1993		1995	6/30/96
						7.4	20.2	0.4	16.4	4.7

Compound Return (%)	10 yr	9 yr	8 yr	7 yr	6 yr	5 yr	4 yr	3 yr	2 yr	1 yr
							11.3	10.4	13.5	11.9

SAXON BALANCED

NO-LOAD

Primary Objective:	Growth & Income
Sponsor:	Saxon
Fund Manager:	Bob Tattersall, Howson Tattersall
Style:	Bottom-up, Value
Size (MMs):	$5.498
RRSP:	100%
Management Expense Ratio:	1.87% (Category Average: 2.54%)

COMMENTS

Bad years in 1987 and again in 1990 are responsible for what appears to be continuous underperformance. However, using a very stringent value-based discipline, Tattersall has done very well with the fund since 1992. Asset allocation is not constrained.

RISK

The fund lost money in ....47 of 114 Months
The fund lost money in ....39 of 112 Quarters
Worst 3 Months ....-19.38% (1987)
Best 3 Months 14.66% (1993)

ASSET ALLOCATION

Industrial products..................17.3%
Natural resources 13.6%
Consumer products................12.6%
Oil & gas.......................................7.9%
Other..48.6%

COMPARISON OF FUND TO INDEXES

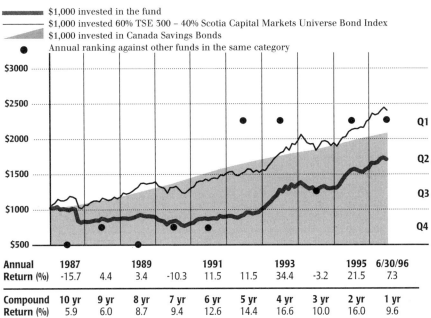

- $1,000 invested in the fund
- $1,000 invested 60% TSE 300 – 40% Scotia Capital Markets Universe Bond Index
- $1,000 invested in Canada Savings Bonds
- Annual ranking against other funds in the same category

Annual Return (%)	1987		1989		1991		1993		1995	6/30/96
	-15.7	4.4	3.4	-10.3	11.5	11.5	34.4	-3.2	21.5	7.3

Compound Return (%)	10 yr	9 yr	8 yr	7 yr	6 yr	5 yr	4 yr	3 yr	2 yr	1 yr
	5.9	6.0	8.7	9.4	12.6	14.4	16.6	10.0	16.0	9.6

SCEPTRE BALANCED GROWTH NO-LOAD

Primary Objective:	Growth & Income
Sponsor:	Sceptre Investment Counsel
Fund Manager:	Lyle Stein
Style:	Bottom-up, Growth
Size (MMs):	$68.586
RRSP:	100%
Management Expense Ratio:	1.57% (Category Average: 2.54%)

COMMENTS

This fund has added value. It has outperformed the average but has done so while maintaining a category-average level of volatility. The management style is value based and has a sector-rotation bias. This fund has no restraints on asset mix.

RISK

The fund lost money in..............37 of 114 Months
The fund lost money in ....26 of 112 Quarters
Worst 3 Months ....-10.18% (1987)
Best 3 Months...................................11.70% (1996)

ASSET ALLOCATION

Equities 62.7%
Gov't. of Canada bonds 20.1%
Corporate bonds.........................9.8%
Cash & equivalents...................7.4%

COMPARISON OF FUND TO INDEXES

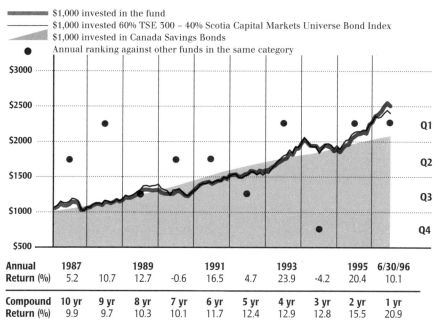

▬▬▬ $1,000 invested in the fund
——— $1,000 invested 60% TSE 300 – 40% Scotia Capital Markets Universe Bond Index
▬▬▬ $1,000 invested in Canada Savings Bonds
● Annual ranking against other funds in the same category

Annual	1987		1989		1991		1993		1995	6/30/96
Return (%)	5.2	10.7	12.7	-0.6	16.5	4.7	23.9	-4.2	20.4	10.1

Compound	10 yr	9 yr	8 yr	7 yr	6 yr	5 yr	4 yr	3 yr	2 yr	1 yr
Return (%)	9.9	9.7	10.3	10.1	11.7	12.4	12.9	12.8	15.5	20.9

SPECTRUM UNITED CDN. PORTFOLIO OF FUNDS LOAD

Primary Objective:	Growth & Income
Sponsor:	Spectrum United Mutual Funds
Fund Manager:	Catherine (Kiki) Delaney, Delaney Capital Management
Style:	Bottom-up, Growth
Size (MMs):	$133.787
RRSP:	100%
Management Expense Ratio:	0.90% (Category Average: 2.54%)

COMMENTS

Formerly the United Canadian Portfolio of Funds, this is a fund of funds. Managed by Spectrum United's investment committee, this fund uses a combination of bonds and Spectrum United bond and equity funds to create a balanced portfolio. Asset mix is not constrained. The MER of the fund is all inclusive. The normal MERs on the underlying funds it holds are waived.

RISK

The fund lost money in ....29 of 91 Months
The fund lost money in ....21 of 89 Quarters
Worst 3 Months ....-6.00% (1994)
Best 3 Months 9.27% (1996)

ASSET ALLOCATION

United Canadian Equity.........30.6%
United Canadian Growth.......17.5%
Bonds...26.0%
Other..25.9%

COMPARISON OF FUND TO INDEXES

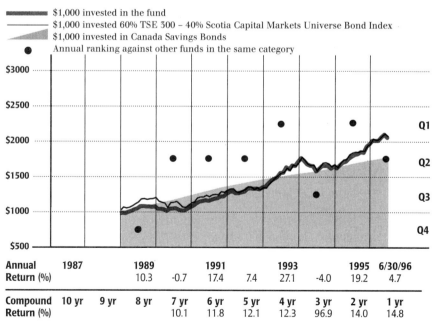

- ▬▬▬ $1,000 invested in the fund
- ───── $1,000 invested 60% TSE 300 – 40% Scotia Capital Markets Universe Bond Index
- ▨▨▨ $1,000 invested in Canada Savings Bonds
- ● Annual ranking against other funds in the same category

Annual Return (%)	1987		1989		1991		1993		1995	6/30/96
			10.3	-0.7	17.4	7.4	27.1	-4.0	19.2	4.7

Compound Return (%)	10 yr	9 yr	8 yr	7 yr	6 yr	5 yr	4 yr	3 yr	2 yr	1 yr
				10.1	11.8	12.1	12.3	96.9	14.0	14.8

TRIMARK INCOME GROWTH   LOAD

Primary Objective:	Growth & Income
Sponsor:	Trimark Investment Management
Fund Manager:	Wally Kusters and Patrick Farmer, Trimark
Style:	Bottom-up, Growth
Size (MMs):	$264.695
RRSP:	100%
Management Expense Ratio:	1.71% (Category Average: 2.54%)

COMMENTS

Trimark is better known as an equity manager. However, Farmer has given Trimark the ability to claim above-average ability in fixed income. Farmer benefits from, as well as assists in, the corporate analysis that is the cornerstone of the Trimark investment style. Kusters applies the Trimark, bottom-up growth equity style. Farmer's style is interest-rate anticipation. This fund is available only on a front-end basis. The DSC (with a higher MER) version is Select Balanced.

RISK

The fund lost money in ....31 of 105 Months
The fund lost money in ....21 of 103 Quarters
Worst 3 Months ....-9.89% (1990)
Best 3 Months 12.26% (1991)

ASSET ALLOCATION

Canadian equities...................40.8%
Bonds......................................30.0%
Foreign equities.....................19.5%
Cash & equivalents..................7.0%
Other..2.7%

COMPARISON OF FUND TO INDEXES

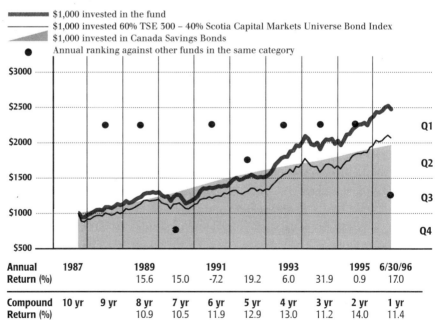

▬▬▬▬ $1,000 invested in the fund
──── $1,000 invested 60% TSE 300 – 40% Scotia Capital Markets Universe Bond Index
▱▱▱▱ $1,000 invested in Canada Savings Bonds
● Annual ranking against other funds in the same category

Annual Return (%)	1987		1989		1991		1993		1995	6/30/96
			15.6	15.0	-7.2	19.2	6.0	31.9	0.9	17.0

Compound Return (%)	10 yr	9 yr	8 yr	7 yr	6 yr	5 yr	4 yr	3 yr	2 yr	1 yr
			10.9	10.5	11.9	12.9	13.0	11.2	14.0	11.4

20/20 AMERICAN TACTICAL ASSET ALLOCATION LOAD

Primary Objective:	Growth & Income
Sponsor:	AGF
Fund Manager:	Team, BZW Barclays
Style:	Top-Down, Growth
Size (MMs):	$287.866
RRSP:	20%
Management Expense Ratio:	2.64% (Category Average: 2.55%)

COMMENTS

This fund utilizes the world-renowned Wells Fargo model. Developed with Nobel Laureate Bill Sharpe, the model looks at the differences in expected returns among stocks, bonds and cash. It then selects the combination that gives the best performance potential with the least amount of potential volatility.

RISK

The fund lost money in ....28 of 93 Months
The fund lost money in ....18 of 91 Quarters
Worst 3 Months ....-3.99% (1994)
Best 3 Months 11.28% (1993)

ASSET ALLOCATION

U.S. equities 50.0%
U.S. bonds...............................49.0%
Cash & equivalents...................1.0%

INTERNATIONAL
BALANCED

COMPARISON OF FUND TO INDEXES

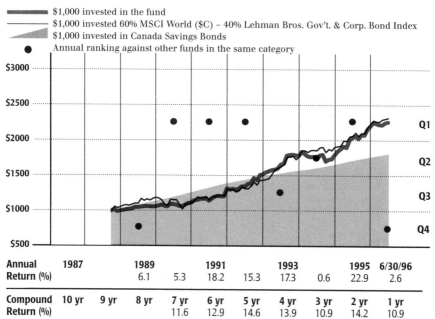

▬▬▬ $1,000 invested in the fund
——— $1,000 invested 60% MSCI World ($C) – 40% Lehman Bros. Gov't. & Corp. Bond Index
◣ $1,000 invested in Canada Savings Bonds
● Annual ranking against other funds in the same category

Annual Return (%)	1987		1989		1991		1993		1995	6/30/96
			6.1	5.3	18.2	15.3	17.3	0.6	22.9	2.6

Compound Return (%)	10 yr	9 yr	8 yr	7 yr	6 yr	5 yr	4 yr	3 yr	2 yr	1 yr
				11.6	12.9	14.6	13.9	10.9	14.2	10.9

ATLAS AMERICAN ADVANTAGE   NO-LOAD

Primary Objective:	Growth & Income
Sponsor:	Atlas Asset Management
Fund Manager:	Richard Glasebrook, Quest for Value
Style:	Bottom-up Growth
Size (MMs):	$5.547
RRSP:	20%
Management Expense Ratio:	2.68% (Category Average: 2.55%)

COMMENTS

Glasebrook is one of the top-rated balanced-fund managers in the U.S. This fund is a clone of the Morningstar five-star-rated (over both three and five years) Oppenheimer Quest Opportunity Value fund. This is relevant for a balance oriented investor, since the Morningstar ranking is a risk adjusted score. The top score, five stars, indicates the fund is in the top 10% of all funds in the category on a risk versus return basis, just what you want in a balanced fund.

RISK

The fund lost money in.................3 of 20 Months
The fund lost money in.............0 of 18 Quarters
Worst 3 Months.................................0.48% (1995)
Best 3 Months 11.64% (1996)

ASSET ALLOCATION

Electronic components...........15.5%
Financial services..................11.0%
Electronic components.............9.6%
Banking...7.7%
Other...56.2%

COMPARISON OF FUND TO INDEXES

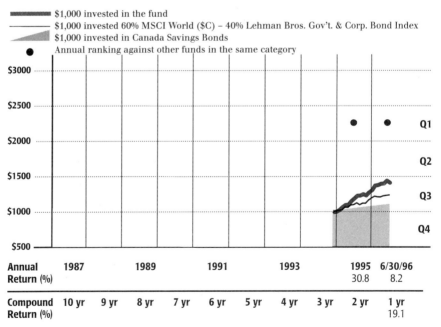

- $1,000 invested in the fund
- $1,000 invested 60% MSCI World ($C) – 40% Lehman Bros. Gov't. & Corp. Bond Index
- $1,000 invested in Canada Savings Bonds
- Annual ranking against other funds in the same category

Annual Return (%)	1987	1989	1991	1993	1995	6/30/96
					30.8	8.2

Compound Return (%)	10 yr	9 yr	8 yr	7 yr	6 yr	5 yr	4 yr	3 yr	2 yr	1 yr
										19.1

C.I. INTERNATIONAL BALANCED RSP <small>LOAD</small>

Primary Objective: Growth & Income
Sponsor: C.I. Mutual Funds
Fund Manager: Bill Sterling, BEA & Associates
Style: Top-Down, Growth
Size (MMs): $103.138
RRSP: 100%
Management Expense Ratio: 2.54% (Category Average: 2.55%)

COMMENTS

While actual fund management is done by a group of managers with regional and/or asset-class specialties, one of the strengths of this fund is Bill Sterling, BEA's global strategist. The addition of Sterling gives BEA the macro expertise it was missing. This fund replicates the C.I. International Balanced fund using BEA's expertise in derivative strategies. This leaves the foreign content portion of the RSP open for more targeted investments.

RISK

The fund lost money in ....3 of 19 Months
The fund lost money in ....0 of 17 Quarters
Worst 3 Months.................................0.69% (1996)
Best 3 Months..................................6.92% (1995)

ASSET ALLOCATION

Europe.......................................26.3%
U.S..20.7%
Japan..12.3%
Latin America 8.8%
Other..31.9%

COMPARISON OF FUND TO INDEXES

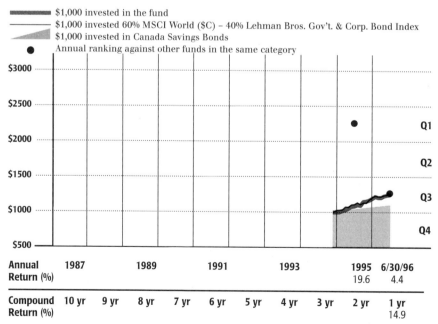

- $1,000 invested in the fund
- $1,000 invested 60% MSCI World ($C) – 40% Lehman Bros. Gov't. & Corp. Bond Index
- $1,000 invested in Canada Savings Bonds
- Annual ranking against other funds in the same category

Annual Return (%)	1987	1989	1991	1993	1995	6/30/96
					19.6	4.4

Compound Return (%)	10 yr	9 yr	8 yr	7 yr	6 yr	5 yr	4 yr	3 yr	2 yr	1 yr
										14.9

GUARDIAN INTERNATIONAL BALANCED A   LOAD

Primary Objective:	Growth & Income
Sponsor:	Guardian Group of Funds
Fund Manager:	Lawrence Linklater, Kleinworst Benson
Style:	Top-Down
Size (MMs):	$8.164
RRSP:	100%
Management Expense Ratio:	2.39% (Category Average: 2.55%)

COMMENTS

This fund maintains roughly a 50-50 split between equities and fixed income. The equity portion is divided again, 35% developed and 15% emerging markets. Bond choices are exclusively AAA rated. This fund also maintains 100% RRSP eligibility by complementing direct foreign investments with derivative strategies.

INTERNATIONAL BALANCED

RISK

The fund lost money in.............13 of 33 Months
The fund lost money in ....11 of 31 Quarters
Worst 3 Months ....-6.02% (1995)
Best 3 Months.................................9.74% (1996)

ASSET ALLOCATION

Bonds...49.0%
Developed markets.................36.0%
Emerging markets..................15.0%

COMPARISON OF FUND TO INDEXES

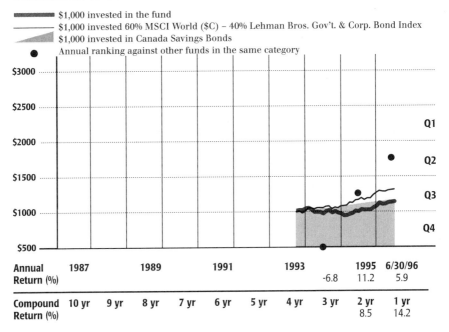

▬▬▬▬ $1,000 invested in the fund
───── $1,000 invested 60% MSCI World ($C) – 40% Lehman Bros. Gov't. & Corp. Bond Index
◢ $1,000 invested in Canada Savings Bonds
● Annual ranking against other funds in the same category

Annual Return (%)	1987	1989	1991	1993	1995	6/30/96
					-6.8 11.2	5.9

Compound Return (%)	10 yr	9 yr	8 yr	7 yr	6 yr	5 yr	4 yr	3 yr	2 yr	1 yr
									8.5	14.2

MERRILL LYNCH WORLD ALLOCATION LOAD

Primary Objective:	Growth & Income
Sponsor:	Investors Group
Fund Manager:	Bryan Ison, Merrill Lynch Asset Management
Style:	Top-Down, Growth
Size (MMs):	$40.200
RRSP:	20%
Management Expense Ratio:	3.08% (Category Average: 2.55%)

COMMENTS

A new fund offered exclusively through Investors Group, this is a clone of the Merrill Lynch Global Allocation Fund in the U.S. This fund has a Morningstar three-star ranking over three years and four-star ranking over five years. This is relevant for a balance oriented investor because the Morningstar ranking is a risk-adjusted score. The Merrill style focuses on value, both in equities and bonds. This will result in a lag in rising markets but a potential for less volatility in choppy markets.

RISK

The fund lost money in..........................of Months
The fund lost money in........................of Quarters
Worst 3 Months ....N/A
Best 3 Months ....N/A

ASSET ALLOCATION

U.S. equities 43.0%
International equities.............29.4%
Cash & equivalents.................16.5%
Other......................................11.1%

COMPARISON OF FUND TO INDEXES

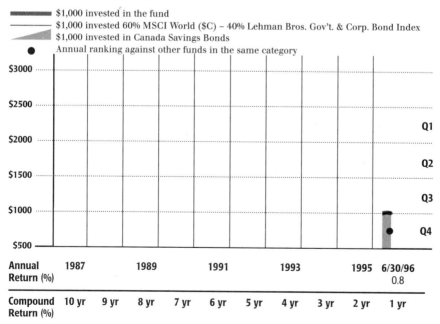

━━━━━━ $1,000 invested in the fund
─────── $1,000 invested 60% MSCI World ($C) – 40% Lehman Bros. Gov't. & Corp. Bond Index
$1,000 invested in Canada Savings Bonds
● Annual ranking against other funds in the same category

Annual Return (%)	1987	1989	1991	1993	1995	6/30/96 0.8

Compound Return (%)	10 yr	9 yr	8 yr	7 yr	6 yr	5 yr	4 yr	3 yr	2 yr	1 yr

UNIVERSAL WORLD BALANCED RRSP <small>LOAD</small>

Primary Objective: Growth & Income
Sponsor: Mackenzie Financial
Fund Manager: Barbara Trebbi & Leslie Ferris, Mackenzie
Style: Top-Down
Size (MMs): $194.618
RRSP: 100%
Management Expense Ratio: 2.43% (Category Average: 2.55%)

COMMENTS

The fund invests in a number of the world's mature markets and selected emerging markets. The fund uses a futures-based derivatives strategy to remain 100% RRSP eligible. Futures are used to mirror the performance of the underlying markets. Emerging market exposure is typically direct using the 20% foreign content the fund is allowed.

RISK

The fund lost money in ....12 of 28 Months
The fund lost money in ....8 of 26 Quarters
Worst 3 Months ....-4.98% (1995)
Best 3 Months.............................9.01% (1996)

ASSET ALLOCATION

Continental Europe................31.0%
Emerging markets...................13.0%
Canada 10.0%
China...0.8%
Other...45.2%

COMPARISON OF FUND TO INDEXES

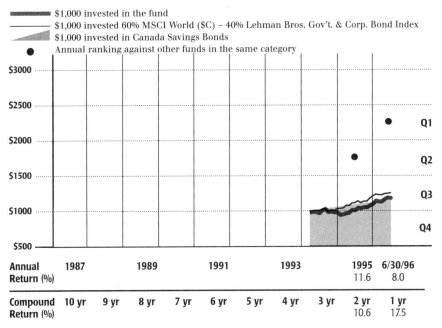

▬▬▬ $1,000 invested in the fund
——— $1,000 invested 60% MSCI World ($C) – 40% Lehman Bros. Gov't. & Corp. Bond Index
▨▨▨ $1,000 invested in Canada Savings Bonds
● Annual ranking against other funds in the same category

Annual Return (%)	1987		1989		1991		1993		1995	6/30/96
									11.6	8.0

Compound Return (%)	10 yr	9 yr	8 yr	7 yr	6 yr	5 yr	4 yr	3 yr	2 yr	1 yr
									10.6	17.5

Index of Smart Funds